C. L. R.

CARIBBEAN

C. L. R. JAMES'S
CARIBBEAN

Edited by Paget Henry and Paul Buhle

▼▼

DUKE UNIVERSITY PRESS   Durham 1992

© 1992 Duke University Press
All rights reserved
Printed in the United States of America
on acid-free paper ∞
Library of Congress Cataloging-in-Publication Data
C. L. R. James's Caribbean / edited by Paget Henry and Paul Buhle.
Includes bibliographical references and index.
ISBN 0-8223-1231-X (cloth : alk. paper).—
ISBN 0-8223-1244-1 (pbk. : alk. paper)
1. James, C. L. R. (Cyril Lionel Robert), 1901– —Homes and
haunts—Caribbean Area. 2. James, C. L. R. (Cyril Lionel Robert),
1901– —Knowledge—Caribbean Area. 3. Authors, Trinidadian—20th
century—Biography. 4. Revolutionaries—Caribbean Area—Biography.
5. Historians—Caribbean Area—Biography. 6. Caribbean Area—
Historiography. 7. Caribbean Area in literature. I. Henry,
Paget. II. Buhle, Paul, 1944–
PR9272.9.J35Z63 1992
818—dc20
[B]   91-42237CIP

Contents

▼▼▼▼▼

Preface
▼▼▼▼

C. L. R. James's success as a writer has been accompanied by a rather strange twist of fate. His writings have brought him worldwide recognition, even celebrity, among a multitude of different audiences, particularly in Britain and the United States. However, because many of his best-known texts focus on the advanced countries, recognition came without an adequate understanding of his work as a whole and of its firm roots in his native Caribbean. This volume addresses the lesser-known Caribbean aspects of James's ouevre, as well as his influence upon the politics and culture of the region. *C. L. R. James's Caribbean* was planned, it should be noted, with the advice and cooperation of James himself for more than a year before his death in May 1989. Rather than attempting a more comprehensive assessment of James's work, we have remained with the original scope of the book.

James's intellectual importance rests, in no small part, upon his formulation of differences and similarities in the "developing" and "advanced" worlds. To his analyses of both types of societies James brought a special sense of urgency. Rooted in the increasing ability of human beings to intervene in the transformation and reproduction of society, the prospects offer both a new chance for decisive improvement and a danger of widescale collapse.

In the case of advanced countries, the capacity for economic or social intervention has long been established. The crises of these societies are underlined by the continuing inability or unwillingness of leaders to mobilize the capacities toward ending class exploitation or race and

ethnic domination and toward halting the erosion of normative foundations. The persistence and worsening of resolvable problems is, in James's
view, the major source of authoritarian and totalitarian tendencies since
the 1920s and 1930s. The advanced countries, James insists, will either
resolve the problems through some form of participatory socialism—
or face barbarism. This is the central theme of *Mariners, Renegades
and Castaways* (1953), which focuses on the advanced capitalist societies. It is also the theme of *State Capitalism and World Revolution*
(1950), which highlights the crisis tendencies of state socialist societies.
The dramatic changes seen since the rise of the Solidarity Movement
in Poland, and of Mikhail Gorbachev in the Soviet Union, have proved
important confirmations of James's hopes and of his warnings.

   In Third World societies, such as the Caribbean, the unfolding post-
colonial crises further dramatize the need for vision and strategies of participatory reconstruction. "The West Indies today," James said in 1964,
"face a future that closely relates them to the present of Haiti and the
Dominican Republic, or, on the other hand, upheaval of the type in
Cuba."[1] Events in the region since the mid 1960s have certainly validated
the claims of his statement. However, in the Caribbean and other Third
World areas the problems to be resolved are quite different from those
of the advanced societies. There they include the preliminary establishment of adequate capabilities for societal intervention and regulation.
These tasks are, in turn, linked to the broader difficulties of transforming
colonial and predominantly agricultural societies into modern industrial
nations. Although this process of transformation gives rise to a number of problems common to much of the Third World, the particular
difficulties to be overcome are shaped by the nature of the pre-colonial
phase and the specifics of their particular colonial experience. To understand James's Caribbean, it is necessary to grasp clearly the nature of
the region's colonial society as he portrayed it, and his proposals for its
transformation.

   In addition to *The Black Jacobins* (1938) James's views of Caribbean
society and its transformation are to be found primarily in *Party Politics
in the West Indies* (1962) in his various essays on the failed attempt at
a federation among the English-speaking territories, and in other essays
on the region as a whole. In these works, James wrote from the perspective of one who saw a Caribbean still in the process of being born.
The personality and identity of this area were first embodied in the
expressive actions of writers, singers, intellectuals, ideologues, musi-

cians, and cricketers from the various but fragmented parts of the region. In the strokes, texts, words, and rhythms of these creative individuals, James saw a prefiguring of the original experiences around which the post-colonial Caribbean would crystalize. Such experiences were most clearly expressed in the achievements of the cricketers and the writers. In his essay "A National Purpose for Caribbean People" James explicitly compares them to the great Russian writers Pushkin, Gogol, Turgenev, Tolstoy, and others, who helped give birth to the identity of the Russian nation.[2] In a similar fashion, Vic Reid, George Lamming, Wilson Harris, V. S. Naipaul, Everton Weekes, Derek Walcott, Garfield Sobers, Mighty Sparrow, and others are great artists who have made possible the emergence of a distinct Caribbean identity. Through their work the region began to see itself as a nation.

James was no mere distant spectator observing these symbolic births, however. On the contrary, he was an active participant. At different points in his life, he has been one of the writers, cricketers, intellectuals, and ideologues who have helped the birth process along. This organic involvement is clear in James's early fictional and expository writings. Among other things, the writing embodies the liberatory hopes and aspirations of the Caribbean working class. It is this commitment to the Caribbean that explains James's periodic returns, and his later writings on the region. In these writings, both as ideologue and intellectual, James relentlessly deconstructed the meanings and arguments that legitimated colonial rule, while he helped to create the new meanings and arguments that would sustain and legitimate the new Caribbean nation. In short, James had deep roots in the Caribbean; he was one of the creative artists in whose imagination the identity of the region came to be.

However, because of the colonial context in which this identity emerged, it was rather ambivalent. This ambivalence stemmed from the fact that colonial cultures tend to be hybrid formations—the results of processes of cultural penetration and control. In the Caribbean, these processes were both extreme and extended, which resulted in comparatively high degrees of Westernization. This Westernization is evident in the game (cricket), the genres (novels and plays), and the ideologies (liberalism and socialism) through which the identity of the emerging nation has been formulated. The very strong European component in the culture of the new nation led James to the extreme but often-repeated statement that "the populations in the British West Indies have no native civilization at all."[3] In less extreme formulations of his position on Caribbean culture and identity, James acknowledged the hybrid nature of Caribbean cultural formations. In "The Presence of Blacks in the Caribbean and Its Impact on Culture," he wrote that "the African . . . had to adapt what he brought with him to the particular circumstances which he found in his environment. . . . But, being a developed person, and with his past, it was natural for him to develop a philosophy and a religion. His philosophy and religion proved to be a combination of what he brought with him and what his new masters sought to impose on him."[4] In either case, the new identity of the Caribbean nation turns out to be highly Westernized.

The ambivalence produced by this asymmetric pattern of cultural hybridization has been the source of two competing interpretations of the recently emerged identity. On the one hand, the extent of de-Africanization has produced images of a people marked by cultural dispossession who have been forced to inhabit cultural worlds that are not their own. Such images of cultural exile as having to write in English or worship in Christian form flow from this interpretation. Although it was not prominent in his works, James took note of this aspect of the Caribbean experience on occasion.

Much more prominent in James's works is an interpretation of Caribbean identity that associates a high degree of Europeanization with a corresponding degree of modernity at the symbolic level. Instead of focusing on the losses that resulted from de-Africanization, James considers the potential gains of Europeanization. Consequently, his scholarly and ideological works constitute a mode of literary praxis that boldly appropriates for the Caribbean nation the modern possibilities that Westernization opens. One never feels that English is a language of exile for James. This is just as true, if not more so, in the case of cricket. On the contrary, one feels that confident claims are made upon these cultural forms as they were being pressed into the service of new Caribbean realities. This attitude toward language and cricket can be extended to such other cultural areas as science, religion, art, and philosophy. James confidently appropriated them for Caribbean service, too. Consequently, the cases of both language and cricket are good indicators of the interpretation of Caribbean identity and culture in James's works.

As early as 1933, in "The Case for West Indian Self-Government," James provided the following portrait of Caribbean people: "Cut off from all contact with Africa for a century and a quarter, they present today the extraordinary spectacle of a people who, in language and social custom, religion, education and outlook, are essentially Western and, indeed, far more advanced in Western culture than many a European community."[5] Twenty-five years later, in "On Federation," James reiterated this view: "People (in the British West Indies) live modern lives. They read modern cheap newspapers, they listen to the radio, they go to the movies. The modern world is pressing in on them from every side, giving rise to modern desires and aspirations."[6] In short, it is not the images of dispossession and exile that predominate in James's work. Rather, it is that of a people actively appropriating the modern possibilities left them by a heritage of Westernization.

No matter how Caribbean identity is interpreted, its prefiguring in the works of great artists is not enough to produce its national realization. Along with such creative embodiment must come institutional and cultural changes of great difficulty and complexity. Colonial institutions must be uprooted and new ones put in their place at the same time that the masses are being educated and acclimated to modern forms of social organization. This is particularly the case in the Caribbean, where the modernity that James recognized at the symbolic level was absent at the institutional and organizational level.

James's analysis of Caribbean institutions was consistent. In terms of productive capacity, the institutions all lagged behind the symbolically shaped expectations and aspirations of Caribbean people. In "The Artist in the Caribbean," James analyzed the nature of regional artistic institutions. He began by suggesting that great artists were products not only of the talents they possessed, but also of the artistic traditions in which they matured. He then posed the question of whether any artistic medium in the Caribbean rests upon a tradition fertile enough to bring an artist to full maturity. James's answer was an unequivocal no. The traditions and institutions upon which artists are reared in the region do not allow them to be "supreme practitioners."[7] To achieve this, artists must go abroad and complete their development by drawing on the traditions of other societies. It was in this context that exile became an important problem for James.

Similarly, in *Party Politics in the West Indies*, James analyzed Caribbean political institutions in terms of the tension between the presence of a modern symbolic orientation and the absence of modern institutional structures capable of meeting the expectations generated by this orientation. At the symbolic level, the defining and ordering of political life had been rooted in the modern ideologies of liberalism, socialism, and Pan-Africanism. However, the institutions and traditions that have supported these experiments in modern politics have not been able to bring them to full maturity. On the contrary, because of their limited governing capabilities, their short histories, and their fragile foundations, such institutions have tended to abort the growth of modern politics.

A final example of this view of Caribbean institutions is the less detailed analyses that James makes of regional economies. In 1958, he described Caribbean people as having "a £500 a year mentality"[8] at a time when local economies generated per capita incomes of about £50 a year. For James, the source of this contradiction was the old plantation system, an outmoded, noncompetitive system of agriculture whose patterns of ownership and external control generated contradictory patterns. In addition to being noncompetitive, the plantation system generated low wages and high levels of unemployment that forced large numbers of Caribbean workers into exile. Consequently, like the artistic and political institutions of Caribbean societies, the economic ones were also in need of systematic modernizing.

In addition to these institutional problems facing the emerging Caribbean nation, difficulties also arose from the fragmentation and balkanization of the region. Insularity, cultural differences, foreign interests, and differences in political status at one time or another have blocked the emergence of the integrated Caribbean nation that James had envisioned. Thus attempts at integration had always been subregional (within linguistic groups), while the continuing colonial or semicolonial status of such territories as the Virgin Islands, Guadeloupe, Aruba, and Puerto Rico posed serious obstacles to regional development. But in spite of such failures as the 1958–62 attempt at federation among the English-speaking territories, James remained hopeful about the prospects for national unification of the entire area. Such a regional federation was, in James's view, the only political framework in which the Caribbean could participate as a genuinely independent member of the modern international community.

In short, James's emerging Caribbean nation had been challenged by a number of major obstacles. Among these, two remain particularly important: the crisis of regionalism and the crisis of post-colonial institutional transformation. Without bold and creative solutions to these problems, the potential nation may not succeed. If the countries of the region do not rise to the challenges that these problems present, they will face the prospect of their own brand of barbarism. Thus, to complete a sketch of James's Caribbean, his contribution to the debates on the transformation of the region must be examined.

Contemporary scholars have analyzed regional transformation in a rather fragmentary fashion. Problems of economic change have been analyzed separately from those of political change, and these two quite separately from problems of cultural change. Since the fifties, a substantial body of literature has emerged in each area. However, with no systematic efforts to translate across the economic, political, and cultural paradigms in use, a comprehensive and integrated vision of post-colonial transformation has been lacking.

Although primarily political in its specialization, it is precisely such a comprehensive and integrated vision of national reconstruction that has been James's major contribution to the problem of Caribbean transformation. The uniqueness of this contribution derived from the fact that James employs a common conceptual framework and a number of common themes in all of his writings on Caribbean transformation. Consequently, systematic continuities and discontinuities occur between the various institutionally specific texts that constitute James's analyses of transformation problems.

Central to all of James's writings on these problems is the necessity to educate the masses so they can participate fully in the responsibilities and privileges of a modern self-regulating society. The theme is present whether James is commenting on economic, political or cultural development. By education, James does not have formal schooling in mind. On the contrary, for the masses it is the educative significance of practical action that is crucial. In making this claim for action, James has been rivaled by only one contemporary thinker, Hannah Arendt, author of the important works *Origins of Totalitarianism* and *On Revolution*. Like Arendt, James views action as a creative medium in which any individual, regardless of social origin, can come to a fuller realization of self. Prior socialization in a number of shared rituals and language games is all that is necessary to start. With these capabilities for speech and action, individuals can come to a deeper knowledge of who they are and what they want by determinate or effective participation in various forms of collective activity. This self-knowledge is further tested by the confirmations and disconfirmations that these actions and self-definitions will evoke from others. This educative potential of collective action is at the foundation of James's argument concerning the social significance of cricket for the Caribbean working class.

However, action is not always educative. Whether or not it is depends on how it is structured, and the terms under which participants are allowed to make contributions and interventions. In James's view, the common factor that links the various institutional approaches to transformation is the educative potential implicit in the organized action that each will require. The more specialized literatures have overlooked this factor. More directly, what James is saying is that an educated population is a necessary foundation for developed or modern institutions. The building or strengthening of the latter in the Caribbean cannot rest only on having the right elites and organizational mechanism in place, but on educating the masses so that they are both willing and capable of participating in the life of these institutions. Without such a popular base, collapse, stagnation, or regression remain possible. Institutional development must rest upon a corresponding growth in the consciousness and self-projection of masses, which can only be achieved through the learning experiences of organized, participatory action.

However, this process of education and growth cannot be separated from specific attempts at post-colonial economic, political, and cultural reform. On the contrary, as the major arenas of organized activities, they can be important agencies for either the education or miseducation of workers. To be educative, the interactive life of the organizations that make up these institutions must develop some of the self-formative dimensions seen in the organization of cricket. For example, the absence of these self-formative and educative experiences from the internal life of the Peoples National Movement (PNM), a popular Trinidadian political party then headed by Dr. Eric Williams, particularly concerned James. In spite of the party's successes at the polls, the absence was the reason James saw it as backward. That is, it was not a genuine mass party. For James, a mass party was one that saw itself not only as a political, but also as a social organization. It operated as a door to a new community social order. However, its leaders recognize that the people rarely know exactly what they want. Consequently, the destination beyond the door the party opened is often only vaguely formulated. Further, this type of party also recognizes that, for the majority, the needed clarification is less likely to come from reading books and more likely from participatory activities that challenge party members and demand creative responses. In this special sense the mass party is a social and not a narrowly political organization.

In a similar fashion, James's critique of the strategies for developing Caribbean economies reflected this concern with the educative significance of organized institutional activity. Given the colonial and plantation nature of these economies, they produced large classes of peasants ("agro-proletarians") for whom economic activity was a process of self-deformation and whose wages were extremely low. Economic transformation for James would have to go beyond just better wages for these peasants; it would not be achieved by simply shifting them into industry. Transformation must also include the reorganization of agricultural production into an educative and self-forming praxis for this class.

In short, James tended to stress the social and educative aspects of whatever mass organizations were needed for institutional transformation. These aspects—especially important for a Caribbean with a comparatively short history and shallow institutional roots—contrast to many post-independence strategies of transformation stressing the manipulation of technical and organizational efficiency in specific institutional areas. We can both figuratively and literally sum up James's critique of existing Caribbean institutions and their urgent need for their reform by saying that, as they exist, "they are not cricket."

Here in essence is James's Caribbean—potentially a federated nation in the making, yet one where societies desperately need institutional transformation, and people need education through both formal instruction and participatory action. Earlier, we saw the important role that James gave to this type of action in the resolution of normative and organizational crises of the advanced societies. Its parallel importance for the transformation of Caribbean societies demonstrates the centrality of the concept for the whole of James's thinking. In the context of the periphery its function is quite different. And yet the significance of participatory action remains the major link between James's theories of transformation for the advanced and developing countries. If the underlying unity of his thought—so often missed because of the unavailability of his writings on the periphery—becomes clear at last through this volume, our hopes for the project will have been fulfilled.

We wish to acknowledge the special contribution of Constance Webb, for granting us permission to use excerpts from three letters of C. L. R. James. We wish to acknowledge Ann duCille, Vincent Richards, and Dominick LaCapra for reading sections of the manuscript; Ellerton Jeffers, Jerome Bleau, Conrad Luke, and Tim Hector for granting interviews on the subject of the Afro-Caribbean Liberation Movement; Sandra Yeghian for typing large sections of the manuscript; and Duke University Press editor Lawrence Malley for seeing the manuscript through production. We are also grateful to the C. L. R. James Society and especially Selwyn Cudjoe for giving new attention to the subject of James and the Caribbean at the C. L. R. James Conference at Wellesley College in April, 1991, and in the *C. L. R. James Journal.*

Notes

1   C. L. R. James, *At the Rendezvous of Victory* (London: Allison and Busby, 1984), 152.
2   James, *Rendezvous of Victory,* 143–50.
3   Ibid., 97.
4   Ibid., 21.
5   C. L. R. James, *The Future in the Present* (London: Allison and Busby, 1977), 25.
6   James, *Rendezvous of Victory,* 97.
7   James, *Future in the Present,* 184.
8   Ibid., 97.

PART I
Portraits
and Self-Portraits

▼▼▼▼▼

C. L. R. James lived long enough, surrounded by intellectuals of all kinds, to have earned many descriptive vignettes of his character. Tributes justifiably dwell upon his attractive personality, including his almost Victorian characterfulness, shrewd wit, and political generosity. And yet James the private man has seemed walled off from James the strategic and cultural intellectual.

In part this lapse is due to James's failure to finish his autobiography and to subsequent legal complications.* But the lapse is also a consequence of the complexities in James's own nature, his ability—as Wilson Harris once said of James's writing—to appear very different in contrasting lights. He summed up so much within himself that perhaps it could not be otherwise. An interview with George Lamming, dean of Carib-

*Anna Grimshaw, James's final secretary, and a distinguished James scholar in her own right, has outlined in several pamphlets James's disappointments in later life and his failure to complete many of his post-1950 projects. The intended autobiography, of which he often spoke, never reached more than a few dictated, fragmentary, often repetitive efforts, and a single revelatory document, "My Life With Women," denied publication here by officials of James's estate despite James's own expressed wishes. See Anna Grimshaw, *The C. L. R. James Archive: A Reader's Guide* (New York: C. L. R. James Institute, 1991); and *C. L. R. James: A Revolutionary Vision for the 20th Century* (New York: C. L. R. James Institute, 1991).

Other very helpful personal accounts can be found in Paul Buhle, ed., *C.L.R. James: His Life and Work* (London: Allison & Busby, 1986; and in *C.L.R. James: The Artist as Revolutionary* (London: Verso, 1989).

bean novelists and James's friend of more than three decades, points up other illuminating contradictions.

Stuart Hall speaks to the self-styling of the public James—and he speaks with a warm personal intimacy as well, knowing James better and owing more to him than does any other renowned critic in the English language. In Hall's portraiture, James personifies or embodies the political and cultural ideas that he projects. This view has much validity to it; certainly James often thought of himself that way.

A different James is disclosed in the sections of three letters, all sent in 1944, to his wife-to-be, Constance Webb, then a young model and aspiring actress. Here, James seeks to explain simply but lucidly his own origins. Attesting to the material crudity of conditions but also to his family's special place (and his own, as a child) in village life, James probes deeper and with less sentimentality than he does in the famous recollective passages of *Beyond a Boundary*. And here, emphasizing his relationship with his family rather than his life with cricket, James gives us a particular view of a father-teacher on the perpetual edge of ruin, and of a mother who holds high public status (not least among neighbors and white administrators) for a Trinidadian nonwhite and nonmulatto. He also gives us unforgettable glimpses into the pathos of the surroundings, for him, and of his protective emotional self-distancing.

One

C. L. R. James: A Portrait
Stuart Hall
▼▼▼▼▼

The life and work of C. L. R. James can be divided into four parts: the early years in Trinidad, the first years in England, the American sojourn, and, finally, James's return to the Caribbean. During all four periods he was intensively active, both politically and creatively.

I will emphasize the political context in which James worked because I think that he has not been accorded his proper due. James was an extremely important political and intellectual figure who is only just beginning to be widely recognized for his achievements. His work has never been critically and theoretically engaged as it should be. Consequently, much writing on James is necessarily explanatory, descriptive, and celebratory. However, major intellectual and political figures are not honored by simply celebration. Honor is accorded by taking his or her ideas seriously and debating them, extending them, quarreling with them, and making them live again. Thus I will raise some interesting but not quite settled questions about James's intellectual and political work. It is not because I think less of him, but because I think so much of him that I think he should be part of a much wider intellectual and political discourse. Paul Buhle's book *C. L. R. James: The Artist as Revolutionary* raises some of those themes, but there is much more to be done.

James was born in Trinidad in 1901; his father was a schoolmaster whose background was of the skilled lower middle class in a colonial British Caribbean society. His mother, an educated woman, had a profound influence upon James and introduced him to books. A great reader, she had a wide variety of books in the home, which was uncommon even among so-called educated people in the Caribbean. It is easy to find people in the Caribbean who are well off but have no tradition of reading. James was thus fortunate in having had early access to books. Some, and there are surprising ones among them, he still read in later years. He confessed to me that he read *Vanity Fair* every year.

Another fortunate event in James's life was that he attended Queens Royal College, one of the large secondary schools for boys that were common in the Caribbean at the time. James received a scholarship, and it provided him with a local variant of an English education. Queens Royal College was not quite an English public school, but it provided an academic education. Students took English examinations, played cricket, and read an English curriculum. James learned the classics there and to read and speak French.

When James left Queens Royal College he thought of himself as a writer. He was hired to teach at the school, and among his students was Eric Williams, later to be one of the first leaders of independent Trinidad. Williams was the founder of the Peoples National Movement (PNM), one of the major parties of Caribbean politics in the sixties. Before that, he wrote a major work on the Caribbean slave trade, *Capitalism and Slavery* (1944), a work responsible for a profound historical reevaluation of the nature of the antislavery movement. The thesis of *Capitalism and Slavery*, Williams's Ph.D. dissertation at Oxford, came from the germ of an idea that James had written on the back of an envelope. Much later in his life when Williams repudiated James, James reminded Williams that he had known him since Williams was a little boy.

By any measure, James was a bold, ambitious, and wide-ranging young man in the colonial society of his native Trinidad. After being educated, he became involved gradually in the artistic and intellectual movements that were developing on the island. He joined with other young writers and began to write short stories. After a collection of the best short stories was sent to him that contained one of his, James began to take himself even more seriously as a writer and soon produced his first novel, *Minty Alley* (1936). The book, about popular life in Trinidad and partly autobiographical, focuses on a young black middle-class esthete in Port of Spain who comes to understand what Trinidadian life is like by listening to ordinary people instead of by writing books.

At the same time, James became involved in the early stages of the Trinidadian labor movement and the movement for national independence. One of the leading figures of the era was Arthur Cipriani, a Corsican. Cipriani's leadership reflected a peculiar feature of Caribbean society, which contains influences from almost everywhere else in the world. That is what is unique about the Caribbean, half of it belongs to everyone else. Thus the fact that a Corsican led a Trinidadian labor movement should not be surprising. Cipriani, who fought in World War I, protested the situation of black soldiers who returned from the war, and he became involved in organizing the Trinidad Working Men's Association. He developed Trinidad's first organized program for workmen's compensation and the limitation of working hours. James worked for this pioneer in the birth of the Trinidadian labor movement. He wrote for the newspaper Cipriani founded and eventually produced his biography. The book, *The Life of Captain Cipriani*, was produced in 1932, just before James left the Caribbean for England, where a portion of it was republished as *The Case for West Indian Self-Government*. Thus James laid claim to the labor movement as a young intellectual in Port of Spain and to the whole development of West Indian nationalism in the interwar period.

Three things are noteworthy about the first phase of James's life. First, James's intellectual formation was through a colonial education. He was educated in a sort of mimickry of an English public school, but the school influenced James in such things as his understanding of cricket. Second, he became linked to the birth of the organized labor movement in the Caribbean. Third, he was part of a small but important and quite ambitious group of young black intellectuals in Port of Spain. It was quite remarkable to consider oneself a writer in Trinidad, a tiny island that had no publishing facilities and no large reading audience. James in particular was very ambitious, and his experiences would be translated into a new political project in the next period of his life.

This second period began with James's departure for Great Britain. He arrived in 1932, still very much committed to making his fortune as a writer. All West Indian writers of James's generation and the next would go to England to work. George Lamming, Sam Selvon, and Wilson Harris all moved to the center of the metropolis; only later in the sixties was the Caribbean public large and organized enough for writers to remain there.

In England, James met another friend, Learie Constantine, the first outstanding black cricketer who made a significant impact on West Indian cricket. Constantine came to England with the West Indian touring team and was the first black cricketer to be employed in the English league cricket. Today, a Puerto Rican ball player comes to the United States and is hired by one of the major league clubs. Then, to be hired by the

Lancashire Cricket Club was an equally important thing. Constantine was not only a great cricketer, but also an important figure in the early formation of a black consciousness movement in Britain.

Even more important for the second phase of James's development was the fact that it was Constantine who introduced him to Neville Cardus, the cricket correspondent for the *Manchester Guardian*. Cardus liked James and discovered that he had a phenomenal memory and knew the scores every touring team had made since about 1901. He got James a job as his substitute on the *Guardian*; when Cardus didn't want to go to matches, James went in his place. Through this connection with Constantine, and his early interest in cricket, James's writing aspirations led him in a new direction—sports writing.

During this period, James also began to develop the project of writing something else about the Caribbean, a history of the slave revolution in Haiti. As he worked on the project, James became involved with British Trotskyism. He read Marx first in the light of the Trotskyist movement. His first Marxist connections were with the political movement of the Trotskyist and neo-Trotskyist groups in England, and through them he encountered the popular literature of Leninist and Marxist texts, which were circulated for people's self-education. James first became involved with a Marxist party called the Independent Labour Party (ILP). The British Labour Party, the major social democratic party, had a different political character. The ILP was an independent leftist socialist party that had long debated the fledgling British Communist Party over whether or not the ILP would join with the Comintern. Eventually the Independent Labour Party decided not to join. Consequently, James's relationship to Marxism was from the first critical of Stalinism and the Comintern. He was never a Stalinist, but encountered Marxism in its non-Stalinist form. As a Trotskyist, he was an independent socialist.

What is James's critique of the forms of Stalinist organizations? Why did he think it important to have Marxist formations outside of the Comintern? This is the beginning of a long critique that belongs to James's "Trotskyism." I put the term in quotation marks because there are many forms of Trotskyism, and James's is just one. But his Trotskyism arose from this moment. It was a critique of the authoritarian forms of Stalinist rule and of the absence of democracy, a critique of a revolution that is not democratic in its form, which does not energize the popular consciousness, and in which the party has been substituted for the people. James was critical of the whole notion of a vanguard party that would accomplish the revolution for the people or tell or educate them about what they should think.

This early critique first took James to the ILP and through that to the smaller Trotskyist groups in British politics. In 1938 he published *World Revolution*, a critique of the history of the Comintern. In it, James examined the ways in which the popular energies of leftist movements throughout the world had been subordinated to the interest of the Soviet Union through the Comintern, and how the Comintern prevented such movements from growing. James also translated from the French a critical biography of Stalin by the important Trotskyist historian Boris Souvarine.

To the interest in cricket and Trotskyism of James's second period must also be added Pan-Africanism, because James was also becoming involved in the revival of the movement in England. Pan-Africanism had a long history before this attempt at revival, a history particularly evident in the work of W. E. B. Du Bois and the Pan-African Congress, which from the early twentieth century was part of American history. Further, the revival was related to the Pan-Africanist elements in Garveyism and the formation of Marcus Garvey's Universal Negro Improvement Association. Consequently, in the 1920s the Pan-African movement shifted some of its activity to London, where James came into contact with it. One of his most intriguing contacts was through George Padmore, an old school friend from Trinidad. Before James came to England, Padmore, whose real name was Malcolm Nurse, left for the United States and joined the Communist Party. An intellectual, he was sent to the Soviet Union, given a position in the Comintern in charge of African and Pan-African affairs, and was later sent back to the West. There he was to organize the black and African elements in the world revolution on behalf of the Comintern. James heard of George Padmore, met him, and discovered that "Padmore" was actually his old friend Malcolm Nurse, snuggled away in a new historical role. In his casual way, James greeted Nurse in the following manner: Hey Malcolm, you are the great George Padmore. I heard that you are the great Comintern man and I am not a Comintern man. We are supposed to be antagonists. I did not know it was you. How are you?

Both this story and the case of James's friendship with Paul Robeson illustrate a striking feature of James's character. In this period, he had a classically Trotskyist way of differentiating among those people with whom he did not agree, a great political skill that Trotskyism had honed.

Trotskyists differentiated among themselves; there was never just one
Trotskyist group, there were at least four or five. James was good at
making such distinctions, but he was also astonishingly good at collaborating with people with whom he did not agree. Thus, Robeson's ties to
the American Communist Party did not prevent James from writing a
play for Robeson, or from thinking well of him.

Malcolm Nurse, as an agent of the Comintern, had a view on the
relationship of the black struggle to both the class struggle and the revolution, and although James did not agree with him, the men still spoke
to each other. James and Padmore were influential in reviving the Pan-
African movement in London. The movement began to grow through
the League of Colored People and through the work of Garvey's first
wife, Amy Ashwood Garvey, who was active in it. James and Padmore
played important roles in the lives of young black African leaders who
were studying in London during the 1930s. James met Kwame Nkrumah
and Jomo Kenyatta, both of whom were heavily influenced by Pan-
Africanism.

The movement was also punctuated by an important development in
international affairs. This was the period of the Abyssinian war, in which
Italy invaded Abyssinia (Ethiopia). The invasion spawned the League
for the Protection of Ethiopia and *Toussaint L'Ouverture*; the play that
James wrote and Robeson performed was staged under the auspices of
the league at a small theater in London.

The remarkable breadth of James's sympathies, as displayed in his
friendships with Robeson and Padmore, was evident in another friendship related to the Abyssinian crisis and the larger Pan-African struggle.
This was James's collaboration with Ras Makonnen, an important Guyanese who was involved in the league. Makonnen was suspicious of the
whole Marxist, Trotskyist historical materialist baggage, but James held
him in high regard and worked with him as an ally. The combination of
a hard edge in James's political positions and the remarkable breadth of
his human sympathies is arresting and unusual. People who hold clear
political positions are frequently thought to be sectarian. James was not
a classic revolutionary sectarian in that sense, however. He was able to
collaborate with a wide range of people.

Completing this second phase of James's life was the publication of
The Black Jacobins in 1938. The book is a major work of historical
scholarship, with a grand majestical sweep. It was the first and most
elaborate history of the major slave revolution in the Caribbean, that in

Haiti. The work is well theorized and wonderfully narrated, with a sense of drama clearly linked to the play James had completed earlier. It can be compared to Trotsky's history of the Russian Revolution. Along with a wonderfully dramatic sense of event, James demonstrates a Marxist understanding of the historical context and sweep of events. He went to France and was the first person to examine the historical records of the Haitian Revolution in the French archives. Consequently, his work contains a history of the Central African people from which slaves first came, as well as a history of the Atlantic slave trade. During this re-search James had an idea that he wrote on the back of an envelope, an idea upon which Eric Williams's dissertation was based. It was against this historical backdrop that the narrative of the eruption of the Haitian Revolution was allowed to unfold.

The Black Jacobins was also informed by James's understanding of the contemporary political scene. Toussaint L'Ouverture, the great leader of the Haitian Revolution, was motivated by the domination that defined the social position of slaves and also by the events of the French Revolu-tion. Because of the latter influence, the black revolutionaries assumed the garb, indeed the uniforms, of the French Revolution and so became Jacobins. L'Ouverture himself was similar to Napoleon. The same thing happened to him that happened to Napoleon: he became seduced into not leading a democratic movement and instead became the charismatic leader of an autocratic one. "Bonapartism" is a Trotskyist concept for what happened to Stalin. L'Ouverture fell from a Bonapartist error and was replaced by Jean-Jacques Dessalines, who was unafraid to be a true political party apparachnik, that is, like Stalin. James reread the Haitian Revolution as a mass uprising in which the leader became trapped in bureaucracy and was slowly transformed into a self-effacing dictator who capitulated, contained, and defused the popular revolution. *The Black Jacobins* is a wonderful book and a fitting conclusion to the second phase of James's life.

The third phase of James's life began when he met J. P. Cannon, a lead-ing American Trotskyist, who invited him to come to the United States in 1938. Although James accepted the invitation thinking that he would be in the United States briefly, his sojourn marked a long and important period of his life. In America, he was partly involved in, and excited by, the Harlem Renaissance. He knew Richard Wright and was a friend of Carl Van Vechten's. He was moved by the music, the film, the fiction, and the popular culture of the era.

More important than such cultural interests was the fact that James was a leading figure in the Trotskyist movement. As a result, he quickly got involved and embroiled in the deep arguments of American Trotskyism. He also began to entertain serious reservations about how Trotskyism understood the relationship between the revolutionary movement and the black struggle. Although James did not want to privilege the black struggle, he did not think Trotskyism or any other Marxist movements, which often made the factor of race too incidental, were correct. James felt that questions of race were subsidiary to questions of class and politics and that to think of imperialism in terms of race is disastrous. But he also argued that to neglect race as incidental would be as grave as to make it the fundamental issue. And when Leon Trotsky invited James to come to Mexico in 1939, that was the issue they debated.

Trotsky compared the black struggle in America to a national struggle inside Eastern Europe; it was a subordinate struggle that, like that of the Poles', would be temporary. Trotsky further suggested that once the revolution had solved it, the black problem would cease. James disagreed, considering the question to be in need of more careful attention. Consequently, he felt that in America the black struggle must have a more pivotal, central role in the constitution of any revolutionary movement than Trotsky's position gave it. He failed to get satisfactory answers from Trotsky and remained unsatisfied by how the theoretical and conceptual relationship between the black struggle and the revolutionary struggle was posed and answered in Trotskyism.

After their meeting, James began to work his way out of organized Trotskyism, although he remained in touch with the movement over a long period and was in and out of the movement's many splits. In 1941, he formed his own tendency, which was called the Johnson-Forest tendency. James called himself "J. R. Johnson," and "Freddy Forest" was the name taken by the extremely intelligent Marxist theoretician Raya Dunayevskaya.

Dunayevskaya was extremely important to James, both in a personal and intellectual sense, because she was deeply and profoundly a Hegelian scholar. Through Dunayevskaya James returned to some of the philosophical foundations of Marxism, and a form of Hegelian Marxism entered his political perspective. *Notes on Dialectics* is one of his most complex and difficult theoretical works. This study of Hegel reinforced the differences and reservations James had developed concerning Trotskyism and culminated in an open break with Trotskyism, later articulated in *State Capitalism and World Revolution* (1950). The book analyzes the degeneration of the revolution in Soviet society as a consequence of bureaucratic deformation. It contains a critique of the Trotskyist position on degeneration, breaks with the whole notion of the vanguard party, and comes down on a particular side of a debate long popular in Trotskyism.

In the 1930s and 1940s any Trotskyist group could be divided in terms of its view of what produced the degeneration of the revolution in the Soviet Union. Was it a "degenerated workers' state"? This position claimed that the revolution was basically all right, but that the excrescences of the particular political forms were responsible for holding it back. Opposed to this view was the state capitalist position that these excrescences had created a deeply bureaucratic system that would require another revolution to overthrow it. In contrast to the degeneration thesis of orthodox Trotskyism, James argued that the Soviet Union was state capitalist. As a result, its internal dynamics must be understood in terms of the growth of a state, and of a party bureaucracy that had become an instrument of capital accumulation rather than of workers' power. The "workers' state" had become the new class enemy. As such, it would have to be overthrown if it maintained this authoritarian substitution of itself in place of a more genuine, proletarian rule. The evolution of a post-Trotskyist position constituted the new political work of this period of James's life.

In addition to the post-Trotskyist analysis, this period was culturally productive. James embarked upon an analysis, which he never completed, of American popular culture. The summation of this work, *Mariners, Renegades and Castaways* (1953), was a book on Herman Melville, a text rather like *Black Jacobins* and structured in much the same way. The revolutionary force is symbolized by the tensions in social relations among the crew of the *Pequod*. This ship is the stage upon which the drama of Melville's *Moby Dick* unfolds. The men down below are the masses; Ahab is a Stalinist figure in control at the top, trying to rule things; and Ishmael is a figure of James himself, an intellectual with a tendency to be pulled toward abstractions, to watch things from the side, and to think about them in theoretical terms but not become involved. The whale's identity is unclear—perhaps nature, chaos, or history. It is an untameable force, energy that the crew tries to harness.

The figurative device that James was most interested in was that of the *Pequod* as a microcosm of labor: the ship is a factory. Melville, James argues, thought of whaling ships as factories and saw factory organization reproduced in how ships' crews worked. Ahab, for example, can also be seen as an entrepreneur, driving the ship forward from the top. Melville elaborately describes the clearly defined division of labor aboard the *Pequod*, that is, who hunted, who creamed off the oil, and other laborious details on how to extract the oil from whales. In all of this James saw how the relationships of production get hold of the forces of production. Hence my suggestion that the whale may be equated with nature; it is matter to be worked upon, harnessed, caught, held, drained, and refined. James's view of the ship as a factory teaming with productive life is a fantastic metaphor. It is also a peculiar one, and a singular interpretation of Melville.

In 1953, James was asked to leave the United States because of his Trotskyist activities. He was imprisoned on Ellis Island and decided to fight the expulsion. As a part of his defense, he made a wonderfully Jamesian gesture: he attempted to present *Mariners, Renegades and Castaways* as testimony to the fact that he was a much better American than the immigration authorities. It was as though he was saying, "You do not understand your greatest artist, Melville, and I do. How can you expel me for un-American activities when I am telling you that next to Shakespeare, here is the greatest use of the English language? It is because you do not understand what your own author is telling you that you can expel me. You should welcome me—not throw me out." The remarkable gesture ended the third phase of James's life.

James was primarily in the Caribbean during the fourth and final phase of his life. He was invited back to the region in 1958 by Eric Williams, who led what was widely understood to be a clearly and skillfully articulated form of anti-imperialist politics through the People's National Movement. Williams was elected overwhelmingly to power and was believed to be the first true leader of an independent, nationalist Trinidadian movement. He astutely made James, his former mentor, the editor of the *Nation*, the PNM's newspaper. He also made James the secretary of the Caribbean Labour Party, which was to bring together all of the left-wing parties of the region. The party was an attempt to constitute a federal socialist movement, a strategic move on Williams's part. During this period James also visited Africa. Nkrumah, then in power in Ghana, regarded him as a mentor. From James's trip came *Nkrumah and the Ghana Revolution* (1977).

After James had worked on the *Nation* for about two years, he and Williams split. Among the causes of friction was a move against Williams, no one knows precisely why, which was made by the Americans. It appears to have involved the American Chaguaramas military base in Trinidad. The lease on the base had run out, and it was generally assumed that it would not be renewed. Williams had always preached about how the North, that is Great Britain and America, had exploited the Caribbean, and the need for regional territories to cut these links and regain independence. He did not throw the Chaguaramas treaty away in the early stages of the controversy, but gave the impression that when the renewal of the treaty came up, he would say enough is enough. In fact, whether or not he was being squeezed economically or in any other fashion, Williams decided to renew the Chaguaramas agreements. James, quite rightly, regarded that renewal as a major point of rupture and used his position on the *Nation* to criticize the decision. It became the source of a major conflict that was at the basis of the break. James was shocked and scandalized when he was repudiated and went on speaking out against Williams. Williams, in turn, brought politics to bear against James to silence him. That story is in a book called *Party Politics in the West Indies* (1962).

Something else happened in this period; James wrote a book on the importance of popular culture, a task that his return to the Caribbean allowed him time to do. The popular activity that he analyzed was the game of cricket, and the book is called *Beyond a Boundary* (1963). In this text he not only wrote about cricket, but he also redefined the game as one of the civilized ways in which the anti-imperialist struggle is played out through sports. James often remarked that the British said that the Empire was won on the playing fields of Eton and would be lost on the playing fields of Lord's Cricket Ground. Just as the British had trained themselves to create the Empire on the playing fields, so on the playing fields they would symbolically lose the Empire.

A second important theme is who would defeat the British on the playing fields. James suggested that it would be the emerging, strong West Indian cricket team and analyzed the social reasons for the team's new strength. It was strong because it had broken down existing team divisions between professionals and nonprofessionals. When the first West Indian touring teams went to England, the first five batsmen were always nonprofessional white West Indians. The blacks, who actually earned a living from playing the game, quite often did not live in the same areas as their white teammates. During the 1950s everyone on the West Indian team had equal status for the first time. They won the first test match after the war and defeated the British. The team included two bowlers, Sonny Ramadhin and A. Valentine, one from Trinidad and one from Jamaica, and three batsmen: Frank Worrell, Clyde Walcott, and Everton Weeks. Out of the team's exploits came the first cricket calypsoes ever sung in Great Britain. They celebrated the defeat of the English and the wonderful performances of Ramadhin and Valentine.

James thus redefined cricket as the playing out of these popular forces. It was more than just the game. What made the West Indian team was not only that they were good at cricket; they were also able to draw on the popular ingenuity and energies of different people. James was sensitive to the unique skills that such players as Worrell or Weeks brought to the game. For him, the cricket team drew on the popular skills and energies of the whole region, and not just those of its upper classes. Thus, *Beyond a Boundary* had a profound and imaginative anti-imperialist message.

James was in love with the game of cricket in the most archetypal way. He thought that W. G. Grace, an English batsman, was a perfect master, epical in the sense that Aeschylus was to drama. And he felt that the traditional stories about cricket, for example, *Tom Brown's School Days*, were masterful. "C. L. R.," I once asked him, "some of your writings about cricket venerate English victorian society, why?" He said, "To organize an effective cricket team is an act of collective mastery. It is an act of social organization. It doesn't matter who is doing it. Through cricket a society raises its capacity to organize its own life, and if you can use an individual like W. G. Grace, a figure of mastery over nature, that is fine. The ability to transform nature into an aesthetic is itself a human accomplishment irrespective of whether the individual is red, white, green or blue."

Thus James's investment in cricket was not just a symbolic replay of how the colonies defeated the metropolitan power. It was a much larger imaginative notion of the game as symbolic of how one talks of the energies of a whole people. He wrote in the same way about calypso, carnival, and about the leading singer in the Trinidadian carnival, Mighty Sparrow. Worrell was to West Indian cricket as Grace was to early cricket, as Shakespeare was to the Elizabethan period, as Melville was to American civilization, and as Sparrow was to carnival. To James, what created the magnificence of any cultural or esthetic product is such a condensation of historical forces. It was the rise of a new class, a new conception of humanity that created the language from which Shakespeare wrote. It was the rise and formation of American civilization with all its contradictions that created the historical moment from which Melville wrote. It was the new drawing together of the energies of the Caribbean people that created the cricket team of the 1950s and allowed Worrell to play with grace. It was the popular energies of calypso music in the Caribbean that created Sparrow as an artist.

These are all instances of the relationship of the artist, the great forces of history, and the historical moment. James steadfastly refused simply to read off cultural things against the economic base. His Hegelianism was a notion connective of historical movement, of whole classes and of esthetic production. He saw such things as one, as not separated into different practices, a notion of collective and creative totality. These were also James's politics. This complex, connective view enabled him to argue against attempts to create a revolutionary movement by making divisions between the black and the white sections of the revolutionary class, or by making divisions between the party and the masses. The movement would be made by the masses, or not made at all. Anything that does not trust the instincts and creative life of the masses would be a deformation, bureaucratic and Stalinist. Another reason why James was not a Stalinist is that he always trusted the masses' cultural and political creative energies. Shakespeare, for example, could only be a great writer because something connected him through the English language to those new energies that were being mobilized.

I once asked James about the three great moments in which he could see a single artist speaking on behalf of a whole historical revolutionary moment. He told me about the Acropolis, even though its architect is unknown. He told me about Shakespeare, and he told me about Picasso's "Guernica." He said, "Look at Picasso. Look at 'Guernica.' A wonderful painting. What is it about? It is about the Spanish people. It is about the energies of the Spanish revolution. When you look at 'Guernica' you see the whole movement, the whole maelstrom of the Spanish revolution encapsulated in an esthetic form." James would take a postcard of "Guernica" to cricket matches, and during intervals when play stopped he would take it out and study it. When play resumed, he would put it away.

The end of the fourth period, 1962, was the end of James's active political life. He returned to live in London and was rediscovered in the United States in the 1960s and 1970s. In particular, *Radical America* discovered his importance, as did many black writers. Others who would study

American slavery discovered the importance of James's work on the history of black revolts. The rediscovery gave him a late legitimation and recognition in the United States during his seventies. His nephew, Darcus Howe, is a leading black intellectual, the editor of one of the major black radical journals in Great Britain, and one of the leading spokespersons for a black documentary television series, "Bandung File." Darcus fixed up a flat for C. L. R. in Brixton, which was where he lived. Paul Buhle's book about him was published in 1988 in London, and James was present at the book's launch. Generally, he hardly moved from the flat. People visited him constantly, visits that reflected the many generations of black political and intellectual figures privileged to talk to James and to know him. Such novelists as George Lamming and Wilson Harris, or young intellectuals who either returned to the Caribbean or remained active in black metropolitan politics all benefited from James's advice and wisdom. Whether or not they agreed with James at first, they were all influenced by him. James was eighty-eight when he died in May of 1989; he was buried in his native Trinidad.

Two

C. L. R. James on the
Caribbean: Three Letters
▼▼▼▼▼

The following letters were sent by James, in 1944, to Constance Webb, a young actress later to become his second wife. The first letter begins as a satire of a typical autobiography; the second begins and ends as a response to a letter from Webb; the third, an excerpt, explains James's personal experiences that led to the development of his characters in the novel *Minty Alley.*—EDS.

No date, July 1944

Autobiography of
a Man
by
Him

Price: Priceless
First Edition. All sold out.

Publisher's Blurp

The publishers have pleasure in presenting the first installment of this autoby. Our readers say that in these troublesome times it provides a necessary escapism. It far exceeds in interest our recent best-seller and American classic: From Log-Cabin to Home Relief. The author wishes his identity to be kept secret. He therefore regrets that everybody knows who he is.

All [the word "ladies" is scratched out] women who wish further details must send stamped and addressed envelopes and photograph. Birth certificate is not necessary but the photograph must be dated. The author will *not* give any press interviews. But he will speak on the radio anytime he is asked and will answer all questions.

Chapter I.

I was born in Jan. 4, 1901. My mother says that I was a very lively child, moving about continuously in the womb. I am very proud of that, though my pride has no scientific basis.

My first memory is at the age of about four. My mother brought myself and my sister, two years younger, in a cab to North Trace. The train brought us to Princess Town and then a cab carried us the six miles to North Trace. My father had gone there to be a village school-master. I sat in the cab looking out. Then I remember in the first days going to the wooden latrine. It was new, built of pine-wood which smelt very strongly as pine does. I remember too that one day my brother and I were allowed by my mother to run out into the street and bathe naked in the rain. I remember too that a teacher at the school boarded with us. I do not remember him at all except that one day a girl, a young woman, came by a cab and my mother hid her in his room. Then he came home from school and she led him smiling mysteriously into the room. I followed. When they saw each other they embraced. I had never seen people kiss for so long a time. I stood amazed. It meant nothing to me, except that they kissed so long.

One night my aunt, my uncle's wife, came to stay with us. She was a beautiful woman—not handsome but beautiful. She and my father went for a walk. I heard him call from the street "We are on the hook," meaning that her arm was hooked in his. I was vaguely aware that my mother did not like it. Those are my first memories—of that house. We left there when I was about six.

Then we moved to another house, nearer the school. It was a small house, shaped like this

6	5	4
	1	3
		2

It was about 25 feet square. Room 1 was not ours. It was a store-room for cocoa, after it had been shelled. Room 6 was (I think) connected with 1. Room 2 was the drawing room. But a paper blind made a little room of 4 for me and my sister. I slept in one bed, she in another. Room 5 was my mother's bed-room. My chief memory is of my mother sitting reading and I lying on the floor near her reading until it was time for me to go to bed—9 o'clock. She was a very tall woman, my colour, with a superb carriage and so handsome that everybody always asked who she was. She dressed in the latest fashion—she had a passion for dress and was herself a finished seamstress. But she was a reader. She read everything that came her way. I can see her now, sitting very straight with the book held high, her pince-nez on her Caucasian nose, reading till long after midnight. If I got up there she was, reading, the book still held high. As she read a book and put it down I picked it up. My father read nothing—a book a year perhaps. My life there until I was nine centered around books and games. When I was about seven I sat up late one night and wrote a poem. About eight verses of four lines each in imitation of a poem in my reading-book. Why I felt to write I do not know. No one wrote that I know. No one had ever said that people wrote. Another day my mother put down *The Last of the Mohicans*. I picked it up and read it. I read as she did—straight through except I saw a chance of playing cricket or shooting with an air-gun. When I finished the Last of the M I got a copy-book and began to write a story of my own. But after two chapters my mother read it and said it was exactly like the L of the M and I stopped. I know now that this was the worse thing she could have done. She should have told me to go on and I would have written it to the end I think. But I don't know.

Books, books, books. There was a rainy season and a dry season and in the rainy season we got fever. So we were sent to Tunapuna to my grand-mother's, every rainy season, for some months. There I used to climb to the top of the wardrobe by way of the window-sill and take down the books. I remember *The Throne of the House of David*. I read it to pieces. And I remember too an extraordinary book—a prize novel, for a prize offered by, I think, the Herald [Tribune] of New York. It was a green book, a modern novel, and it had style. I didn't know what style was. But it is one of my most powerful memories—the strange effect this calm, de-tached writing had on me. I must have been about seven. Long before that I had appropriated my mother's Shakespeare. I couldn't read it all. But there was a picture at the head of each play with two lines or so describing the picture, giving the act and scene. I looked up each one, over and over again and read the whole scene. The one I remember, the only one, is the quarrel between Brutus and Cassius. My father bought me the Pickwick Papers and I read that too when I was about seven. When I didn't read I played cricket or ran races or went shooting birds with my air-gun, or shot at a tin-cup or a bottle. I was a dead shot at about seven and for long after—with my air-gun and after a time I didn't use to aim but shot from the stomach. I wasn't aware of my physical surroundings. They didn't change sufficiently—the wet season wasn't very different from the dry. I wasn't aware of social distinctions. We were all Negroes. The house in Tunapuna had two rooms, one divided by a paper blind. My two aunts and my grandmother lived there. They were very poor. The house was about 12 feet by 18 feet. There were holes in the floor, the house was so old. It had a thatched roof, and the rain came in. My aunts were in their early twenties. My grandmother was about sixty-five. They washed clothes for a living and my aunts also were seamstresses. Very good seamstresses they were. But they had a very hard time. I remember chiefly the fleas at nights. Never seemed to sleep when I was there. But my father sent money and we were well fed.

I shall try to keep my impressions in harmony with my age. I lived in North Trace and in the wet season I went to Tunapuna. I went to school and read and played and read. I don't know that I thought of anything else until April 26 1909 when I was eight—a great day in my life.

But until then there were some personal developments. I thought my parents knew everything and were always right. I still remember that one day—I was walking across the drawing-room in North Trace—it broke in upon me that I had a judgment of my own opposed to theirs. I was about seven.

Then came the Sunday cricket. Some Chinese people lived near to us and there were boys, Kelvin, Buller, George, and Aldrick. We played every day and Saturday. But they had a grocery store and were busy selling on Saturday. On Sunday afternoons there was a big game in the grass patch behind the house and all around came to see. My mother, who was a Puritan, said I was not to play on Sundays. So on Sundays I sat in the drawing-room and listened to the game. God. How my heart used to hurt me. Every Sunday. Then to make matters worse my father would go and play. My mother said he could do as he pleased—he was a man. I was to stay in. I felt bitterly the injustice of it.

Bitter too were my experiences with my brother [Eric]. He was the last and about five when I was eight. He was a sickly boy and lazy and not too much inclined to play. When I had no books to read, for I read them without stopping until I was finished, I would beg him to play with me. Sometimes he came. Now at cricket one bowls the ball and the other bats. Then when the batsman is out the other takes his place. My brother would never play unless I allowed him to bat first. If he got out at once he would say he wasn't playing any more. I used to cry bitter tears (I remember them now). It wasn't fair. He had cheated me, and the idea revolted me. I complained to my mother. She sometimes compelled him to play—a stupid thing. He would play for a while. I was batting away. Then he would stop before getting me out and once more the bitterness began. I gave him two innings to my one. No use. He always cheated me. He cheated naturally and I was naturally honest and fair-minded. I believe those days left an indelible mark on me. I went about a lot. Wherever he went, to play cricket himself, to see friends, to see games, my father took me. Everybody said I was a handsome, bright boy, but I merely remember that. It had no effect on me. I was happy I think but for the sense of injustice I have described. I didn't love my parents. I loved nobody. I didn't hate them. I had no grievances. I just didn't feel to them as I was supposed to. Once when my mother was near death I cried because everyone was crying and I thought I ought to cry. But I knew I was faking. They were very kind to me. Simply I was like that. I had sex experiences but I do not feel to go into those as an honest statement demands some intimacy. I think so, at least. I believed in God and went to Church regularly. But it was routine. I was very well trained. My mother saw to that—respect for elders, good manners at table, modesty and self-respect. My father made about forty or fifty dollars a month and was always desperately in debt. But he always dressed my mother well and we never needed anything. My mother kept us scrupulously clean and kept the house the same as did my aunts. I was somehow aware that we were not common people or laborers. We kept a servant, a girl sometimes, sometimes a woman. White people meant little to me. The clergyman in North Trace was white—a Mr. Reeves, an Englishman, and he drank I remember. His wife was stylish and like most of the white women wore a veil. The colored people I knew didn't wear veils. Only white people wore them. But my mother wore one. And I used to hear my parents talking about the way in which her clothes compared with Mrs. Reeves's at church. My father played the harmonium at church and took the choir-practice and he and Reeves ran the church. One day the Reeves's invited my mother to lunch. It was an occasion. The white parson had invited her to lunch. There was great preparation and for days afterwards it was discussed. But I had no strong feelings on the subject. They were white and somehow special, but my father was the schoolmaster and I was his son and everybody made much of me. There were some white planters in the district, a few, who used to speak in a friendly way to my father. There was a German named Conrad. I don't remember him but I remember his wife—a tall, slim, elegant, handsome woman. I heard my father say once that she called herself Mrs. Conrad but he didn't think they were married. One day, my mother was very ill and she came to see us. I remember how well she carried herself and the dress going up to her ears with whale-bones in the neck. She was a mysterious woman. I don't think she kept company with the few whites in the district but I am not sure.

There was also a girl once—a girl about eleven—brown-skinned, very handsome. I remember her to this day and if I were an artist I could draw her picture easily. One day all of us were playing police and thief— your cops and robbers. We ran into the forest; found ourselves alone and stood looking at each other—just looking for two or three minutes. She and I understood what we were thinking. Then the others came and the moment passed.

There was another curious episode. I got hold of an English history book by a man called Ransome. It was dry fact but I read it from cover to cover over and over again. But the English always won all the battles. I resented it fiercely. I used to read and re-read the few battles they had lost. I conceived a fanatical admiration for Napoleon. A friend of my father's had a picture of Napoleon pasted on his wall. It was always a great day when my father took me there specially to see it. I used to stand and watch it—enthralled. Why I do not know. Nobody ever discussed history or literature or writing with me. But I read that history and hated the British for always winning and loved Napoleon. So I lived my life till I was eight years old and four months. I was a happy boy I think, active and very intelligent. My parents worked hard on me when I was ill as I was not infrequently. I had no love for anyone. I went to school, did my work, read all books and played. On April 20 my father began to teach me for a scholarship. Next time I'll tell you about my father and what he was and how he taught me. I hope you find this interesting. The life of the people, the physical landscape, the ideas, meant nothing to me. Later they came home to me. In time I shall describe them, but only when I became aware of them. If I may, I say that in a different environment I would have been a different child. I learnt everything. But there wasn't too much for me to learn except in books.

September 13, 1944

Your letter was fine. One day I'll show it to you. Very simple, very clear, very confident. Now I am just going to continue my autobiography. Off to the West Indies 1908 (you'll get another letter to-morrow). You remember North Trace—the little village, and the schoolhouse and my parents and me, and my brother and sister. The schoolhouse was about eighty feet by forty, with a few maps on the wall and benches. Everything was very primitive. There were about 120 children, boys and girls, most of them bare-footed for they were very poor, Negroes and mulattoes chiefly. Few white children came to such schools and when they did not for long. There were some Indians and a few Chinese, for the island has a very cosmopolitan population. My father was the Head Master and there was a Head Mistress. She was always in charge of the infants. Then there were about half-a-dozen other teachers of varying degrees of ignorance. The school was divided into standards, Standard I, II, III, etc., up to Standard VII. We were taught Reading, Writing, Arithmetic, Geography, Singing, and Drill, a form of physical culture. The chief thing about the school was the yearly examination and to this day that examination and everything connected with it stands out in my memory.

First of all the pay of the head teacher depended upon it. He was a government teacher, but his pay was divided into three parts. About thirty dollars a month was the regular pay. Then every three months he received a capitation grant—so much per head for those who attended. This might bring in about thirty odd dollars a quarter. Then the examination was marked very good, good, or fair, as the case might be. Very good meant so much per pupil, good meant less, and so on. This could come to a tidy sum—about 100 dollars, known as "the bonus." And a series of good capitations and a good "bonus" meant not only money, but promotion to bigger schools in the towns. Furthermore the bonus was a lump sum—you could do things with it. All life was governed by these financial circumstances.

The examination lasted one day. They were carried on by an Inspector of Schools and his assistant, a woman, who examined the infants. They, in 1909, were always white. For months we prepared and then on the day they came. The examiners took a kind of tour. North Trace to-day, Princess Town the next day and to place after place day after day. The chief part of the examination was the written part; all the standards had for example Arithmetic Cards with sums on them. Now my father was an able, conscientious teacher. But the teachers took no risks with their bonus. The cards were imported by the examiner from England. Groups of teachers got together and imported cards from every maker of cards in England. They all had all possible cards. When the tour began, the first teacher passed the word along that this year, Mr. Robinson was using Craul's cards or Johnson's as the case might be. At once the teachers all along that route had their pupils furiously working out those cards over and over again so that when the day came and they were handed out each pupil knew his sums already. If the cards were of a kind which had different sums for each pupil, then we were so arranged that we got the cards we had prepared for. If we didn't get them, we changed them, with the help of the teacher. No arrangement or rearrangement of the boys and girls could stop this. Same with the geography and the grammar. Thus there was this cheating going on in every school, scores of them, for miles and miles all over the different circuits. The curious thing is that no one considered it immoral. I never did until I was about twenty. I never thought of it. Teachers and pupils all cooperated to pass the examination and do well. My father was not lazy. He taught hard and well, but he was not going to take the chance of getting a good instead of a very good. So it was everywhere.

On the great day the Inspector and his assistant came. They were usually very incompetent. They never discovered that they were being cheated. They all had weaknesses. One loved singing. My father therefore always had some fine songs for him. Another one fancied himself as a military man. My father gave him a long and special drill. You could be sure that he would give a V.G. Then a clever teacher would give them lunch—a wonderful lunch with champagne. One of them always got tipsy. He would be sure to give a V.G. and so on and so on.

I remember only one of the examiners—a Miss Doyle. She was, guess what, you will never guess, a beautiful woman. This sounds trivial. I assure you it was not. She was small, dark-brown hair, slender, elegant, quick in her movements. (It is thirty-five years ago now and I saw her once.) But everybody in the teaching business on that circuit spoke of her. When she came in there was a murmur of admiration. The women teachers raved over her. When the examination was discussed, her beauty was always mentioned, as a constituent part. There was no lasciviousness about it, no envy. The teachers were servile to the inspector because he was authority. They loved her because she was lovely and gracious. It was a glimpse of something "artistic" in a dull, drab world. Part of the charm was her speech, nothing very wonderful perhaps in itself but standing out against the dull heavy rustic accents. My father was not servile—he had a formidable dignity against all white people. But he was a careful, shrewd man. On examination day some or most teachers wore their best clothes. He did not. He wore a plain white tunic. Let the inspector be dazzling and the best-dressed man in the show. I remember his deportment during the exam, as we called it—a mixture of dignity and deference. He always got V.G.

All the bonus and all the capitation came to him. But he gave substantial sums to the staff. They knew that he would and worked hard. Some head teachers were mean and kept it all for themselves. He never did and if he had wanted to, my mother would have raised cain. Later, many years later, this business of capitation, etc., was stopped. The authorities condemned it and paid a man his full salary every month. Everyone agreed that it improved matters all round. But the thing I have described went on for many many years all over the island.

Of the teachers I remember little. There was a man called Leben—a black fellow who always wore tight shoes. Often they were so tight he had to cut a hole at the side. Why he wore them so tight God only knows. Perhaps the local cobbler just couldn't get them right. I know I often suffered martyrdom from badly made shoes. The other teacher I remember was a Miss Todd. She also was an experience. She was not handsome, but she was brown, and very very stylish. She had a face like Miriam Hopkins, with a broad mouth; and she had a mole. She was my father's head mistress for years and there was an affair between them. I only worked it out years after. But altho' my mother knew she could only hint to my father that she did. I was always vaguely aware that something was going on but what it was I didn't know.

So for a year or two I read books and played games and went to church and was one of the 100-odd children who came from miles around to the school. I was the schoolmaster's son and therefore had status. I was bright as a new shilling and everybody said I would be sure to be something one day. It didn't matter to me. I just lived along. Then on April 26,

1909 my father called me and said he was going to teach me specially for a scholarship. I said Yes. I didn't know. I didn't care. But things happened. I'll describe them next time.

Now I hope you'll go straight off to sleep with your mind drained of your troubles for the time being. See me one Monday morning I think it was, all clean and scrubbed, over thirty years ago, at 8 o'clock, with my father beginning special training of me. An hour before school 8–9 and an hour after 3–4. You were not born then, darling. New York, California, Los Angeles, Hollywood were not in existence. If they were, I wouldn't have known. A little island 50 miles long by 30 broad, a little remote village, a little school, and in it, a little boy looking at his father and waiting to be taught. The years would pass and I would get to know a lot of things, and meet a lot of people, but chiefly I would get to know Marxism and meet you. It began on April 21, 1909. Whenever you feel for some distraction let me know. I'll tell you about it as Scheherazade told the tales of the Arabian nights.

No date, 1944

What is a poet? I'll explain. When I lived in the W. Indies I lodged once with a woman, a Mrs. Roach. She was not educated. She spoke English with the French patois accent of the peasant people. She was a gentle-woman, but language was not her strong point. She had a brother, a drinking, shuffling, guitar-playing idler, Francis. Francis would not work and what was worse got himself one day into trouble with the police for keeping a brothel or helping to keep one. Mr. Roach was the City Cashier, and this would have meant a terrific scandal. And Mrs R, a woman with a high sense of social propriety and a very moral woman in addition, was outraged. Passing through the yard I heard and saw her talking to Francis.

She had a shawl around her shoulders and she stood straight like a tragic actress. She said "Our parents brought us up together Francis, spent time and money on us. But from youth you went your gambling, guitar-playing way. Wine and women, that has been your life. You have disgraced yourself and disgraced us enough; and now you may have to go to jail for keeping a brothel. Look at the white hairs on your head, Francis? Are you never going to change? Thank God, our dear parents don't live to see you as you are," etc., etc.

She had never spoken like that before. I never heard her speak that way again. But for the moment she had uninterrupted fluency, a wonderful rhythm, dramatic pauses, etc. I, a very literary person in those days, listened amazed. What caused it? Intense emotion, it was bursting in her, a subject she knew well, had long meditated upon. At various times she had said this and thought that about Francis; other people had discussed it with her. Then under a powerful stimulus, this last disgrace, she became for the moment a poet. She was on a very high level of emotion and to batter Francis into some sort of discipline she needed a very high level of expression. She found it. Perhaps for once in her life—perhaps two or three times. Then she slipped back to her old level.

Three

C. L. R. James: West Indian
George Lamming interviewed
by Paul Buhle

▼▼▼▼▼

[*The following interview was conducted with the West Indian writer George Lamming in Barbados on November 25, 1987.*—EDS.]

P. B.: Can you describe James's influence on you and the other West Indians in England during the 1950s?

G. L.: I think that his friendships among West Indians in England were pretty general. He had a seminar thing, a generation who used to go to Staverton Road, and who were concerned with transforming the Caribbean society. In some cases there were people who had no political connections, and the importance of those meetings [was] in helping them relate to professions. It was a pervasive influence over a number of people. All that they had in common was the deep need to contribute to the process of change. It was not so different from James's relations to Africans in 1930's London.

This is really how I see James, not as a political man but as a teacher—in the old philosophical sense of teaching. The interesting thing about James—if you were doing him fictionally—is that in James's political history, there is a certain pattern. James has a consistent career of breakaway, breakaway, breakaway. I don't think of breakaway in a negative sense, but in which the teacher who does believe in the idea breaks away from groups the moment that group is not sharing the idea. James has no period of consistency with any organization for any length of time, right up to the PNM. We could analyze the reasons.

How I see him, really, is the predicament of the restless imagination, the imagination which cannot and does not settle, which is always driven towards opening and exploring new frontiers, making each frontier an unprecedented revelation. James has a way of speaking in superlatives about the particular thing—"Never in my life," "Never before,"—which, in reflection, is not that extraordinary, but is *made* extraordinary in the moment of perceiving.

He met me when I had a very big reputation. I did not hold him in awe. Having hardly heard of him, apart from *Black Jacobins*, once I had picked up the translation of the Souvarine biography of Stalin. Even when I met him I would not have read *Captain Cipriani*, although I had heard of it. But as I got to know him I became very aware of a special quality [which influenced my writing].

If you read *Age of Innocence* and *Season of Adventure*, two things are working there. One is the creative power of mass, the central character is usually the mass more than the individual. The creative power of the mass, in *Season of Adventure*, that the drums bring out is not too far away from what James sees as spontaneous confrontation. There's another reference to him in *Age of Innocence*, a description, a reflection of the relation of the teacher to the artist. There is an element of James in that passage, too.

P. B.: How was the West Indian left from the 1950s influenced by Nello [C. L. R.]?

G. L.: I don't know if you can pinpoint it. You will have to think of James's influence really in terms of the way he has influenced a debate about the ways in which masses will organize themselves for the transformation of the society. There is a position of James which would not have met with widespread approval, but had in some ways to be *answered* all the time. You see, you can have an influence at work, not that the influence makes the person think in the direction but the influence works by making the person think how they're going to argue about it. So James's position is a position as a Marxist. James is a Marxist. And he's quite unapologetic, and calls himself a Marxist and Leninist. But James abandons the concept of a vanguard party, that the revolutionizing of a mass requires as a condition something called a vanguard party. That would have been the position of all of the Marxist parties in region with the exception of the WPA. The WPA never had a leader. There was some form of collective leadership, but not in the way that [Cheddi] Jagan was the leader of the PPP or [Trevor] Monroe was the leader of the WPJ. And to this day they have retained that sense of a collective leadership.

P. B.: Were there others as influenced as Walter Rodney by James, personally?

G. L.: Most of the generation of Walter Rodney, that whole generation, was reading James and arguing about *Black Jacobins* and arguing about James's evaluation of what happened in Trinidad and so forth. It was very much on their agenda. I don't know about influence, but he was always on the agenda of [Eusi] Kwayana. I wouldn't be so much concerned with defining something called "influence." I don't think any of them would see themselves or want to claim discipleship, but what one can very safely say, is that James has been a pervasive influence on the political thought and intellectual argument throughout the Caribbean. That could be said without any reservation.

James was being invited. He has spoken at mass rallies in the political parties of Barbados, on the platform (wisely I thought at the time) of the Barbados Labour Party because of some special interest he had, historical interest in Grantly Adams. James had a sort of Victorian loyalty toward Adams. And there is a very interesting document of James's, I haven't seen a copy of it for some time, in which they asked James to give an analysis of the condition of the party. There it is, as a document, in which he made very remarkable predictions that did in fact come true, either very early in the 1960s or late 1950s, when he had come back from England. It was not made generally available, it was a party document.

He'd given a series of lectures to campus audiences in Jamaica, he had spoken in Guyana. So apart from texts, James became a figure that aroused great curiosity, great intellectual curiosity, at a level much wider than just political action.

P. B.: Was he a voice in the wilderness?

G. L.: I don't think he seemed a voice in the wilderness at all. When James was functioning in that way, he was very inspirational. In Trinidad, there was a feeling at that time, had James in a way played that differently, he might have influenced the direction of politics during the PNM. I think James made certain tactical errors—this is my own view. James did not, in my view, give a correct assessment to the meaning of that twenty-five years' absence. He returned to the terrain as though he were out for a year or eighteen months. And therefore because of his old and close association to Williams, [he] overlooked, in a way, the meanings that this would have for people who were around Williams, that he would be seen as someone who was preempting other people. That was something that would have to be watched. James may have gone for too high a profile too soon, and might indeed have [had] more influence in shaping the underground subsoil of the PNM had he worked more from behind the scenes. Having worked in front of the scenes, he then found himself coming into collision with Williams's supporters. So that when he came into collision with Williams, he was really without support, because the supporters then closed ranks.

The other thing I thought was a mistake was that after the break with Williams, the open break without any possibilities of reconciliation, James automatically entered the battle of political rivalry with Williams. Challenging Williams to election, contesting election, turning this matter into a gladiatorial contest between himself and Williams, which he could not win. But which also [was] fundamentally in contradiction to James's position that what was more important was the building of movements, not getting parties ready for election. You do not build a movement in six months, you do not build a movement in three years. Without the base of movement, but just with this notion that by some magic of personality there will be a spontaneous response of something called a mass [movement]—that was a fundamental error. When the gladiatorial show was over, the next move was departure.

P. B.: He answered my questions along the same line by emphasizing that up to this point Williams had always done what he said.

G. L.: But this was also a misjudgment. What he didn't understand but should have understood was that the Williams, in the relation of disciple and mentor, was not a Williams who exercised power. And the Williams he knew as the man who exercised power would not have the same relations that he had before. That was a misjudgment. But I think that James embodied, in a way, an attribute of a certain type of intellectual, that James believed in the force of ideas. If you were able to communicate ideas, ideas had the force of moving mass. And he had the overwhelming confidence in his capacity to make ideas function as a force. But you would find people in Trinidad who thought perhaps that had it been worked in a different way, the possibility existed that a serious left within the PNM could develop to challenge the authority of Williams, not on an individual basis of leadership but on a mass basis of what is to be the direction of this movement. Today the PNM is not a movement. It just became a party, came to office, supervised over the deterioration and demoralization of people, over the largest scale of corruption in the history of the country. Nobody really knows what will happen to the PNM after that sort of rejection.

P. B.: What about C. L. R.'s influence on Michael Manley?

G. L.: The influence in the case of Manley, who again could not be described as a Marxist, would be intellectually, of a Marxist persuasion, persuaded in some ways by the central ideas. James at that time [the late 1950s and early 1960s] was moving more and more back to his original base. James was arguing, almost evangelizing, about what he sees as the uniqueness of a Caribbean civilization having taken shape in this archipelago. That appeals to everybody in a certain way. And while this has not really been explored, the basis is there. You can follow the nature of the struggle for survival, to see how from point A or point B it is Cuba we are talking about or Guyana or Puerto Rico. You are going to find these correspondences between men who are trying to define the reality. It is unique in the history of human society, this is the point that is going to be, the uniqueness of something created here, waiting to be realized, to be elaborated.

That kind of message went home both to, on the one side, a political figure like Manley who does not only want to speak for Jamaica but to speak to the region, and that sort of message would have gone home on the other side to a certain type of academic who wants to give more than a provincial or parochial dimension to his area of inquiry of the Caribbean waiting to be explored and elaborated. I think that is what I mean by a pervasive influence. He did that, was able to do it, because of this *range* of curiosity. He was unusual.

James had a synoptic vision that was not exclusively based on the politics of victory. It was also concerned with what James thought was a unique sensibility in the Caribbean that would have to produce an unusual kind of literature, a unique sensibility that, if men started to work, would produce an unusual social science. It would not be the social science of metropolitan conventional institutions. It would [also have] a different kind of creative artist, a different kind of political activist. And that would come not by nature or by special gifts of God, but by the uniqueness in composition and formation of the society itself. That here was a society that probably did not have a precedent.

He has a view on the Caribbean and the Non-Aligned Movement that you have to have reservations about. James never really abandoned, to this day, in spite of all that has happened, the idea that the supreme good fortune of the Caribbean was its link to European civilization—that was the thing—and its link to what he would regard as the major languages. This is the problem of what we would call the Euro-centered James. And related to that, James believed that [link] gave the developed intellect in the region a very special advantage vis-à-vis something called the Third World, in the sense that it was universalized by the very nature of the European influence upon it. What he would mean is that if you had a Caribbean as one, a federated Caribbean as one, that region would have had the intellectual resources that could have been very decisive in its influence on African leadership. He means of course the case of [George] Padmore and [Kwame] Nkrumah, and that would multiply with whomever would be the Martinican equivalent of influence on French Africa and so forth. This is one of the things he would have in mind. There are people who would not buy that. People who say that the evolution of the African intellectual has its own interpretation of Europe was inevitable. There would be an African sensibility and an African mold of perceiving reality that would find serious deficiencies in the Caribbean.

That vision of Pan-Africanism is still there, it depends upon how you interpret it. Common historical experience links Africa and people from African descent, and that fundamental experience has been the European colonization, the experience of imperialism, and the struggle to dismantle it. Whether they come from English- or French-speaking Africa, English- or French-speaking Caribbean, there is that continuity as long as imperialism survives, a struggle that is qualitatively similar. They talk a common language, they are in that sense Pan-Africans. They have a lot of pooling in the exchange, [such as] the great influence that [Amilcar] Cabral had on Rodney's interpretation of Marx within the context of an underdeveloped society. Those linkages were there. Certain Afro-Americans have come to see the colonial dimension of their experience through their encounter with West Indians speaking about the colonial problem vis-à-vis European experience. I think that the concept of Pan-African movement of ideas is still very seminal.

P. B.: James's influence, not directly but indirectly, seemed to reach toward a new potential at the end of the 1970s and beginning of the 1980s.

G. L.: Between 1979 and 1983, there was an extraordinary idealism and enthusiastic boldness of commitment right through the region. Those four years did something to ignite and activate people in all kinds of fields. But the tragedy that [the Grenadan] Revolution took such a fall, it traumatized the left—and we have not yet quite recovered the meaning of that event.

P. B.: And what about the force described as the New Culture movement? How does it relate to James's political interpretations, over the years, of music and culture generally?

G. L.: Some of the most progressive responses to the neocolonial situation have come through the creative expression of music, from Jamaica to Trinidad. The dominance of Sparrow, Marley in the Eastern Caribbean. And the Rastafarian movement. Now that can be interpreted as a very conscious rejection of the established structures.

There are two forces at work in James, not only the mold of the Victorian. The point James used to make from time to time has now passed into general currency. Because of the size of islands, we did not have an experience of the kind of social distance that isolated any one element from the other. James was growing up as a middle-class boy, a schoolmaster's son, but he was looking out the window at working-class boys playing cricket. They were not five hundred miles away. This reciprocal influence across class lines was permanent and continuing. The greatest cricketers were the poorest boys. But there was an enormous reservoir of gifts of all kinds, locked up and fighting to break out of this artificial package. It's breaking out in the Marleys, breaking out in the Sparrows, breaking out in the Rastafarians, and then you see in a sense it's breaking out within the middle class, with the sons who are going communist and who don't want that whole bourgeois thing. I don't think it's a contradiction, there's an area of experience always influenced by the gifts of those from down below, whether in the area of sports or other areas of entertainments. And this was also capable of demonstrating itself in various forms of political leadership if the lid could be blown off.

What seems to be new is that there is an increasing awareness that the cultural act exists not only in the old petit-bourgeois sense, but united with a very strong force of liberation. Increasingly you find in the trade union movement, in political parties, that a political struggle—if it is really going to have a continuing vitality and sustenance—has always to have a cultural base and cultural expression. I don't know where you pinpoint "new," but it's stronger today than it would have been twenty-five or thirty years ago, and very much on the rise.

It is tied up with what is older. If you were speaking of nationalism, then you were speaking of some spirit, some distinctive quality, of the people, that could not really be respected if it were just a replication of political institutions and political forms which they had inherited from the imperial power. It would have to have an expression more distinctive than the political institutions were.

Even in the 1950s there was going to be among writers of a certain kind, [certain critical changes in] . . . what they call the novel and so on. They were not interested in the novel as such but a very different organization of narrative. You are writing prose narrative but it is not really connected to those established forms with a central character. For people like myself, [the novel] has no central character. It may be the place and not the person. There is a movement of presences and so on. What you have to deal with now is the pattern of that organization and not the old conventional forms of finding the point of causality from beginning to end. They may not be able to formulate it, but that conscious breakaway is even more evident in the verse, the poetry. So you have recently what is almost an abandonment of the text. (In dub poetry, the poet is performer to a large audience, to music.) Then in the theater, a very outstanding example, the Sistren Theatre [in Jamaica] which actually uses theater to document the domestic circumstances of workers, to document the workplace whether it is agriculture or these new branch plant industries and so on. There is a sense, a concept of the organic function of cultural expression. The intuitive link between this and the political ramifications is being worked out, and what is coming. So that is, I would say, very very much on the agenda.

I think that the immediate task is to regionalize that struggle, that cultural struggle. And to deal with what we have now. This is topic number one, even among people not thinking at the same level that we're talking at. People are becoming aware that the overwhelming dominance of North American mass culture will destroy the society if there is not what one would call a force of cultural resistance to that. A lot of cultural expression is now informed by that need to be a force of cultural resistance to that dominance. How do you capture the heads of people who become quite mesmerized by the images coming out. Today, 50 percent of Caribbean television is North American. There's not anything wrong with that but the nature of the product. It is stupifying its victims and, more dangerous, it creates a concept of consumerism and standard of living that is actually in conflict with the productive capacity of the society.

I think what we're trying to do is multidisciplinary. The compartmentalization has to be broken. What we do is to bring together those coming from very different occupational and intellectual experience to address a central one. We can bring together an economist and a theater person and ask, In what ways can theater serve strategies of national planning? You may do it with theater and the historian, In what ways can theater be put to the history that you are doing? These are the linkages we are seeking to make. My contribution has been to bring this kind of discussion into political organizations, to address political party conferences raising this theme. Bringing them onto the terrain of how do you conceive of sovereignty, how does your party conceive of cultural policy.

P. B.: And James's role in all this?

G. L.: I would say that the totality of James's life and work, as it came to be known in the Caribbean, assumed the role of a pervasive influence on all aspects of intellectual and social activity in the region. You then, perhaps, have to ask individual people in what way did that work. One is on quite safe ground to speak of it as a pervasive influence, there is no discussion within social science and so on: What you are going to do, what would be the new relations, what kind of social order, all of these discussions, how do you deal with the structures and institutions of a political movement in terms of leader and led since the political culture will not accept a concept of an elitist vanguard which is a head with a belly that is somewhere else. What is the university doing restructuring the intellectual environment—I don't think you could have a discussion on any area of this seriously in which he would not be quoted, without a reference to him. Not necessarily agreement, but how do we deal with the problem. That would be true of people whether they were right or left.

PART II
The Early
Trinidadian Years

▼▼▼▼▼

What little is known of James's early literary development—apart from his fiction—comes from a very few sources. Passages in *Beyond a Boundary* describe James and his friends very much in passing. The file of his circle's publications, *Trinidad* and *The Beacon*, offers a sense of his collaborators and the sensibility they shared. But much remains unexplored.

How was it possible for a writer to achieve such an extraordinary sensibility in a society with no apparent tradition of literary culture, no tertiary scholarly institutions of importance outside Queen's Royal College, and no prominent mentors?

Clearly, as a young writer C. L. R. James drew upon several powerful heritages. His mother's literary learning and interests were highlighted in *Beyond a Boundary*. Her influence gains new resonance in the interview included, which James granted about his family and his writing. By 1930, James had also been a schoolteacher, an amateur theatrical producer, and perhaps most important to his actual writing practice, a cricket reporter. Yet it is astonishing that he should have completed the novel *Minty Alley* by 1927 (although it saw print only nine years later) and that he should have written a handful of short stories with such boldness of subject and brilliant eye for detail. As his devotee and an important scholar of slavery, George Rawick, pointed out, James had learned a second culture which he combined with his own, making him "bifocal," intensely conscious of both. *

*Unpublished interview of Rawick by David Roediger, kindly lent us by the inter-

But in a breathtaking essay, Selwyn Cudjoe has also pointed to unrecognized sources that must have played an important role for James and his entire milieu. Later in life, James often reflected that he had just begun to understand what he could not have seen when the European models had suffused his aesthetic sense of tradition.[†] Through Cudjoe's illuminations, the Caribbean background and nature of James's work becomes, for the first time perhaps, demonstrable and decisive. We are too late for James himself to confirm the precise influences, but these efforts to fill in the missing spaces would have interested him immensely.

---

viewer. For a valuable reflection upon Rawick's work and influence inspired by James, see Don Fitz and David Roediger, eds., *Within the Shell of the Old . . . A Salute to George Rawick* (St. Louis: WD Press, 1990). Rawick's student, George Lipsitz, in turn has become the key explorer of multicultural "bi-focality," in the Jamesian tradition. See his *Time Passages* (Minneapolis: University of Minnesota Press, 1990).

[†]"Interview," in *C. L. R. James: His Life and Work*, 167.

Four

The Audacity of It All: C. L. R. James's
Trinidadian Background
Selwyn Cudjoe

▼▼▼▼▼

Time would pass, old empires would fall and new ones take their place,
the relations of countries and the relations of classes had to change, be-
fore I discovered that it is not quality of goods and utility which matter,
but movement; not where you are or what you have, but where you have
come from, where you are going and the rate at which you are getting
there.—C. L. R. James, Beyond a Boundary

Cyril Lionel Robert James, born in Tunapuna, Trinidad, West Indies
in 1901, emerged as one of the most distinguished intellectuals of the
twentieth century. In seeking to understand the manner in which James
developed, it is necessary to understand the social, cultural, and intellectual forces that shaped his life. When James arrived in London in 1932
at the age of thirty-one, he was already a mature individual. Although
he learned a lot in London, in his subsequent travels, his work with different organizations, and in meeting innumerable thinkers and workers
from throughout the world, the world of work and ideas that engrossed
him for more than the first third of his life continued to be important
to his overall development. Thus, if James's life spanned the twentieth
century, he was surely made by all the social, cultural, and political
forces that made nineteenth-century Trinidad, an examination of which
is important to understand the man and his work.

Sociohistorical Conditions

The socioeconomic environment from which James came was important in shaping the man he became. Like George Padmore and Sylvester
Williams, James came from the Tunapuna-Tacarigua-Arouca area, one of
the most economically advanced areas of nineteenth-century Trinidad.[1]
Tacarigua, which existed as a *encominenda* from 1674, continued to play
an important part in the economic development of the society well into
the twentieth century. Three years after Sir Ralph Abercromby captured
Trinidad for the English in 1797, the Tacarigua-Arouca area consisted of
fourteen sugar factories, the fourth-largest number in the country. There
were also nine light distilleries in the area and two coffee mills. The area
possessed the fourth-largest population of the society and, with the exception of the Naparimas, had the highest percentage of Africans of any
of Trinidad's communities.

From 1800 to 1900, Tacarigua emerged as one of the richest communities in the country. The Orange Grove Sugar Estates there likewise
emerged as one of the richest sugar estates in the country. The owner,
William Burnley, was one of the richest and most influential men in the
society and possessed approximately a thousand slaves.[2] When slavery
was abolished in 1833, Burnley received approximately £50,000 of the
£1,039,119 allocated by the British parliament as payment to the slave-
holders of Trinidad. Even after slavery was abolished, within the period
from 1835 to 1840, Burnley continued to profit from the colonial situation, making a profit of £28,275 within the period.[3] More importantly,
the Tacarigua-Tunapuna-Arouca enclave continued to possess the highest concentration of sugar estates in the island and also became one of
the most active areas politically.

When apprenticeship ended, Africans began to bargain with their
former masters for better wages and to develop their communities.[4] As a
result, Trinidad offered the highest wages in the British Caribbean during
the 1840s.[5] Not only were there empty lands for the asking, but there was
also a shortage of laborers. Because the Trinidadian legislature was controlled by planters, immigration became the primary way this shortage
was met. From 1839 to 1850, 10,278 West Indians, quite a few of them
from Barbados, immigrated to Trinidad, bringing with them innumerable
skills that would be used in the sugar industry and in society in general.
This trend in immigration continued for most of the second half of the
nineteenth century and, in the process, brought from Barbados both of

James's grandfathers. James notes that his maternal grandfather came to Trinidad around 1868. Of his paternal grandfather, he says, "[He] worked as a pan boiler on a sugar estate, a responsible job involving the critical transition of the boiling cane-juice from liquid into sugar. It was a post in those days usually held by white men. This meant that my grandfather had raised himself above the mass of poverty, dirt, ignorance and vice which in those far-off days surrounded the islands of black lower middle-class respectability like a sea ever threatening to engulf them."[6]

Through hard work, James's father went on to become a teacher. Although James eventually became a star pupil at Queen's Royal College, one of the leading schools on the island at the time, he also did his stint at one of the sugar estates in the area.[7]

The Cultural Dimension

The area to which James's grandparents came was characterized by a great deal of African (and later East Indian) cultural and social practices used to contest foreign rule and cultural hegemony on the island. Even though James alludes to the English periodicals that came to his home and his fascination with English literature, the influence of African religions and culture upon his life seems to have been elided in his attempt to demonstrate that he hadn't learned about European literature under "a mango tree." His silence in this area seems to have been a strategic move to deal with the more pressing problem of demonstrating how much the origins of his work are to be found within Western European thought and civilization.[8] Indeed, *Minty Alley*, the novel that James wrote before he went to England (even though it was published in England), does not deal with English characters such as he encountered in *Vanity Fair* or the other English novels he imbibed in Trinidad. Instead, it is set in the barrack-yards of Port of Spain, with characters who represent the element of society that held onto the indigenous cultural practices of the island. Whether or not James wished to acknowledge these influences, they played an important part in his development and need to be accounted for.

The second half of the nineteenth century in Trinidad was characterized by a fierce sense of nationalism manifested via cultural practices. Chief among these practices was the annual Carnival celebration which, until 1834, was confined to the upper class. After Emancipation, Carnival was taken over by the masses and for the remainder of the century became the dominant manifestation of popular culture. Official attempts from as early as 1857 to stop Carnival resulted in serious disturbances, the worst of which, the Canboulay riots, took place in 1881. According to Andrew Pearse, this confrontation resulted in "a pitched battle between the Police and the organised masqueraders, in which the interest of many groups within the community became involved, and which was a national issue of the greatest importance."[9] In fact, the 1881 riot demonstrated that Carnival had assumed a distinctive national character and possessed a great deal of social significance. Indeed, it was "the singers, drummers, dancers, stickmen, prostitutes, matadors, bad-johns, dunois, makos and corner-boys, that is to say the jamette class, who dominated carnival," and who were ready to defend their ways of life.[10]

In 1884, another important demonstration of the power of the people's culture, the Hosea riots, took place in San Fernando when the government passed legislation to confine the predominantly East Indian Hosea celebrations to the sugar estates and to prevent them from entering Port of Spain and San Fernando. The East Indians, together with a number of Africans, refused to accept these regulations. When they sought to enter San Fernando, police opened fire and killed twelve Indians and wounded more than a hundred persons.[11] Once more, another segment of the population showed its determination to express a particular experience and to defy the oppressor class.

These instances of cultural resistance demonstrated people's desire to control their destinies. Indeed, such defiance led in part to the movement for constitutional reform that began at the latter part of the 1880s and continued to the end of the century. When, therefore, the governor of the island suspended the Port of Spain city council in 1898 because its members would not allow themselves to be bullied, it took Norman Le Blanc, a calypsonian, to lead the attack against the government. Le Blanc sang: "Jerningham the governor, / It's a fastness in you, / It's a rudeness in you / To breakup the laws of the Borough Council."[12]

In fact, the second part of the nineteenth century became a time when ordinary Trinidadians came into their own and began to assert themselves through their cultural practices. James may have learned a lot through English periodicals, but a vibrant culture was taking shape on the island as society asserted its specificity and people spoke of the need to control their affairs. Although James chose not to mention the impact of such cultural influences, the entirety of his contribution suggests that he understood this culture's impact upon the shaping of his adult response to the world. At any rate, his response to and affection for the Mighty Sparrow demonstrated his understanding of the role that cultural resistance played in the development of society.

The Intellectual Dimension

By far the most decisive impact on James's early development was the vigorous intellectual life of Trinidad. One year before he left for England in 1932 he wrote the following encomium to Maxwell Phillip (1829–88), the first black solicitor general and creative writer of Trinidad:

> He went to school in San Fernando and there showed at once those two qualities which so distinguished him in afterlife—natural ability, and intense application. As a child he walked along the seashore and like Demosthenes, of whom he read, pitched his voice above the roar of the waves, to develop his powers of delivery. When he was fourteen his friends, recognising what he was worth, decided to give him an education and sent him to the Jesuit College at St. Mary's, Blairs, "on the bank of the Dee." There he stayed for six years, and his career is a lasting witness to the soundness and thoroughness of the Jesuit teaching. For Mr. Phillip was all his life an educated and scholarly man. There he learned Latin and Greek, French, Spanish and Italian, and a master of those languages he remained until the end. Like his great rival for intellectual primacy, Mr. Charles Warner, he read a few lines of the classics every morning of his life and so kept his knowledge fresh. His facility in French was perhaps not so extraordinary at the time when educated persons in Trinidad commonly spoke both languages; his powers in Spanish have already been indicated and there is the testimony of a Spanish priest who said that unlike so many people in Trinidad who spoke Spanish, Mr. Phillip's Spanish was that of a Spaniard. When he started to practise at the bar, seeing that Hindustani would be useful to him he soon mastered it. At St. Mary's too, he learnt the principles of the Roman Catholic religion, and was always a faithful servant of that Church. He was happy at school. When he built his house in Maraval, he called it Loyola, after St. Ignatius, the founder of that body of men who had given his mind information and direction.

He came back to Trinidad and entered the Solicitor's office. But in 1851 he raised some money and went back to Great Britain, this time to read for the bar.

While in England he had occasion to write his father asking for help. It seems that his father refused, or at least neglected the appeal and Maxwell Phillip never forgave him. It was about this time too that he wrote and published *Emmanuel Appadocca* which I shall write about on some future occasion.[13]

James ended his piece by noting that "perhaps the greatest of all creoles lie in the Lapeyrouse Cemetery."[14] James, it would seem, was intent on recognizing the intellectual brilliance of Maxwell Phillip, whose scholarly reputation was known throughout the Caribbean, and the contributions that he made to the development of jurisprudence in Trinidad.[15] Indeed, Phillip was regarded as "an authority upon all matters relating Spanish jurisprudence [in the island]."[16] Although James never wrote about Phillip's *Emmanuel Appadocca*, it is clear he was aware of the intellectual tradition that Phillip represented, a tradition that informed James's idea of the scholarly vocation. That is why when we speak of James's intellectual development it is well to note that he was a part of an intellectual tradition with strong roots in a society that prized learning and promoted a critical approach to scholarship. In suggesting that Phillip lay forgotten in Lapeyrouse Cemetery, James may have been thinking of the countless other black men who lay forgotten after making so many contributions to the intellectual development of their society.[17] Although he did not set out consciously to rectify that shameful neglect, his entire life demonstrated his commitment to Phillip's ideals: the development of natural ability, intense application to work, and commitment to intellectual excellence. Not that James saw intellectual excellence as an end in itself, but he recognized the ennobling qualities that the pursuit of the intellectual life produced and the importance of its application to the liberation struggle of working people.

Who, then, was Maxwell Phillip? As James noted, Phillip was the most distinguished Trinidadian jurist of the nineteenth century. In the course of his career, he became "one of the most prominent members of the bar, which was distinguished throughout the West Indies for its talent and ability."[18] He was an unofficial member of the Legislative Council, the mayor of Port of Spain, the solicitor general of the island, and acted on numerous occasions as attorney general of Trinidad. In the 1880s he turned down the opportunity to become the chief justice of Ghana (the Gold Coast), and in 1888 he proposed and carried forward the motion by which Trinidad and Tobago became a political unit.

In 1854, he published *Emmanuel Appadocca*, a book James promised to write about but never did. Although it is one of the most important historical romances of Trinidad (perhaps the only such Trinidadian work of the nineteenth century), the most important aspect of the book is why it was written in the first place. As Phillip noted, it was written in the aftermath of the U.S. government's passage of the Fugitive Slave Law in 1851, when black immigration into Trinidad was rife.[19] Phillip was aroused by the cruel manner in which African Americans were treated by their government.

> This work has been written at a moment when the feelings of the Author are roused up to a high pitch of indignant excitement, by a statement of the cruel manner in which the slave-holders of America deal with their slave-children. Not being able to imagine that even that dissolver of natural bonds—slavery—can shade over the heidousness [sic] of begetting children for the purpose of turning them out into the fields to labour at the lash's sting, he has ventured to sketch out the line of conduct, which a high-spirited and sensitive person would probably follow, if he found himself picking cotton under spurring encouragement of "Jimboes" or "Quimboes" on this own father's plantation.[20]

It is ironic that in 1843, Phillip went to London and studied at St. Mary's Catholic College, Blairs, Scotland. In 1849, he returned to Trinidad, spent two years, and then returned to London in 1851. Upon his arrival, he heard about the passage of the Fugitive Slave Law and, without ever traveling to the United States, decided to write a romance to instruct African Americans on how to respond to slavery. Phillip certainly wanted African Americans to know that the people of the Caribbean felt a similar repugnance against slavery and shared in the solidarity of their cause.

It is instructive to contrast Phillip's behavior with James's some eighty years later. In James's case, he had read virtually nothing about Marxism–Leninism before he departed for London in 1932. However, he went to London, read Karl Marx's *Communist Manifesto*, joined the Trotskyist Party, and within three years (together with some friends) wrote a manu- script that condemned the behavior of Stalin on the grounds that Stalin's

Marxism was not in keeping with the tenets of Marx or Lenin. When asked why he wrote the book, James declared calmly, "no one else wanted to write it."[21] He had never seen the Soviet Union but felt comfortable enough to offer advice to his comrades there and to demonstrate his solidarity.[22] This "bold-faceness" (perhaps audaciousness) would characterize the behavior of other Trinidadian intellectuals as they worked their way across the world stage and contributed to world understanding. Phillip and James were cut from the same cloth.[23]

For James, however, the example of Maxwell Phillip was important for two reasons. Apart from establishing that there was a long intellectual tradition in Trinidad and Tobago of which James would be an important part eventually, it also demonstrated that from early in the island's social development Trinidadian intellectuals were never merely inward-looking but were propelled by contemporary intellectual currents to look outward, a fact that goes back to the beginning of the nineteenth century.[24]

Another important Trinidadian intellectual of the nineteenth century was John Jacob Thomas. As Phillip was writing *Emmanuel Appadocca*, Lord Harris, governor of Trinidad (1846–54), was putting in place a free primary educational system for the island. Thomas, a contemporary of Phillip's and something of an intellectual guide of James's, would receive the rudiments of his primary education from this system. In 1858, Thomas entered a normal school in Woodbrook and two years later became the principal of the ward school in Savonetta in the ward of Couva. In 1866, Thomas took the civil service examination, topped the list of students, and was appointed third locker clerk in the Receiver-General's Office in 1867. By 1869, this self-taught man was made secretary to both the board of education and the council of Queen's Collegiate School, the college James attended. His training, however, had prepared him to understand the educational system and the attempts of the colonial polity to impose its values upon an evolving colonial society.

In 1869, two events had important impacts upon the direction of the social and cultural practices of Trinidad. The first was the publication of the Kenan Report, a document that arose from the desire of Governor Arthur Gordon (1866–70), to examine the educational system of Trinidad and to shape it to fit the needs of the colonial power. A systematic critique, the Kenan Report became the intellectual instrument that shaped the development of society for much of the rest of the nineteenth century. Until that time, the laws of Trinidad were predominantly Spanish, a majority of people spoke a French patois, and Roman Catholicism was the predominant religion of the ruling class (in fact, a violent struggle was occurring between Roman and English Catholicism), whereas African religious and cultural practices were preferred at the bottom of society. The aim of the colonial authorities, via the Kenan Report, was to Anglicize society as quickly as possible.

While Gordon was busy receiving Kenan's report, Thomas published *The Theory and Practice of Creole Grammar*, the second important event of 1869. It may be too much of a leap of the imagination to interpret Thomas's action as a conscious response to Gordon's action, yet one cannot read *Theory and Practice of Creole Grammar* without recognizing it as a counterdiscourse—in fact, it was a direct challenge to Gordon's official attempts. Whatever Thomas's hidden agenda, it is clear that he saw the value and integrity of the language of the masses and sought to recognize it properly by making it respectable. In addition, by recognizing the distilled wisdom in folk language, Thomas indicated the presence of a philosophical apparatus through which the masses interpreted the world. He felt so strongly about this matter that at the time of his death in 1889 he was preparing a second, enlarged edition of the text, to be called *Gramme Creyol: Being the Theory and Practice of Creole Grammar*. In it, he intended to include "an entirely new system of spelling, an historical and philological survey, more proverbs and examples of Creole from Haiti and New Orleans, Martinique and Mauritius."[25]

Apart from his philological work, Thomas also involved himself in shaping the literary and cultural production of his society by participating actively in the literary life of Trinidad in the 1870s. He was the secretary of the *Trinidad Monthly*, the first known literary journal of the country, that appeared sporadically in 1871 and 1872, spearheaded the formation of the Trinidad Athenaeum, a literary society that arose in 1872, and later edited the *Trinidad Review*, another literary magazine.

Given his vast energies and many talents, Thomas was one of the many Trinidadians who felt the need to organize and preserve the cultural bounty of their society. He collected local folk songs and wrote a manuscript on slavery, which unfortunately were not published. When, therefore, James Anthony Froude, Regius Professor of Modern History at Oxford and "one of the greatest intellectuals of this time," published *The English in the West Indies* in 1887, a work that sought to diminish the achievements of black people in the Caribbean, Thomas was poised exquisitely to respond. Not only was Thomas more aware than

Froude of the Caribbean and African-American situation, but according to James he also demonstrated "a social conception and a historical
method, which was vastly superior to that of the highly educated and
famous English historian and writer."[26]

James learned two things from Thomas. First, history possesses "a
controlling LAW." As James noted, if one had no sense of historical law,
then anything one chose to speak about "becomes not only non-sense,
i.e. has no sense, but is usually a defense of property and privilege, which
is exactly what Froude . . . made it."[27] Second, for James, Thomas was the
quintessential West Indian intellectual (as James entitled his introduction to *Froudacity*), the one person who represented the highest intellectual ideal and achievement of West Indian society in the nineteenth
century. But, as James pointed out so carefully:

> The work of John Jacob Thomas, the Trinidad schoolmaster, with-
> out European or university education of any kind, shows that the
> impact which the West Indian writers, our writers of fiction and
> the politicians and political writers of the day, have made upon the
> consciousness of the civilization of Western Europe and the United
> States, is the result not of the work of certain brilliant individual
> men, but is due in reality to our historical past, the situation in
> which our historical past has placed us. This historical situation has
> produced a particular type of social and intellectual activity which
> we can define as West Indian. This is what I think we can learn
> definitely from this book.[28]

In this context, it would be useful to contrast Thomas's behavior with
Phillip's and James's. Here was an obscure headmaster from an obscure
village in Trinidad, without the benefit of a formal education, taking on
one of the most respectable English intellectuals of the time and, if we
are to accept James's analysis (and I do), besting this English professor
at what he did best—interpreting historical data. One can only wonder
at the audacity of it all. Yet, that was James's genius; he understood that
Thomas was a product of a particular social system and body of ideas. In
the Appendix to *The Black Jacobins* James discusses with even greater
clarity the specifics of the West Indian personality.[29]

The last example of this important intellectual tradition to which
James was indebted comes from the novel of A. R. F. Webber, a Toba-
gonian who emigrated to Guyana in 1899 and wrote, among other works,
Those That Be in Bondage, the first novel of Trinidad and Tobago, before

his untimely death in 1932. More importantly, Webber was one of the earliest socialists in the Caribbean. He accompanied Hubert Crichlow, the father of West Indian trade-unionism, to London in 1930 and dedicated his life to struggling for the rights of the working people of Guyana and the Caribbean. He also led the fight for self-government and the freedom of the press in Guyana and worked actively toward bringing the Caribbean together as one political unit. Long before James discussed the problems of the negative influence of the colonial expatriate in the Caribbean in *The Case for West Indian Self-Government*, Webber addressed that theme in *Those That Be in Bondage*. Phillip did the same in *Emmanuel Appadocca*. James may not have read Webber's work, but he certainly was aware of Webber's activity because Webber was an active colleague of Arthur Cipriani, C. D. Rawle, and T. A. Marryshow, all active participants in the struggle for West Indian self-government. More important, together with Cipriani and Tito Achong, Webber addressed a massive meeting on these matters in 1926 at the Princes Building in Port of Spain; a meeting James must have known about given his political inclination and his interest in the life of Captain Cipriani.

Yet, the important thing about Webber's novel was its philosophical resonances that were to reappear (perhaps re-echo) in James's philosophical works. In his review of *Those That Be in Bondage*, Wilson Harris, one of the leading minds of the Caribbean, observes two major tendencies in Webber's novel. First, he identifies Webber's place in the intellectual tradition of Trinidad and the psychological aspect of "bondage."

When one reflects on the distinguished body of writing that has come from Trinidadian-born authors who include C. L. R. James, Alfred Mendes, Ralph de Boissiere, V. S. Naipaul, Samuel Selvon, Earl Lovelace and others one looks to the "first" in such a faculty of design for seeds of impulse both ominous and instructive within the medium of the twentieth century that spans areas of colonialism and post-colonialism, empires and revolutions.

Webber's vision of "bondage"—though apparently rooted in political and economic legacies—is determined by a psychology of fate, fate so restrictive that the characters in his novel seem unable to breach certain formulae, certain structures of ornament. Ornament therefore—in the guise of public school "chivalry" or transparent, escapist convention—becomes the decoy of frenzy or unconscious/subconscious violence built into the body politic. The morality of

the plantation is as ineffectual as the morality of protest in which
the rebel Karin [one of the characters of the novel] is involved like a
blind puppet.[30]

Second, Harris notes the "associative parallels" between Herman Melville's *The Confidence Man* and *Those That Be in Bondage* and then
argues that St. Aldwyn, another character in Webber's novel, "may well
be the first appearance of the trickster in written West Indian literature in the twentieth century. . . . For the role of the trickster, as it
emerges here, possesses a parallel with anancy, folkloric constellation,
part-saviour, part-nihilist." Harris then examines the several allusions
in the text to the "great Napoleon":

> Such allusions may have appeared idiosyncratic until St. Aldwyn
> reinforces the pattern by speaking of the Kaiser of Germany and
> prophesying in the year 1913 on the river steamer in the Demerara
> River where he saves Harold [the major protagonist of the work],
> that the "fiercer wills of the Nihilists" will prevail over "the lovable
> soul of the Czar of Russia."
>   It is the trickster apparition of St. Aldwyn which jolts us into per-
> ceiving a strand in the novel that subsists upon a dark sometimes
> flamboyant admiration for Napoleonic and Czarist figures of destiny.
> That such "masters" are inherently doomed yet remain a source of
> hero-worship tells us something about the convention of the novel,
> the conventional dress or restricted ambience, in which the eruptive
> capacity of the trickster to stand outside rigged institutions, rigged
> ceremonies, etc., etc., becomes hypothetical if not an illusion.[31]

In what way, then, did Webber anticipate James? It seems to me that
James's work suggests that after he completed *The Invading Socialist
Society* in 1947 he had not quite annihilated the ideas of Trotsky and
Trotskyism. He had dealt more with the practical, polemical matters
that arose in his day-to-day conflicts with Trotskyism, but not with the
source of the conflict. To do so, he had to go back to Hegel and Marx
and to the origins of dialectical thinking. As far as James saw it, the rise
of Nazism and the specter of Stalinism had driven the world into confusion. Civilization was in crisis, the world was without direction, and
bourgeois theorists could show no direction. James responded through
his most important theoretical works, "Dialectical Materialism and the

Fate of Humanity" and *Notes on Dialectics* (1948). I will confine my remarks to the former essay.

Written at a time when the twin scourges of Nazism and Stalinism had left their imprint upon the world, a philosophical work such as "Dialectical Materialism and the Fate of Humanity" was needed more than ever to assist in understanding the general crisis of humanity. In it, James sets forth his attack against Stalinism and the Nazi state apparatus. He argues that, for Marxists, "the fundamental logical law is the contradictory nature of all phenomena and first of all human society. The dialectic teaches that in all forms of society we have known, the increasing development of material wealth brings with it the increasing degradation of the large mass of humanity. Capitalism, being the greatest wealth-producing system so far known, has carried his contradiction to a pitch never before known. Thus it is that the moment when the world system of capitalism has demonstrated the greatest productive power in history is exactly the period when barbarism threatens to engulf the whole of society."[32] Because Nazism and Stalinism were in fact the negation of democracy, they had to be destroyed. In philosophical terms, they had to be negated by the proletarian revolution or socialism achieved the inevitability of the negation of the negation, the third and most important law of the dialectic, according to James. The history of the working-class movement had prepared the world for such an inevitability.

Webber never dreamed of working out this problematic in such advanced detail (he could not), but Harris's point is that embedded in what he calls "the faculty of design" of that early Trinidadian novel is the capacity to see, perhaps anticipate, Nazism and Stalinism. For James, West Indian creative writers always saw far beyond anything that historians or the politicians could see. West Indians, he argued, were "a modern people," and its authors carried within them those seeds of modernity.

It seems to me that a few conclusions can be drawn from such intellectual activity. (1) In Trinidad and Tobago in the nineteenth and early twentieth centuries there existed an active intellectual tradition that sought to interpret the social and cultural experiences of its people. (2) Although these thinkers were aware of the inner complexities of their society, they always looked outward to understand the larger design of things. (3) They were not afraid to take on the mighty minds of the time and make their views known. (4) Their interests spanned the globe: slavery in the United States, rabid negrophobia among some British intellectuals, and a groping to understand the laws of social development as they understood them within the context of their history and their time.

James situated himself within these intellectual currents and drew upon this legacy when he began to interpret and understand Trinidad and, later, the world beyond. Although Phillip, Thomas, and Webber traveled the world (Phillip to England and Europe, Thomas to England, and Webber to England and the United States), they all returned to their societies. James's sojourn lasted much longer and spanned a larger world. Even though he returned occasionally to Trinidad (he tried to settle there at the end of his life), the Trinidadian society of the 1980s had become too small for him. Indeed, his oeuvre reflects the breadth of his travel, his radical departure from the concerns of his literary ancestors, and his more systematic engagement with some of the central issues of his time.

Like Phillip, Thomas, and Webber, James remained a self-educated person. In fact, much of the burden of *Beyond a Boundary* revolves around a discussion of a young colonial who is determined to educate himself in his own way despite the wishes of his parents and teachers. This truism holds for James, Phillip, Thomas, and Webber. Indeed, this capacity for self-development and the bold desire to pursue the truth remained a major preoccupation of these early intellectuals. As James noted, when he arrived in London in 1932, politics and political associations were the furthest things from his mind. However, two months after his arrival he unearthed the signs of his future direction after talks with Sir Learie Nicholas Constantine, the famous West Indian cricketer with whom he lived during those early years in Nelson, Lancashire. As he describes his early relationship with Constantine: "Up to that time [1932] I doubt if he and I had ever talked for five consecutive minutes on West Indian politics. Within five weeks we had unearthed the politician in each other. Within five months we were supplementing each other in working partnership which had West Indian self-government as its goal."[33]

James may have known very little about the world that he was about to enter when he left Queen's Royal College in 1916, but his early life in Trinidad had fostered a particular way of looking at the world. Moreover, the basic impulse of his early education pushed him to his ultimate political position: making the world more responsive to the demands of the disinherited. In time, he learned to see the choice facing humanity as one between socialist humanism or capitalist barbarism, a truism that seems to ring true even in the heady happenings of today's world. As Samir Amin notes in *Eurocentrism*:

Eurocentrism has led the world into a serious impasse. If the West remains locked into the position that it has dictated in every area of political relationships, most notably North-South and East-West relationships, the risks of violent conflicts and of an increase in brutal racist positions will grow. A more humane future—one that is universalist and respectful of all—is not an ineluctable necessity, destined to impose itself; it is only an objectively necessary possibility, for which one must strive. The option remains true and thus necessarily socialist universalism or Eurocentric capitalist barbarism.[34]

James arrived at this point long before Amin. His entire education propelled him toward the recognition of this truth. He would have understood only too well the events that are taking place in socialist countries and South Africa. After all, he predicted these transformations long before anyone else did. However, it was deep within the bosom of his society, in the struggles of his people and their constant quest for dignity, where his response to his world was shaped and where he was prepared for the work he undertook for most of the twentieth century.

Notes

1   Tacarigua, one of the first four *encomiendas* under the Spanish system, had existed since 1674. The villages of Tunapuna and Arouca arose quickly after the period of apprenticeship (1838) and were settled by former slaves. As Donald Woods notes, "In the closing months of 1846, surveyors were laying out lots around its [Arouca's] central savannah which was kept as common land, like the village greens in England. These were the first planned townships after emancipation." *Trinidad in Transition* (London: Oxford University Press, 1968), 94.

2   In *The Loss of El Dorado* (New York: Vintage Books, 1984) V. S. Naipaul describes (338) the manner in which Burnley made his fortune. Arriving in Trinidad penniless around 1810, he began to lay the foundation of his wealth by plundering widows and orphans. Most of the money collected from the estates of the men who died on the island began to disappear. According to Naipaul, "All property in dispute and all dead men's estates and moneys had been passing into the hands of an official called the despositario. Since [George] Smith's [a kind of chief justice] arrival property worth £180,000 had so passed, and only £4,000 had been given back. The despositario was a young man called William Burnley."

3   See Selwyn R. Cudjoe, *Movement of the People* (Ithaca: Calaloux, 1983), 97–120 for a discussion of the social and economic development of Tacarigua from 1800 to 1850.

4   See William Burnley, *Observations on the Present Condition of the Island of*

Trinidad (London: Longman, Brown, Proudhon, Green and Longmans, 1842), for a discussion of this question.

5   Woods, *Trinidad in Transition*, 59.

6   C. L. R. James, *Beyond a Boundary* (New York: Pantheon, 1983), 17.

7   James, *Beyond a Boundary*, 23.

8   "Discovering Literature in Trinidad: The 1930s," in C. L. R. James, *Spheres of Existence* (Westport: Lawrence Hill, 1980), 238.

9   Andrew Pearse, "Carnival in the Nineteenth Century," in *Trinidad Carnival* (Port of Spain: Paria, 1988), 30.

10   Pearse, "Carnival," 39. It is important to note that Carnival (or "the culture of carnival," as I call it in another context) possesses a literary dimension. As I have noted elsewhere, "verbal compositions, [that is] the calypso, the parodies of the official life, the robber talk of the midnight robbers, the language of the stick fighters, and so on" constitute the literary elements of Carnival. See Selwyn R. Cudjoe, *V. S. Naipaul: A Materialist Reading* (Amherst: University of Massachusetts Press, 1988), 248.

11   See Eric Williams, *A History of the People of Trinidad and Tobago* (Port of Spain: PNM Publishing, 1962), 187–90 for a discussion of these disturbances.

12   Quoted in Williams, *A History of the People*, 180.

13   C. L. R. James, "Michel Maxwell Phillip: 1829–1888," in *From Trinidad*, ed. Reinhard W. Sander (New York: Africana Publishing, 1978), 254–45.

14   James, "Michel Maxwell Phillip," 269.

15   See the biographical sketches of Phillip in the second edition of *Emmanuel Appadocca* (Port of Spain: Mole, Brother, 1883), v–viii, and Bridget Brereton, "Michel Maxwell Phillip (1829–1888): Savant of the Centurion," *Antillia* 1 (April 1989): 6–20.

16   Phillip, *Emmanuel Appadocca*, vi. Although Trinidad was wrested from the Spanish in 1799, Spanish law was retained well into the nineteenth century.

17   See, for example, James's comment on Chief Justice Conrad Reeves of Barbados, whom he felt was "a very distinguished" West Indian whom should be known about. "But," he concluded, "we don't bother about these things, we continue to learn about [David] Pitt and [William] Wilberforce and Gladstone and Joseph Conrad and God knows who else, but we don't pay attention to our own people. Conrad more than ever is a very important character, at least in West Indian history." John Jacob Thomas, *Froudacity: West Indian Fables by James Anthony Froude* (London: New Beacon, 1969), 36.

18   Phillip, *Emmanuel Appadocca*, v.

19   Donald Woods, *Trinidad in Transition: The Years After Slavery* (London: Oxford University Press, 1968), 66–68.

20   Maxwell Phillip, *Emmanuel Appadocca: Or, the Blighted Life*, 1st ed., vol. 1 (London: Charles J. Skeet, 1854).

21   Author interview with C. L. R. James, May 1983.

22   C. L. R. James, *World Revolution, 1917–1936* (Nendeln: Kraus Reprint, 1970).

23   In an interesting interchange with John Bracey, Jr., St. Clair Drake speaks of what he calls James's "West Indian arrogance": "I think in dealing with Africans and with Afro-Americans there has been, among those old-timers way back, a bit of

what I call West Indian arrogance, and for all of C. L. R. James's great qualities he has a bit of this too." George Shepperson and St. Clair Drake, "The Fifth Pan-African Conference, 1954 and the All People's Congress, 1958," *Contributions in Black Studies: A Journal of African and Afro-American Studies* 8 (1986–87): 57.

24 See, for example, Naipaul, *The Loss of El Dorado*, and J. B. Phillipe, *Free Mulatto* (London, 1824, repr. Port of Spain: Paria, 1987).

25 Thomas, *Froudacity*, 21.

26 Ibid., 27, 26.

27 Ibid., 32; see also Wilson Harris's response to James's interpretation of Thomas's position. Harris argues that "Thomas does not really overwhelm Froude. The duel which they fought is nevertheless a very instructive one in pointing up the historical stasis which afflicts the West Indian sensibility and which may only be breached in complex creative perspectives for which the historical convention would appear to possess no criteria." Wilson Harris, *History, Fable and Myth in the Caribbean and Guianas* (Georgetown: National History and Arts Council, Ministry of Education and Culture, 1970), 8.

28 Harris, *History, Fable and Myth*, 27.

29 See *The Black Jacobins* (New York: Vintage, 1962). As James notes in the Appendix: "Wherever the sugar plantation and slavery existed, they imposed a pattern. It is an original pattern, not European, not African, not a part of the American main, not native in any conceivable sense of that word, but West Indian, *sui generis*, with no parallels anywhere else" (391–92).

30 Wilson Harris, "A. R. F. Webber," *Callaloo* (forthcoming).

31 Harris, "A. R. F. Webber."

32 James, *Spheres of Existence*, 72.

33 James, *Beyond a Boundary*, 120.

34 Simir Amin, *Eurocentrism* (New York: Monthly Review Press, 1989), 151–52.

Five
The Making of a Literary Life
C. L. R. James interviewed
by Paul Buhle
▼▼▼▼▼

[*This dialog combines several conversations in Brixton, London, during May and September 1987.*]

P. B.: Did you ever have any doubt about dedicating *Minty Alley* to your mother?

C. L. R.: No doubt. She was the *center* of my life. I followed literature because of her. When she put a book down I picked it up. She was an unusual woman, who in 1900, at the beginning of the century, was reading every book she could put her hands on. She was an educated person, in literary matters and in the social world. She spoke good English and she wrote it. There was no trace of vulgarity. She had a certain style and elegance which she had learned, and which she transferred to me. My brother didn't have it at all.

P. B.: Did she encourage your first writing?

C. L. R.: When I was a small boy, no more than seven or eight, I wrote stories, and she didn't encourage but she thought it was good for me to be doing that. Once I started to write and publish, she was very interested, and collected the material, and kept me going at it.

P. B.: Was she more encouraging than your father?

C. L. R.: My father was a philistine of note. He said, "That is all very well, but what money?" He was cautious because the government paid you and then, the important thing was when you reach a certain age, you get a pension. And if you didn't you were lost. The brown skin might do it but the black man had better get a government post. My father thought that was the correct thing to do, and I should follow that always. But my mother said, "Leave him alone, the boy going this way." And when [my writing] began to gain recognition abroad, she told my father, "You see!"

p. b.: She helped you through your early years as a professional writer?

c. l. r.: Without her, I didn't know what would have happened to me. Because in those dark days, she said go ahead and she insisted that I be encouraged. She passed me some money and said, "Go on boy." She supported me all through. My father said "Well, where are you going?" I began writing not what the public wanted but my own. He didn't like the writing business too much, but if I was going to write, I should write something that the newspapers would accept. But I was doing this individual work, and my mother said, "No. He wants to write." And passed a few dollars to me on the quiet.

p. b.: Was she scandalized by the sexual themes and language in your early fiction?

c. l. r.: She wasn't scandalized. She said it's not impropriety. The boy [is] not advocating. He's saying, "This is what happened."

p. b.: Did she ever offer criticisms?

c. l. r.: One of the stories, she told me, was merely imitating an English author. Before I wrote and was successful, one of the early ones. She said this is merely that one transferred to Trinidad.

p. b.: What did she think of *Minty Alley*?

c. l. r.: She was very pleased. She thought it was fine. She read it and she was very pleased. To write for black people in the Caribbean was a distinction. And here was I writing well, and she was very pleased. But she wasn't one to get excited.

p. b.: She followed your career abroad?

c. l. r.: She'd send messages—write me a letter, How are you and so on. But she made it clear—while I was pursuing this, which nobody else was doing, to be a Caribbean writer—she insisted, he wants to go that way, let him go, while my father turned up his nose and said, "Why doesn't he become a teacher?"

She took ill and died. But she had the satisfaction that I was writing and not taking part in the struggle for material things. She insisted that I be supported. And she was able in time to realize that I had made good. I was established in Britain and the United States before she died.

p. b.: Was she sympathetic to the political writings, *Captain Cipriani* and *Black Jacobins*?

c. l. r.: She was sympathetic to everything that I did.

p. b.: Let's talk a little about the 1920s. You say very little in *Beyond a*

Boundary about that period in your life, as if your personal life is absent from age twenty to thirty. What were you doing with your time?

C. L. R.: Reading books, that's what I was doing. Literature and history. And I not only read as the ordinary West Indian read, but I went to the library and found all sorts of books on history and classical studies. Somebody had put all the books there. When they asked, I don't know who it was, to make a list for the library, he put a classical list in there and then no one used to read them. I came and saw them and began to read and I read everything and I had a fantastic memory so that in time, before long, when anyone in Trinidad wanted to know something about literature, they came to me. James was the man. [Also] I was teaching practically after I left college. I was teaching at a high school. Then I went over to Queen's Royal College.

P. B.: Did you find teaching satisfying?

C. L. R.: I found it rather exhausting. But I couldn't leave it alone. What happened was, contact with the students and other teachers who looked upon me as somebody who could give them information which the average person didn't have. So I was pressed from these sides to keep going and gathering [material].

P. B.: Did you teach West Indian history at all?

C. L. R.: Yes, I was one of the pioneers in that field. Insisting that there *was* a West Indian history. I didn't gather much of it together, but what there was, I said, we have to do.

P. B.: Was there resistance to that idea?

C. L. R.: No, there wasn't resistance. There was indifference, to begin with, but among some of the younger people coming up, they grabbed onto it and went on. Oh yes.

P. B.: Was it a struggle to live on the salary?

C. L. R.: No. After a time, they paid me well. They looked upon me as an exceptional person. Everybody knew that if I had worked at it I would have won a scholarship and gone away to England. But I stayed here and was the person to whom they applied for knowledge of literature, history, local history and so forth. I was very much considered and offered ample opportunity to do something. And when there was money to be made they came to me and said, "James." I was someone young who they fancied to help them.

P. B.: This is the period when you met Eric Williams?

C. L. R.: He was in short pants. He was fighting for a scholarship, and I coached him.

P. B.: And what did you do on weekends?

C. L. R.: In a typical weekend I was playing cricket. Saturday, regularly and Sunday. I was a fanatic you see. And during the football season I continued to play cricket while playing football. So those are the games that I played and the books that I read. Reading and playing cricket and football.

P. B.: Were you interested in music?

C. L. R.: I was very curious. I was a classical man, but I was a calypso man too. And I was the first one to write an essay, saying all that calypso, that is music, it's ours. I'm very pleased about that.

P. B.: You had a record player to listen to music?

C. L. R.: In the 1920s I had a little box, a gramophone. I was listening to DeBussey, Mozart's piano concerto and so on.

P. B.: Were there records by calypsonians?

C. L. R.: The records of calypsonians mostly came later, but I picked up those fairly early, too. One or two people had them made and they gave me copies. They were not publicly sold until later.

P. B.: Did you have any friends among the Calypsonians?

C. L. R.: They came to me and talked to me all the time, because I was the one who wrote about them. And I said, "Look, these people are artists, local artists." So they came to talk, to tell me, and I would talk to them and go and hear them. That was quite something in those days. Alfred Mendes followed along. He had money you know.

P. B.: Did you listen to American jazz records at his house?

C. L. R.: We heard them, yes, we heard everything. Particularly Louis Armstrong was one of my favorites.

P. B.: Did you dance?

C. L. R.: My brother, he could dance. When he danced people danced around him looking at him and some of them would stop and he could be in a corner dancing and they would surround him and the girls [thought] a dance with him was really something. I wasn't distinguished as a dancer. But I danced and was swept away by the calypso as everyone else, it was quite a sensation.

I was very unusual in that although I was a man of literature and music of the classical style, I used to go to the tents and hear calypso and write about it. That was a duality no one had done before. I started it and the rest followed.

P. B.: How did you come to know Captain Cipriani? Did he encourage you to take part in his political activity?

C. L. R.: No he didn't. I was regarded as a literature person. And furthermore I was in public service. It was unwise for me to. [But] I was the person they could depend upon. Everybody knew I was sympathetic to them. They used to think that James was a very bright boy. When they wanted a piece of writing they came to me and that was an understanding. James was part of the movement, he didn't put himself forward, but he was part. Cipriani would come to me and ask me what about this and so on. I would speak on behalf of the movement.

P. B.: Did you ever speak publicly?

C. L. R.: I would speak, yes, I wouldn't be aggressive with it, but when I got up to speak everybody knew that I was supporting Cipriani and he accepted that. I would say that man Cipriani, he is the man who has our future. Oh yes.

P. B.: Did you write for *The Labour Leader*?

C. L. R.: I wrote for the paper, but about sport. I wrote one or two things. [Later] I went into it and said, "Mr. Cipriani, I would like to write about you," and he said, "By all means." And he [gave] me all the material and I wrote the biography of Captain Cipriani after I went to England, but he had sponsored it.

P. B.: When you became political, you left behind the idea for a novel about the West Indies that you never wrote. What would have been the plot?

C. L. R.: It would have been my school days, my father teaching me in the elementary school, then I go to QRC, then I became a teacher in secondary schools. My life, but it would have been different because when my father began, we lived in the country. So I would be describing life in the country and the people there, and then he came to Port of Spain, and I came to Port of Spain and life at QRC. And then I left that and became a part of the life of the black middle class. So it might seem to be my personal life, but in reality it would have been different stages of the form of existence of black people in the Caribbean.

P. B.: Do you regret that you weren't able to write that novel?

C. L. R.: I don't regret but I am sorry. I am not miserable about it because I left all this writing to take part in political activity.

P. B.: Did you have the least inkling in the 1920s that you would become *primarily* a political figure?

C. L. R.: None, none whatever.

PART III
Textual Explorations

▼▼▼▼▼

In this section, we enter theoretical territories of a different nature and of more recent discovery. Poststructuralist readings of James and other anti-colonial writers such as Fanon have raised or perhaps sharpened many new problems of interpretation. In the past, discourses about these writers were read primarily in Marxist, nationalist, and racial terms. But with the general passing of colonialism and the ensuing crisis of the Third World, the post-colonial states's monopolization of definitions of freedom, justice, and cultural and racial identity have been increasingly difficult to maintain.

A newer academic discourse has proceeded with a radical uncoupling of liberation and self-definition from the projects of the post-colonial nation-state. This divorce has also prompted rejections of the notions of race, freedom, identity, and political praxis which legitimated the birth of the same state. The works of Edward Said, Gayatri Chakravorty Spivak, Homi Bhabha, Neil Lazarus, Paul Gilroy, Sylvia Wynter, and Sandra Drake, among others, contain plentiful examples of this approach.

Separated from strategic and ideological confines of nationalist mobilization, the concepts of popular democracy, gender, and racial identity are emancipated, free to be reconstituted and redeployed. They gain status, with the above critics, as open signifiers, semio-linguistic constructions with capacities for play and reorientation that must not be monopolized by elites but instead freely used by pluralities of popularly constituted groups. Against this backdrop of open signifiers rather than (and opposed to) the nation-state, political praxis can be thematized.

And yet no simple, straightforward road opens to an awaiting higher truth. The turn away from the state and toward the realm of language and signifiers could not have been conceived without structuralism and post-structuralism. The two approaches have provided theoretical bases for identifying and analyzing signifiers. This intellectual shift is particularly relevant for a reading of James. Noted post-Marxists such as Cornelius Castoriadis and Jean-François Lyotard were in fact key intellectuals in the 1950s French group *Socialisme ou Barbarie*, which shared a common political orientation and fraternal contacts with James's Detroit-based Correspondence and Facing Reality organizations. Castoriadis and Lyotard, along with Jean Baudrillard and Michel Foucault, have been major figures in the uncoupling of liberation projects from the familiar Marxist formulation and their theoretical recasting on the model of the open signifier.*

The essays by Wynter and Lazarus deftly apply the semiotic approach to a number of James's texts. In doing so they demonstrate the remarkable openness of these texts by revealing the creative tension within their Marxist assumptions. This openness, so rare in older Marxist thinkers and so appealing in James, has prompted critic Sandra Drake to identify James as a precocious postmodernist.† In the essay by Henry and Buhle the mode of analysis has been reversed: an evaluation of the post-structuralist reading of post-colonial discourses is attempted through the Jamesian mirror.

*This is not to say that James agreed with the *political* evolution of Castoriadis and Lyotard after the 1950s.
†Sandra Drake, *Wilson Harris and the Modern Tradition: A New Architecture of the World* (Westport, Conn.: Greenwood 1986).

Six

*Beyond the Categories of the
Master Conception: The Counterdoctrine
of the Jamesian Poiesis
Sylvia Wynter*

▼▼▼▼▼

C. L. R. James is an exceedingly complex and subtle thinker. His thought moves on several levels and covers a wide variety of domains. This chapter focuses on the deconstructive thrusts in James's works and the counterdoctrine that they produced. James's deconstructive efforts radiate in several directions, simultaneously exploding the theoretical esthetic and metaphorical foundations of the doctrines that sustained Western imperialism. However, James also directed many of these critical darts at earlier formulations of his own thinking, thus subverting their very foundations.

One result of this extended critical analysis has been a methodology that employs a pluri-conceptual framework. In this framework the dynamics of multiple modes of domination arising from such factors as gender, color, race, class, and education are nondogmatically integrated. Consequently, it challenges not only the basic categories of colonial liberalism, but also the labor-centric categories of orthodox Marxism. Displacing but also reincorporating the latter's notion of labor exploitation is a dynamic conception of domination as a process that operates along a number of dimensions. Against these various faces of domination, James pits the creative determination of women, workers, dominated races, and other groups to resist and affirm themselves.

I will call this pluri-conceptual framework the "pieza framework," and will explore its importance for James's fictional and autobiographical writings. This exploration is done in five basic steps. The first is a semiotic analysis of the master conceptions that legitimated European projects of global capital accumulation. The second outlines James's de-legitimating critique of these master conceptions from the standpoint of his pieza framework. The third examines James's fiction in relation to this framework. The fourth provides a brief summary of the framework, and the final step takes up the implications for a contemporary praxis.

The Legitimating Concepts of Global Capital Accumulation

The homology between the historical and the fictional universe is not realized at the level of a particular element but at the level of the system. It is the fictional system in its *ensemble* which produces an effect of reality.—Pierre Macherey, 1972

The novel, in its true pedagogical function, Pierre Macherey argues, is not the product of a doctrine, not the form-giving mechanism to an already preestablished content. It is, rather, the condition of possibility of the emergence of a doctrine.

The Jamesian poiesis, taken as a system, the theoretics providing a reference for the esthetics and vice-versa, provides the condition of possibility for the emergence of a Jamesian doctrine, one that subverts its own center—the labor conceptual framework. This doctrine—pointing as it does toward a global model of multiple modes of accumulation and of multiple concomitant modes of coercion—begins the relativization of the Marxian factory model of exploitation; it projects the future through conceptions of the past and representations of the now, which lends coherence to all the Jamesian writings. These conceptions of past and present are rooted in a popular pluri-conceptual framework whose praxis erupted in the global national revolutions of the postwar period and in the social revolution of the sixties.

The "doctrine" produced by the autosociography of *Beyond a Boundary* constitutes that act of definition which is itself a part of the social universe it defines.[1] James acts as both the instrument of discovery and of definition because of that self-imposed marginality he chose for himself when, as a bright young scholarship winner, he failed to stay the course by violating the central interdiction, that is, keep your eye on the course and tailor your actions, choices, and desires to fit the course.[2] The stubborn young boy was pushed into theoretical and esthetic marginality when he blurred the categories—an intellectual wanting to play cricket, a scholarship winner reading for discovery rather than to pass examinations. These rebellious acts disturbed the governing categories of the colonial bourgeois cultural model, the categories of head/body, reason/instinct, and transgressed the separation between them. The young James lived his revolt against the governing bourgeois "mythology," the mythology with which it attempted to stem the subversive consequences of its own conceptual code, its literature, its organized sports, its globally constructed network of accumulation; the global revolution it had launched upon the world and which it attempted and attempts to control by the development of the metaphorics that subtends both its thought systems and its social system.

To grasp the significance of the counterdoctrine that emerges from the Jamesian theoretics and aesthetics taken as a whole, and of the questioning that counterdoctrine represents to the dictatorship of the master conceptions of Liberalism and Marxism, it is necessary to look at the semiotic foundations of bourgeois thought, the monarchical system of power it delegitimated, and the liberal state it helped to establish.

To be effective, systems of power must be discursively legitimated. This is not to say that power is originally a set of institutional structures that are subsequently legitimated. On the contrary, it is to suggest the equiprimordiality of structure and cultural conceptions in the genesis of power. These cultural conceptions, encoded in language and other signifying systems, shape the development of political structures and are also shaped by them. The cultural aspects of power are as original as the structural aspects; each serves as a code for the other's development. It is from these elementary cultural conceptions that complex legitimating discourses are constructed.

To establish its system of power, the European bourgeoisie had to displace the monarchy and the hegemony of the aristocratic classes. To do this, it was not enough to gain politicoeconomic dominance. It was also necessary to replace the formal monarchical system of signification with a cultural model that "selected" its values as normative. The elementary cultural conceptions upon which the monarchical system of signification rested can be designated as the "symbolics of blood."[3] They gave order to a social structure whose hierarchy was based on the principle of the possession of noble blood or the nonpossession of noble blood. It constituted what Bateson has called an abduction system.[4] Based on the fantasy of blood, this system legitimated the aristocracy's ownership of landed wealth, and the marginalizing of mercantile and artisanal-industrial life activities. Further, this abduction system legitimated both the categories of clerico-feudal thought and the macro-metaphor of the Ptolemaic universe and the hierarchical categories of its social order; legitimated in fact its politicoreligious polis, as totemism legitimated the politicoreligious world of traditional societies.

It was these elementary cultural conceptions of power and their abductive extensions that had to be uprooted by the bourgeoisie if the whole system of monarchical power was to be overthrown. The rise of the liberal state and bourgeois hegemony were the results not only of a revolution in economic production, but also in the cultural conceptions of power. If the organizing and legitimating discourses of the aristocracy were based on the symbolics of blood, those of the bourgeoisie were based on the metaphorics of natural reason and lack of natural reason. This represented a displacement of theological justification by the new notion of natural right. This notion was a construction within an abduction system that was based on an analogy with a representation of nature as opposed to concrete nature in the case of totemism.

Abductive extension of this state of nature metaphor provided the categories that structured the middle class social order, particularly its system of power and prestige. Accumulated property (capital) displaced "landed wealth" as the source of legitimacy, and this new property was represented in the Lockean formulation as having been acquired in the state-of-nature outside the "compact" of the state-of-society. Those who had property only revealed the high degree of "natural reason" that nature had endowed them with; those who lacked property revealed the degrees of lack of reason that nature had endowed them with. Thus after the English Civil War, to protect their newly acquired property, the Independents forced through and the Levellers acquiesced a social division based on men-of-property. Men-of-property-as-men-of-reason got the vote, and were governed only by their consent and were therefore "autonomous." The "servants and almstakers," dependent on others, without property, without natural reason, were excluded from the vote. They became the signifier of the body to the signifier of the reason of the propertied. The central division of categories was repeated at the level of the individual. This head/reason part of the meta-natural state-of-nature government controlled his body/instincts, part of brute-nature, that part of nature which lacked the reason of nature-as-ideal-model.

The colonial systems of power established abroad were also shaped by these cultural conceptions. Thus, if internally, the servants and alms-takers category represented lack of reason in relation to the middle class, then at the global level, it was nonWestern cultures and peoples that represented varying degrees of the lack of reason. In the great chain of being which was thus erected, the zero-term-of-reason and therefore of social being was the "Negro": the zero-term-of-culture, the cultures that merged with brute nature as the "Negro" merged with the apes, were the cultures of Africa. Consequently, the cultural categories of the colonial social orders embodied the ratio of human value represented by each group. In this ratio, value for the bourgeoisie had replaced the blue blood of the nobility as the status-organizing principle.

In sum, the governing cultural categories of the social orders in both center and periphery became the governing categories of their systems of knowledge and of aesthetics. Further, both knowledge and aesthetics systems constituted the sociocultural environment as an environment which encoded its conceptions in the very structure of social relations. These structural encodings of cultural conceptions are made possible by the fact the structure serves as the abduction system for the thought-systems and vice-versa. Consequently, for fundamental change to take place, it must take place both in the conception and in the pattern of relations. Such changes must therefore call into question both the structure of social reality and the structure of its analogical epistemology; they must involve "shifting our whole system of abductions. [To do this] we must pass through the threat of that chaos where thought becomes impossible."[5]

The Jamesian journey took place through the Scylla and Charybdis of that chaos. His poiesis has been a constant and sustained attempt to shift "the system of abduction" first of colonial Liberalism, later of Stalinist and Trotskyist Marxism, and, overall, of the bourgeois cultural model and its underlying head/body, reason/instinct metaphorics.

Delegitimating the Master Conceptions

[This] class [the bourgeoisie] must be seen . . . as being occupied, from the eighteenth century on . . . with forming a specific body . . . a class body with its health, hygiene descent and race. . . . There

were doubtless many reasons for this. . . . First of all, there was a
transposition into different forms of the methods employed by the
nobility for marking and maintaining its caste distinction . . . for the
aristocracy had also asserted the special character of its body . . . in
the form of *blood.*—Foucault, *The History of Sexuality,* vol. 1

James was aided in the task of deconstructing these conceptions by his
identity as Negro. Here one must contradict James and suggest that it
is not only nor even primarily because he is an adherent of the Leninist
"policy" that his solution to the Negro question emphasizes the autonomy of the race question, however much he insists on the hegemony
of the labor question. Rather, it is because of the multiplicity of his consciousness, a multiplicity shaped by the complex structures of both the
British-Trinidadian social system and the historical processes that had
shaped this system.

The Jamesian consciousness growing up, as adult, was molded by
the "morphogenetic fantasies"[6] that shaped an intricate permutation of
color, levels of education, levels of wealth, and levels of "culture." It
was a permutation in which these specific systems of values themselves
took value from the a priori categories based on the abductive system
of a Head/Body, Reason/Instinct analogy. These multiple permutations
gave rise to multiple identities: to the "ecumenicism" then of being a
Negro—of being Caliban.

The relatively small number of white settlers in British colonial Trinidad lead to a social hierarchy based on a cultural model in which the
heraldry of degrees of whiteness permutated with other value systems
and translated the race question into a color question. The latter was,
however, premised on the former, that is, on the social value of whiteness, the non-value of blackness. Black as the original sin could however be "redeemed" by degrees of education and wealth. The latter could
"make up for" degrees of blackness, which could devalue levels of education and of wealth. Whiteness functioned—exactly as money—as the
Marxian general equivalent of value.

This social hierarchy was unlike the rigid prescriptive white/black
categories of the United States "native model." As Asmaron Legesse has
pointed out, "one of the many immutable prescriptive rules in America
is the classification of human beings into Blacks and Whites. These are
mutually exclusive categories in the sense that one cannot be both Black
and White at the same time. One cannot help but be impressed by the

rigidity of this native model. It denies the fact that Blacks and Whites enter into elaborate illicit sexual liaisons. The myth of the two races is preserved by the simple rule that all the offsprings of interracial unions are automatically classified as Blacks."[7]

In Trinidad, color, wealth, education, and culture dynamically interacted not only as markers of differential social status, but also as legitimating value systems in which the ratio of distribution of the national wealth—engendered through the life activities of production, consumption, and circulation of all Trinidadians—was a ratio adjusted to the degrees of color/wealth, or education, one had accumulated. In other words, the living standards for each group was equated with the group's value standing in the pluri-defined social totem pole.

A central motif of *Beyond a Boundary* is the analytics of the permutation of race/education/culture and skill. Ownership of "White-value" paid dividends in the kinds of jobs that were reserved for whiteness regardless of merit; jobs that were logically equated with mental (head/reason) rather than with manual (body/instinct) labor. And James gives several examples of this in *Beyond a Boundary*.[8]

Color, then, acted as another kind of merit, an unearned social merit. A system of color value existed side by side with capital value, education value, merit value, and labor value. To single out any of these factors was to negate the complex laws of the functioning of the social order, the multiple modes of coercion and power relations existing at all levels of the social system. Because of the multiple modes of coercion and of exploitation, the factory model was only one of many models. Thus there could be no mono-conceptual framework—no pure revolutionary subject, no single locus of the Great Refusal, no single "correct" line.

Given the pluri-consciousness of the Jamesian identity—a Negro yet British, a colonial native yet culturally a part of the public school code, attached to the cause of the proletariat yet a member of the middle class, a Marxian yet a Puritan, an intellectual who plays cricket, of African descent yet Western, a Trotskyist and Pan-Africanist, a Marxist yet a supporter of black studies, a West Indian majority black yet an American minority black—it was evident that the Negro question, and the figure of Matthew Bondsman that lurked behind it, could not be solved by an either/or—that is, by either race or class, proletariat or bondsman labor, or *damnes de la terre*, Pan-African nationalism or labor internationalism. The quest for a frame to contain them all came to constitute the Jamesian poiesis.

The Jamesian "magical agent" lay in the fact that he had lived all the contradictions. The problematic of race and nationalism, of class and culture was not new. Indeed, this problematic links the individual quest of the young James for theoretical autonomy with the quest of Trinidad for national independence and cultural autonomy. In the structuring motifs of *Beyond a Boundary*, this problematic also mediates Jamesian theoretics and esthetics, fusing them into a counterdoctrine. It is this counterdoctrine that then reveals that the national and racial questions were questions repressed by the master conception of liberalism, repressed precisely in those areas in which the liberal conception realized itself at its best, that is, in its articulation of the "public school code" through the ritual code of cricket: "a straight bat and it isn't cricket became the watchwords of manners and virtue and the guardians of freedom and power" (*B.B.*, 163).

Thus the "literary" system of *Beyond a Boundary* uses James's personal quest for cognitive awareness of the laws of the social order's functioning to reveal the existence of racism and nationalism as a living, breathing part of his social reality and the repressive exclusion of this reality from the "Eden" of the school, its life determined by the public school code.

This code saved the young James from the naked racial distinctions that so harshly mark the American social order. The public school code insisted that the category that separated the colonizer ruling whites from the ruled natives was reason and its lack, rather than merely race. Reason/merit was the prescriptive category; not blatantly race as in the "native model" of the United States. As James recalls: "this school was a colony ruled autocratically by Englishmen. What then of the National Question? It did not exist for me. Our principal . . . was an Englishman of the nineteenth century. [No] more devoted conscientious and self-sacrificing individual ever worked in the colonies . . . [He] was beloved by generations of boys and was held in respectful admiration throughout the colony" (*B.B.*, 38).

For the headmaster as for the other masters, all of whom lived up to and doctrinally passed on the public school code,[9] questions of race and of nationalism were at best marginal—as for orthodox Marxians—at worst, not cricket to discuss. The operating of this code also made it possible for a scattering of talented native individuals to be cooptable into the lower levels of the ruling elements, but never quite up to the level of the British.

James's schoolmasters were able, for awhile at least, to universalize this code—the apogee of the British Empire as a cultural order was concomitant with this moment of universalization—because they themselves lived up to the "vision of life" embodied in the code. They held strictly to its rules, subordinating their personal prejudices and interests to its demands.

In the context of the code, while there was no question that the colonial relation between Englishmen and natives was in the nature of things, at the individual level things had to be different. Here racial or national origin could not matter. Merit, talent, and the ability to play the game could be found among the exceptional class of natives. These natives could be recruited into the ruling group, could share in the vision of life, and could come to be bound by it, too, to play by the rules.[10]

The schoolmasters did their duty according to the categorical imperative of what was cricket and what was not. It wasn't cricket to harp on race—a chap couldn't help being black. What mattered was his natural talent, that he kept a straight bat and kept to the rules. Not the party line, but the public school code.

The race question did not have to be agitated. It was there. But in our little Eden, it never troubled us. If the masters were so successful in instilling and maintaining their British principles as the idea and the norm, (however much individuals might fall away) it was because within the school and particularly on the playing field, they practiced them themselves. . . . They were correct in the letter and in the spirit. When I went back to the college to teach . . . the then principal, a Mr. A. M. Lower, a man of pronounced Tory, not to say chauvinist ideas amazed me by the interest he took in me. Once in an expansive moment . . . he muttered: "We do our work and in time you people will take over. . . . That must have been about 1924 and it was the first and only time in some fifteen years that I heard a word about the national or the racial question. (*B.B.*, 39)

Here the voyage-quest motif of *Beyond a Boundary* functions at the level of theoretical awareness. James was never to free himself from the public school code, nor did he want to.[11] He would, however, have to free himself from the master conception that underlay the code, the conception that effected the separation of the "native" elite from the native masses, binding the loyalty of the former not to their own reality but to that of their colonizers.

The Jamesian quest for autonomy would have to struggle against a conception that had accorded the elite, and he among them, a place of privilege, a conception that provided the pastoral protection of code and school against the existential brutalization to which a Matthew Bondsman was condemned, that conceded for a few an Eden in which both mind and body fused, cricket as well as *Vanity Fair*, that excluded the Caliban niggerdom from this life, and that excluded those like Bondsman as the absolute zero of social and metaphysical value.

The paradox was that the public school code, quickened by the revivifying sweep of Marx's critique of the social order, of Thackeray's critique of the aristocracy, was to be related to the Jamesian concern. He would be haunted and impelled by the thought that the differential of life value accorded by the social order to his own life, and to that of Matthew Bondsman, simply "wasn't cricket." Nor was the conception that legitimated such a differential flawed not only by its repression of the key questions of race, nationalism, and class, but also through its representation of the status-quo as in the very "nature of things." "It was only long years after that I understood the limitation on spirit, vision and self-respect which was imposed on us by the fact that our master, our curriculum, our code of morals, everything, began from the basis that Britain was the source of all light and leading, and our business was to admire, wonder, imitate, learn; our criterion of success was to have succeeded in approaching that distant ideal—to attain it was of course impossible. Both masters and boys accepted it as the very nature of things. . . . As for me, it was the beacon that beckoned me on" (B.B., 39)

Here eventually and once again, the Jamesian poiesis would constitute its own ground, Caliban establish his own identity, in a sustained act of separation from the very "beacon that had lead him on." Yet this beacon was also to provide him with the tools of thought to question its presuppositions. Like Caliban, he could use the language he had been taught to push into regions Prospero never knew. The tools of thought were such that, violating the interdiction that "decent chaps" do not question the social "nature of things," James could begin his series of sociohistorical actions by posing the repressed question. The national question was theme and motif of his first book, *The Life of Captain Cipriani*, a part of which was reprinted as *The Case for West Indian Self-Government*.

The national question was also to form part of an even more fundamental question—that of the autonomy of the body category. As such, it initiated a calling in question of the abduction system on the basis of whose analogy the entire polis rested. If, as Cornelius Castoriadis tells us, his *Socialisme ou Barbarie* group was to base its theoretical evolution on the fact that, at a certain moment, they pulled the right string, that of "bureaucratization, and . . . simply and ruthlessly kept pulling,"[12] the string that the Jamesian poiesis pulled was the centrally related question of autonomy, the autonomy of the body categories. Pulling this string, James called into question the entire "socially legitimated collective representations," the social imaginaire (Castoriadis)[13] on the basis of which both the mode of social relations (i.e., *bourgeoisism*) and its economic expressions private property capitalism and nationalized property socialism, are legitimated. The question of autonomy once posited, James would stand in its truth. It is here that the doctrine that emerges from *Beyond a Boundary* puts into free play the great heresy of the Jamesian poiesis.

The Jamesian Fictional System and the Pieza Conceptual Frame

He was genuinely shocked at what Philemon had so carelessly revealed. . . . He had gone on his way, taking it all for granted. To what sacrifices had he put the good woman to feed him regularly while the rest of the household starved. He would have to do something about it.—James, *Minty Alley*

In the Jamesian ensemble, the theoretics is the politics. The politics, that is, the mode of being together in the polis, is shaped by the struggle of groups and individuals to maintain or redefine the terms of their relations to bourgeois domination. The perpetuation of the middle class as a ruling group is a form of politics that deploys recursively both the categories of the esthetics/theoretics and of the economic "as a tactic, a detour, an alibi."[14]

Thus an esthetic differential value set up between fine and non-fine arts replicates, and thereby stabilizes and legitimates, the differential value empirically expressed between the life value of the middle class and the life value of the popular forces. This differential value is then validly expressed in the differential of reward, that is, of the differential between the consumption ratio of the middle classes and the consumption ratio of the popular forces.

The esthetic categories of an art critic like Bernard Berenson, diffused through education, act effectively to inculcate in the non-middle class a sense of their own inferiority, of their own lower life value. In effect, what is diffused, encoded in these critical categories is a mode of measurement according to which both the distribution of the material wealth accumulated and of the new life chances afforded by this global process are accepted as legitimate and valid.

In other words, the categories both of bourgeois esthetics and of its theoretics provide above all a cultural law of value in which the ratio of value between the head/reason and the body/instinct categories legitimates the system of differential rewards necessary to the telos of the accumulation of value, the telos upon which the global middle class bases its class domination, whether in capital or labor form. This continuity between capitalist and Stalinist forms of social organization was important in James's thinking. Thus, he pointed out that "the philosophy of the planned economy and one-party state is distinguishable from that of the bourgeoisie only by its more complete rationalism. . . . It consciously seeks to plan and organize the division of labor as the means to further accumulation of capital. . . . It is a product of the modern mass movement, created by the centralization of capital, and holds its position only because of this movement. At the same time, it cannot conceive the necessity for abolishing the division of labour in production. By a remorseless logic, therefore, representation of the proletariat turns into its opposite, administration over the proletariat."[15] Because of this law of cultural value, the capital and labor conceptual frames cannot by themselves provide scientifically exact modes of measurement or accurate ratios of distribution. Only modes and ratios are seen as valid and are represented as such through the mythologies of the market and the party line.

As Jean Baudrillard suggests, the capital conceptual frame and the labor conceptual frame, which define either capital in the case of the first or labor in the case of the second as the single or primary determinant of value, both function through their privileging of the production end of the multiple processes to set up a mode of calculation that ensures middle-class hegemony through the legitimated accumulation of not only material goods but also power, wealth, and multiple life opportunities.

In *Beyond a Boundary*, the organizational structure implicitly juxtaposes Bondsman and Sir Donald Bradman, both equally talented as cricketers, yet the latter is offered all opportunity to realize his powers, to swim with the current in order to achieve fame and fortune while

Bondsman ends in an obscurity only redeemed by memory, by the stroke he left imprinted in young James's consciousness. A model is thus set up to reveal the existence of an objective ratio of distribution of life value and of opportunities to realize one's powers. In the fictional system of James's novel *Minty Alley* and short story "Triumph," this model emerges to provide the lineaments of a new popular theoretics, of an alternative conceptual frame.

The interplay of color and class in the fictional system of *Minty Alley* reveals patterns of interactions in which a parallel between the global order and the social order of Trinidad, between the middle-class esthetic canons and the non-middle-class ones, between the canonization of the first and the stigmatization of the second, can be clearly discerned. In these patterns are lawlike equivalences between the hierarchical degrees of social value, whether measured in terms of the possession of capital, profession, skills, jobs, whiteness, education, fine arts, "good English," or good hair, and the ratio of distribution of life chances. Between the social value ascribed by the "imaginaire social" and its cultural law of value are the opportunities provided either to "realize one's powers" or to negate this realization, even to debase these powers in a blind quest for self-affirmation, for an aggressive escape, as in the case of Bondsman, from the incredible pressures of this relentless stigmatization.

The fictional systems of both *Minty Alley* and of "Triumph" constitute the site of the yard, that is, a tenement house, overcrowded, its life spilling out into the yard, where people jostle each other, and most are jobless or underemployed in a world ruled by chance and instability. These are people whose societies are reserve societies drawn into the system when the profits of single crops boom, and expelled when the single crop booms burst. In this world, a job becomes not a matter of course, a right, but a magical possession. The identity of labor is not the norm. It is rather a privileged status, as Fanon points out. Bondsman, the Lumpen, and the *damnes de la terre* are the norm. In the value code of the hegemonic system, most of the dwellers of the yard are condemned like Bondsman to accept their inculcated zero value of identity, their own nothingness.

Here the heresy of the Jamesian poiesis places the contradiction not between the progressive productive forces and the backward relations of production as in the labor conceptual frame, but rather in the contradiction between the thrust of men and women to realize their powers, to take their humanity upon account and the mode of social relations that blocks this thrust in order to perpetuate its classarchy. In 1950 the Jamesian theoretics arrived at the following conclusion: "It is not the world of nature that confronts man as an alien power to be overcome. It is the alien power that he has himself created. . . . The end towards which mankind is inexorably developing by the constant overcoming of internal antagonisms is not the enjoyment, ownership or use of goods, but self-realization, creativity based upon the incorporation into the individual personality of the whole previous development of humanity. Freedom is creative universality, not utility."[16]

Similarly, the fictional system of his novel had already enacted this doctrine—the imperative nature of the popular quest for self-realization, for creative universality, and for freedom rather than for utility, as the quest for that by which people live.

The fictional characters of Minty Alley and of "Triumph" refuse to accept their value of nothingness. Their lives are spent in constant combat to refuse this negation of their being, to affirm, by any means, fair or foul, usually the latter, that they have a life value and have powers that must be realized. They do this come hell or high water, and to hell with the consequences.

The setting of the drama that they enact is both the global network of accumulation in which they are inserted and the interplay of color, class, and culture value in the context of which they act out their parts. For example, the Nurse, almost white and with a profession however dubious her certification, exercises a certain dominance in the yard. When the showdown comes between herself and Mrs. Rouse, the owner of the house, over whom should have the macho sweet-man Benoit, the Nurse wins hands down. She realizes her own powers and affirms her identity within the only way open in the structure of the system, by defeating someone else. She knows that Benoit will have calculated the points that place her higher on the totem pole than Mrs. Rouse, that is, her color value and her job profession value. Like Mamitz at the end of the short story "Triumph," who plasters her room with dollar notes given to her by her butcher boyfriend and flaunts the pork and chicken cooking in her pot, affirming her "dollar value" as a kept woman and her superiority over her rivals, the Nurse realizes her identity along the lines prescribed by the formal system of signification, on which bourgeois classarchy is based.

The yard and its dwellers, although living partly in an alternative popular cosmology—Benoit gives the Nurse a magic bath to help her find a job and Mamitz's friend gives her a magic bath to help her find her kind of job, a steady man who can provide in exchange for the labor power of her sexual favors—have had to partly internalize the code of value of the ruling bourgeois in order to survive. And in that conception, as Sparrow puts it in a calypso, "it is dog eat dog and only the fittest survive." The doctrine that emerges from the Jamesian fiction includes, among other things, five points.

1. What rules in Trinidad is not so much a ruling group as a ruling conception, a "morality of mores" which, internalized to greater or lesser degrees at all levels[17] is a value system based on the acceptance by all of the higher differential value of the middle class. In *Minty Alley*, after the middle-class Mr. Haynes has had intimate sexual relations with Maisie, the young niece of Mrs. Rouse, she still calls him "Mr. Haynes" and he sees nothing strange in this because the middle class exists as the "reference group," as the general equivalent of social value.

2. The entire social structure is based on the acceptance and implementation of power-relations as the normative mode of relations. For example, Maisie is determined to keep Philemon in her lower place as a "servant" and as a "coolie" (i.e., East Indian indentured labor), yet Maisie is kept in hers by a system that codes her joblessness, refusing her any role but that of a servant. Yet keeping other groups of people below one's own group enables one to realize that differential value central to identity in its middle-class form.

3. The "factory-model of exploitation" and the labor-conceptual framework has little explanatory power with respect to the modes of social coercion and domination, modes that work invisibly, like fate, not only to structure the hierarchical categories of the Trinidadian and the global system, but also to coerce individuals and groups into the categories for which they have been deterministically selected by the ruling value system, by the internalized ruling conception.

4. The system of capital accumulation is not only carried out through labor activity, but through the life activities of the popular groups as workers, as consumers, or merely as signifiers of non-value, that is, those like Matthew Bondsman who serve as the "refuse" of the system, as the symbolic inversion of norm value, the liminal category that defines the norm from which social value is reckoned and the mode of measurement of the consumption ratio legitimated.

5. The fictional system of *Minty Alley* enables the emergence of an invisible model of global accumulation, the model whose dynamic needs

to lock each category into its relative place so that the social system can serve as the empirical abduction system of the mode of distribution of differential rewards based on a hierarchical identity system. This global model of accumulation, unlike the factory model of exploitation of the labor conceptual frame, can encompass both the proletariat and the multiple groups and groupings whose mode of coercion and oppression are outside the explanatory power of the labor conceptual frame.

In the frame of the later code, those like Bondsman and the ghetto shanty-town archipelago stand condemned, stigmatized as the lumpen, as "non-productive labor" that is not really exploited. So, too, do Mrs. Rouse of *Minty Alley* and Mamitz of "Triumph" in the strictly orthodox Marxian canons.

Mrs. Rouse, baking cakes and supplying them to the shops, using the hired labor of Philemon and of the yard boy—although she lives on the edge of poverty as they do, eating as little as they do—would definitely be stigmatized in such canons as a Kulak. That is, she would be put in the class of Russian traders who grow rich not by their own labors, but through the labor of others. Solzhenitsyn has shown the way in which this category was used as the moral antithesis of the proletariat to make vast numbers of peasants into exploitable objects. The same would be true of Mamitz, the kept woman selling her sexual labor. She exchanges her sexual labor not only for the chicken and pork in the pot with which she affirms her triumph over her rivals in the yard. Through this exchange she is able to realize her powers in the only avenues open to her strata, both in the global system of social role allocation and in its local Trinidadian variant. In orthodox Marxian canons, such a self-affirmation would be stigmatized as antisocial, the very negation of the "new man" that socialism builds.

In such a conceptual frame, what happens to those like Bondsman—except they are represented as "victims" or sufferers[18]—cannot logically be of any concern. They are "outside of history. Nor can what happens to Philemon and to the others of the yard in *Minty Alley* and in "Triumph" be of significance. Yet these are the characters through whom the fictional system reveals the concept of levels of consumption ratio and the dynamics of a global system of social savings accumulated through low cost, not of labor alone but of the lower categories of human lives. These categories reveal the increasingly minimal levels of consumption of food, clothes, shelter, and education to which those like Philemon and Bondsman are condemned in a global system whose objective telos is the hegemony of the process of accumulation.

In this spare, taut novel, James's most beautifully portrayed character is Philemon, the East Indian coolie servant, the lowest on the totem pole. A startling aristocracy of spirit illuminates Philemon, the aristocracy and grace of a spirit possible only to the truly nonaccumulative psyche. The brief scene in which the young middle-class hero, Haynes, realizes the sparse "eating" of the others in the yard that makes possible his own well-prepared meals has a double significance. First, it extends the Marxian theory of labor value into the pluri-frame of life value and puts the Negro question and the Bondsman contradiction into appropriate frames. Second, this scene also reveals a central aspect of the multiple mechanisms of the process of accumulation as it is carried out through multiple modes of empirical and cultural coercion at all levels of the social order, even at the level of the reserve lives of Bondsman and Philemon.

What the fictional system of *Minty Alley* reveals is precisely the single underlying keel, not of the whaling ship this time, but of the process that had sent the ship to sea in the first place, the bourgeois telos of accumulation, both of capital (the owners) and of self-realization (Ahab), the telos in which they have co-opted all the isolates of the globe, either as active or tacit consenters.

Philemon is a tacit consenter, and so at first is Haynes. The trajectory of the novel startles him into questioning. Haynes, normally shut off as a middle-class Trinidadian from the people of *Minty Alley* due to financial circumstances, violates the middle-class interdiction of separation and chooses "down." He takes a room at No. 2 Minty Alley. During his interactions there, he stumbles upon the realization of the social crime that makes his own standard of living possible. It is one of the most powerful and moving scenes of a novel whose taut spareness in its portrayal of Philemon would not find its like until Roger Mais's Rastafarian *Brother Man* in the 1950s.

Haynes, in conversation, with Philemon, finds out that sometimes, except for his own meal, there are days when no food is cooked at all in No. 2 Minty Alley.

"Not cook at all for the day!" It was incredible.
"Why! That is nothing."

"But hasn't she to cook for me?"

"Yes, but that is different. She must cook for you. You give her money."

"And what do you all eat?"

"Any little thing. We cook sometimes. But if we only get money to make cake for the parlours, we can't get anything."

"But why don't you credit at the shop?" said Haynes, and knew even before he was told that he had asked a stupid question.

But never once . . . was any meal late. . . . . Morning, noon and night everything was ready punctually on the table for him. . . . He had gone on his way taking it all for granted. To what sacrifices had he put the good woman to feed him regularly while the rest of the household starved.[19]

Haynes/James was to spend a lifetime doing something about this social crime. The doctrine of the Jamesian fictional system, as well as of the "blurred genre" of *Beyond a Boundary*, therefore goes beyond the Jamesian theoretics, that is, beyond his independent Marxism, in that it altogether displaces the labor conceptual framework (still a middle-class conceptual framework bound to the laws of its code of knowledge) with a popular esthetics, a popular conceptual framework.

Toward a Pieza Conceptual Frame

In fact, the veiled slavery of the wage workers in Europe needed, for its pedestal, slavery, pure and simple.—Marx, *Capital*, vol. 1

If we use Matthew Bondsman and the Negro question as a point of departure it is possible to sketch the lineaments of the new popular theoretical frame, the new unifying idea that emerges from the Jamesian poiesis. This idea takes us on the stage of the Jamesian journey that lead back to Africa, back to the seminal importance of the Atlantic slave trade. The latter in particular takes us back to a painfully constructed multilayered system of global domination characterized by a plurality of points or bases of resistance. As Wallerstein has pointed out, "in the sixteenth century, there was the differential of the core of the European world economy versus its peripheral areas, within the European core between the states, within states between regions and strata, within regions be-

tween city and country, and . . . within more local units. The solidarity of
the system was based on ultimately this unequal development, since the
multi-layered complexity provided the possibility of the multi-layered
identification."[20] These details are crucial for any attempt to displace
the metonymic substitution of the last phase of this global system for
its entire historical development. In other words, they are crucial for
any attempt to deconstruct the masterdom of capital and labor mono-
conceptions or mono-conceptual frames.

In displacing these conceptions, James developed a pieza theoretic
framework in which the pieza served as a general equivalent of value
for the variety of groups whose labor could be exploited within the capitalist world system. The pieza was the name given by the Portuguese,
during the slave trade, to the African who functioned as the standard
measure. He was a man of twenty-five years, approximately, in good
health, calculated to give a certain amount of physical labor. He served
as the general equivalent of physical labor value against which all the
others could be measured—with, for example, three teenagers equaling
one pieza, and older men and women thrown in a job lot as refuse. In
the Jamesian system, the pieza becomes an ever-more general category
of value, establishing equivalences between a wider variety of oppressed
labor power.

The starting point for James's displacement/incorporation of the labor
conceptual framework is his insistence on the seminal importance of
the trade in African slaves. In particular, he wants to end its repression
in normative Western conceptual frames. Along with this repositioning
of Africans, James also resolves the class/race and class/sex dispute by
revealing each as aspects of the language of the other.

Second, the pieza framework required a repositioning of the mode of
production in relation to the mode of domination. The former becomes
a subset of the latter. That is, economic exploitation only follows on,
and does not precede, the mode of domination set in motion by the
imaginaire social of the bourgeoisie. Consequently, the capitalist mode
of production is a subset of the bourgeois mode of accumulation which
constitutes the basis of middle-class hegemony.

Third, what Wallerstein has called the world system was constituted
by James as above all a single network of accumulation. This network can
be divided into three phases: (1) circulation for accumulation; (2) production for accumulation; and (3) consumption for accumulation. In each

of these phases, the pieza—the source of extractive value—is different. In the first, it was the African slave; in the second, the working class; and in the third and current phase, it has been the consumer. Just as the pieza role reduced the African from the specificity of his/her multiple identities to quantifiable Negro labor, so too has this role in different ways reduced the working class and consumers to productive value through unending cycles of consumption. Thus, in all three phases, the piezas (blacks, labor, consumers) were locked into passive, coerced identity roles, as well as a social rather than a technical division of labor. This division of labor was legitimated as natural by the metaphorics of the head/body opposition, and as historical by the representation of the party's vanguard as the consciousness of the proletariat.

Fourth, this international network of accumulation leads to the abductive elaboration of a differential ratio of distribution of goods and of rewards, which in turn provides additional legitimacy. The institutionalizing of this ratio results in its lawlike functioning to code differentiated identities, which will need the differential ratio of rewards in order to realize status identity, as opposed to simple identity. Consequently, this ratio functions to separate layers of identities, and must be changed into a ratio that supports a greater sharing of common experiential grounds.

Further, the cultural categories that legitimate this ratio also distort and minimize the contributions of various pieza groups to the process of global capital accumulation. Within the discursive constructions of this categorical framework, accumulation is represented largely as resulting from production, as opposed to the coordination of the broader life activities of the peoples of the globe. Thus it minimizes their real productive activities, their participation in processes of exchange, and their lifestyles and cultural patterns. This displacement of the mirror of accumulation by the mirror of production is sustained by the same categorical system that displaced and repressed the importance of African slavery in the first phase of capitalist development. It is also the same categorical system that in the present constitutes black piezas— the Matthew Bondsmen of the world—as useless and therefore expendable.

Finally, because it recognizes the historical constitution and subordination of a variety of piezas, this framework recognizes multiple points of resistance. These points of resistance need to be specifically coded as trans-race, trans-class, trans-group, to enable a popular cultural revolution to emerge from the whole body of the people. Thus, rather than the Negro or women's struggle being included under the rubric of labor, the rubric of pieza includes all the experimental categories of the coerced, the non-norm. The mode of oppression must dictate the specific mode of organization to fight that oppression. There is no universalized mode of organization which is scientifically correct since the modes of oppression are multiple. Michel Foucault and Gilles Deleuze made the same point:

> as soon as we struggle against *exploitation*, the proletariat *not only leads the struggle*, but also defines its targets, its methods, and the places and instruments for confrontation; and to ally oneself with the proletariat is to accept its positions, its ideology and its motives *for combat. This means total identification.* But if the fight is directed against power, then all those on whom power is exercised to their detriment, all who find it intolerable, can begin the struggle on their own terrain and on the basis of their proper activity (or passivity). In engaging in a struggle that concerns their own interests, whose objectives they clearly understand, *and whose methods* only they can determine, they enter into a revolutionary process.[21]

Whatever the Game: A Praxis for Matthew Bondsman

> I hope this book will convince . . . that it isn't cricket to sell a game at baseball or basketball or whatever the game may be. This hail and farewell to the ancestral creed may be of some use . . . and in any case it can do no harm.—James, *B.B.*

The "cultural revolution" which responds to the radicalized logic of capital, to "indepth" imperialism, is not the developed form of an economic-political revolution. It acts on the basis of a reversal of "materialist" logic. . . . Species, race, sex, age, language, culture, signs of either an anthropological or cultural type—all these criteria are criteria of difference, of signification and of code. It is a simplistic hypothesis that makes them all "descendents" in the last instance, of economic exploitation. On the contrary it is truer to say that this hypothesis is itself only a rationalization of *an order of domination* reproduced through it.—Baudrillard, *The Mirror of Production*

A pluri-conceptual theoretics, a universal based on the particular (Cesaire) is the logical result and outcome of the Jamesian poiesis. It is the product of the journey that he took to bridge that early separation between himself and Matthew Bondsman, of the effort to chart the lineaments of their common distress and of their common destiny.

Such a pluri-conceptual theoretics leads necessarily to a praxis that is correspondingly plural in nature. More specifically, it is a praxis that will not sell out the game because of blind or strategic commitments to particular monoconceptual frames. It is in this context that we must understand James's act of separating himself from the 6th Pan-African Congress, a congress he had worked hard to organize. He negated both the congress and its doctrine and moved the national and the class question into the wider dimensions of the popular question.

The doctrine that had come out of the congress was astonishing. When Sekou Touré described Pan-Africanism as a "kind of racism based on a so-called Black Nation," he was backed by Mozambique's Frelimo:

> The Vice-President of *Frelimo* reiterated President Samora Machel's denunciation of Black Power and warning against the "fascist" tendency of defining the enemy on the basis of skin color. And from Julius Nyerere himself, "If we react to the continued need to defend our position as Black men by regarding ourselves as different from the rest of mankind, we shall weaken ourselves." Observer Lerone Bennett reports the leader of one delegation as expressing to him personally a concern about "being committed to questionable political positions by the perceptions of Black Americans who were, he said, obsessed by race." [22]

The final declaration of the congress summed up the definitive triumph of the Marxist-Leninist interpretation of the African and black experience: "The General Declaration of the Congress fully endorsed the Marxist, or progressive position as it has come to be called, and pronounced definitively and astonishingly that Pan Africanism therefore excludes all racial, tribal, ethnic, religious or national considerations." [23]

The identity of racism, capitalism, and imperialism undid the Jamesian dialectic of the autonomy of the black question. It undid it, even if under the hegemony of the labor conceptual frame (i.e., the frame of the struggle against capitalism) that firmly subordinated racism to laborism. This enabled the repression of the popular question, both in its black expression in the United States and in its class expression in Africa itself, that is, the growing disillusionment of the popular masses with their increasingly totalitarian elites.

The Negro question, a question compelled to challenge not only the economic expression of bourgeoisism, (Capitalism) but also bourgeoisism itself; to challenge its *imaginaire social*, one in which the "Negro" functioned as the central symbolic inversion of human value, had always imperatively been a popular rather than a primarily national or class question. As such, its mode of revolutionary transformation would have to question bourgeois hegemony itself, and the new African elites are the new bourgeoisie.

As the earlier *comprador* bourgeoisie had locked themselves into a liberal macro-conception and served as the satellite areas of the West, so the new *pensador* bourgeoisie ensured their class hegemony by locking themselves into the master conception of a Stalinist Marxism and its legitimated totalitarian formulations. Thus they and some of the governing elites in the Caribbean logically refused to allow any nongovernment-sponsored delegations to attend the conference.

Although James was specially invited, he refused to attend. He made no fanfare. But in his talk in 1976 to the First Congress of all African writers, in Dakar, Senegal, he first dismissed the conference and then in his plans for the Seventh Pan-African Congress transformed the Pan-African national quest into a popular quest and laid the explicit basis of a popular theoretics.

His plans are explicit because the implicit theoretics is there everywhere in the Jamesian poiesis. These plans parallel James's return to the calypso tents and the reevaluation of Sparrow's art. In particular, the recognition that his art had evolved its own conception of the world, its own forms, and its own imagery was a violation of a childhood interdiction that marked the crucial rubicon of James's return to Bondsman.

Similar in its significance was his quick salute to the seminal significance of the popular theoretics involved in Fanon's constitution of the hitherto invisible Bondsman—*les damnes de la terre*—as an agent of history. His recognition of the thrust was the new dramatic spectacle of the popular forces in the streets, in motion, demanding a reinvention of the world, and reinventing for themselves a counter-imaginaire. Thus James was one of the first to see the significance of the great Orphic heresy of the Rastafarians, to understand that Bondsman today would be a Rastafarian, to understand under the apparent absurdities of their alternative cosmology, a determined refusal of the "great fictions that pour in upon them from every side." He was also among the first to grasp that they were reinventing the imaginaire social, refusing that of Babylon, and creating a new vision of life for the whole body of people.

It was from outside the productive process, from those expelled from it, liminal to its categories, that the revivifying prescriptions must emerge, as they emerged from the Roman Catacombs of a dying world—from them and the men of the word, the diffusors who provide the unifying frame, the theoretics of their symbolics. So James concluded his review of Fanon: "the work done by Black intellectuals, stimulated by the needs of the black people, had better be understood by the condemned of the earth, whether they are in Africa, the United States or Europe. Because if the condemned of the earth do not understand their pasts, and know the responsibilities that lie upon them in the future, all on the earth will be condemned. That is the kind of world we live in."[24]

In sketching his plans for the Seventh Pan-African Congress, James, who had struggled with Nkrumah for national independence, now struggled with the uneducated masses to initiate a popular social transformation. The act of separation from the ruling elites was discreet. It was there, nevertheless. Thus, refusing to "sell the game" even for the sake of his past comradeship with the now firmly installed ruling elites, James zeroed in on the clash of interest between the African elite and the peasantry. "There is an African elite in every African territory which had adopted the ways and ideas of Western civilization and is living at the expense of the African peasant. And we, in talking about the Seventh Pan-African Congress must make it clear that this African elite is what we have to deal with, and that the African peasant must be our main concern." He then insisted on the centrality of the *damnes de la terre: "We have to be concerned with the masses of the population. . . .* The masses of the population matter in a way that they did not matter twenty-five years ago. . . . We of the Conference are looking forward to a new relation of leaders and masses in Africa and in countries of African descent." He then takes away the "national basis," projecting a series of federations: "In other words, we are not going to hold a conference and hold up the national state as an ideal anymore. That belongs to the last century."[25]

James's proposed federations are: (1) A West African Federation, a southern African Federation with Angola and Mozambique; (2) a West African Federation with Uganda, Kenya, and Tanzania; and (3) a North African Federation, Morocco, Tunisia, Algeria, and Libya. Here he reinvents Pan-Africanism in contemporary terms but above all conceptualizes like Padmore long ago, and Cesaire later, a relation in which the solidarity of the labor code, that is, of the world proletariat, must not negate the imperative solidarity of the African people. The road to the universal passes through the realization of the particular—at least in the popular conceptual frame.

The great unifying forms of our times are no longer, as in the case of cricket, coded, under the hegemony of middle-class cultural mores. What we are experiencing is a cultural shift of historical magnitude, a shift that James pointed to in the lectures on modern politics given in Trinidad. The great unifying cultural forms of our times, beginning with the jazz culture and its derivatives, are popular. This is the significance of calypso and Carnival, of the reggae and Rastafarianism. This is the significance of the Jamesian poiesis. In the dimensions of the popular code of knowledge that our work as functional intellectuals, rather than as a ruling element, now lies. We, too, must initiate the return that James spelled out at the end of his talk to the writers' congress:

> Our repudiation of the national state, our repudiation of the elite, our respect for the great mass of the population and the dominant role that it would play in the reconstruction of society, our recognition that our elitism is morally responsible for what is happening to the ordinary man, our recognition of the capacity they have in them, our recognition of the need to release the enormous energies of the mass of people, in particular in women and peasants, such a congress could be the Seventh for Pan-Africanism, but—for that very reason—the first of new world-wide social order.[26]

He gives the theoretic representation esthetic dimensions by quoting George Lamming's lament for that separation of experience that marked out a different destiny for Lamming's own version of Matthew Bondsman—Powell. Powell is now a thief, murderer, and rapist; Lamming, stamped by the heraldry of education, escaped Powell's fate by becoming a writer. Yet Lamming knows in his bones that his escape from the ghetto of nonrealization of his powers had impelled Powell to realize his power of action in the only ways open to him, to measure up if negatively. Lamming mourns the price of this separate peace. James quotes:

> I believe deep in my bones, that the mad impulse which drives Powell to his criminal defeat, was largely my doing. I would not have this explained away by talk about environment, nor can I allow

my own moral infirmity to be transferred to a foreign conscience labelled imperialism. Powell still resides somewhere in my heart, with a dubious love. Some strange nameless shadow of regret, and yet the deepest nostalgia, for I have never felt myself to be an honest part of anything since the world of his childhood deserted me.[27]

The significant form, the "flow of motion" of Bondsman batting, was, for James, his memory of another Powell. And on the basis of that memory James makes, in *Beyond a Boundary*, an esthetic demand that by itself redefines the mode of desire, the code of what humanity lives by.

If *Beyond a Boundary* as genre cuts across the lines set up and drawn between the individual and the social, as theory and as esthetic, then the chapter referred to as the Summa of the Jamesian poiesis completes the Jamesian quest for Bondsman. It sets the frame in which we know Bondsman differently from the start, because we know ourselves more. We know in the frustrated nonrealization of Bondsman's powers the loss to be personal. There is no way to cut that loss, no way to deal it. The division of this "coordinated" loss cannot be made—the loss that is universal. It can no more be done than a scientifically accurate division of the cumulative economic value of human/coexistence and global fitting together can be done. Then as now the lines are arbitrary and logical only in relation to the bourgeois social imaginary.

This bourgeois imaginaire social—creative in its time, purely destructive in its decline, dangerous now with the atom split, the social solidarity of humanity and the biosphere we inhabit—has become the primary imperative. It calls for an imaginaire social able to link everyone. Thus we live the dark age of its meaninglessness as James points out at the end of *Beyond a Boundary* (190):

> What little remains of "It isn't cricket" is being stifled by the envy, the hatred, the malice and the uncharitableness, the sharelessness of the memoirs written by some of the cricketers themselves. Compared with these books, Sir Donald's ruthless autobiography of a dozen years ago now reads like a Victorian novel. How to blind one's eye to all this? Body-line was only a link in a chain. Modern society took a turn downwards in 1929 and "It isn't cricket" is one of the casualties. There is no need to despair of cricket. Much, much more than cricket is at stake, in fact everything is at stake. If and when society regenerates itself, cricket will do the same. The owl of

Minerva flies only at dusk. And it cannot get much darker without becoming night impenetrable.

The Jamesian summa of a popular esthetics opens a sunlit clearing in our present impenetrability: a vision of life that unfurls new vistas on a livable future, both for ourselves and for the socio-biosphere we inhabit. "Prolegomena," James writes of Grace, "is a tough word but my purpose being what it is, it is the only one I can honestly use. It means the social, political, literary and other antecedents of some outstanding figure in the arts and sciences. Grasp the fact that a whole nation had prepared the way for him and you begin to see his status as a national embodiment" (*B.B.*, 168). The same can be said of James—with one crucial difference. If W. G. Grace embodied a national process, James embodies an entire world historical process. And so, too, does his poiesis. With its ease and certainty of phrase, its refusal at whatever price to fake the game, it establishes the new identity of Caliban. The region is not only new. It evokes a shared "Ah!" of recognition and delight.

Notes

1   C. L. R. James, *Beyond a Boundary* (London: Hutchinson, 1963). Further references to this book [*B.B.*] will be given parenthetically.

2   "All I wanted was to play cricket and soccer, not merely to play *but to live the life*, and nothing could stop me. When all my tricks and plans and evasions failed, I just went and played and said *to hell with the consequences*. Two people lived in me. One, *the rebel against all family and school discipline and order; the other, a Puritan who would have cut off a finger sooner than do anything contrary to the ethics of the game.* To complicate my troubled life with my distracted family, the Queen's Royal College fed the other two of my obsessions, English literature. . . . I discovered in the college library that besides *Vanity Fair*, Thackeray had written thirty-six other volumes. . . . After Thackeray there was the whole bunch of English novelists . . . the poets. But in the public library in town there was everything" (*B.B.*, 37) (italics mine).

3   Michel Foucault, *The History of Sexuality* (New York: Random House, 1978), 1:36.

4   Gregory Bateson has emphasized the centrality of abduction systems to all human thought and representation. He calls abduction the "lateral extension of abstract components of description. . . . Metaphor, dream, parable, allegory, the whole of art, the whole of science, the whole of religion, the whole of poetry, totemism (as already mentioned), the organization of facts in comparative anatomy—all these

are instances or aggregates of instances of abduction, within the human mental sphere." See *Mind and Nature* (New York: Dutton, 1979), 142.

5   Bateson, *Mind and Nature*, 143.

6   Ibid., 140.

7   Asmaron Legesse, *Gada: Three Approaches to the Study of African Society* (New York: Free Press, 1973), 258.

8   "My father's father . . . as a mature man worked as a panboiler on a sugar estate, a responsible job involving the critical transition of the boiling cane juice from liquid into sugar. It was a post in those days usually held by white men" (*B.B.*, 17) (italics mine).

9   "It [the public school code] came doctrinally from the masters, who for two generations, from the foundation of the school, had been Oxford and Cambridge men. . . . [Inside] the classroom the code had little success. . . . [We] lied and cheated without any sense of shame. . . . But as soon as we stepped onto the cricket or football field, more particularly the cricket field, all was changed. We were a motley crew. The children of some white officials and businessmen, middle-class blacks and mulattos, Chinese boys, some of whose parents still spoke broken English, Indian boys, some of whose parents could speak no English at all, and some poor black boys who had won exhibitions or whose parents had starved and toiled on plots of agricultural land and were spending their hard-earned money on giving the eldest boy an education" (*B.B.*, 34–35).

10   James came to be bound by the "vision of life," by the rules: "Before very long I acquired a discipline for which the only name is Puritan. I never cheated, I never appealed for a decision unless I thought the batsman was out, I never argued with the umpire, I never jeered at a defeated opponent, I never gave to a friend a vote or a place which by any stretch of imagination could be seen as belonging to any enemy or to a stranger. My defeats and disappointments I took as stoically as I could. If I caught myself complaining or making excuses I pulled up" (*B.B.*, 35).

11   As he points out, to acquire the code he paid a price—the forfeiture of reaching the room at the top and the title of Honourable. "[In] order to acquire this code, I was driven to evasions, disobedience, open rebelliousness, continuous lies and even stealing. . . . I was not a vicious boy. All I wanted was to play cricket and soccer, not merely to play but to live the life" (*B.B.*, 36–37).

12   Dick Howard, *The Marxian Legacy* (London: Macmillan, 1977), 265.

13   Howard, *The Marxian Legacy*.

14   Jean Baudrillard, *The Mirror of Production* (St. Louis: Telos, 1975), 142.

15   C. L. R. James, *State Capitalism and World Revolution* (Chicago: Charles Kerr, 1986), 115–16.

16   James, *State Capitalism*, 117.

17   Cf. "The tremendous labor of that which I have called 'morality of mores' . . . *the labor performed by man upon himself* during the greater part of the existence of the human race, his entire *prehistoric* labor, finds in this its meaning, its great justification, notwithstanding the severity, tyranny, stupidity and idiocy involved in it: *with the aid of the morality of mores* and the social straitjacket, man was actually *made* calculable." Walter Kaufman, ed., *The Basic Writings of Nietzsche* (New York: Modern Library, 1968), 495 (italics mine).

18 As in the Jamaican situation under Manley where the representation of the jobless as "sufferers" not only perverted Marxism, which insisted on the contribution of labor and on its right to a decent standard of living, but also enabled the rise of redemptive messiahs who realize their own powers through manipulation of a peculiarly ugly blend of Marxist Labourism and black (in its biological rather than social category sense) nationalism.

19 C. L. R. James, *Minty Alley* (London: Secker and Warburg, 1936), 168–70.

20 Immanuel Wallerstein, *The Modern World System* (New York: Academic Press, 1974), 64.

21 Michel Foucault, *Power/Knowledge* (New York: Pantheon, 1980), 31 (italics mine).

22 K. Henry, "The Formative Influences in Earlier Twentieth-Century Responses to America," (unpublished paper, 1976).

23 Ibid.

24 C. L. R. James, "On the Origins," *Radical America* 2 (August 1968):29.

25 C. L. R. James, *At the Rendezvous of Victory* (London: Allison and Busby, 1984), 247, 246.

26 Ibid., 250.

27 Ibid., 249.

Seven

Cricket and National Culture in the Writings of C. L. R. James

Neil Lazarus

▼▼▼▼▼

To begin an essay, intended for publication in the United States, on the subject of C. L. R. James and cricket is inevitably to feel oneself under the shadow of an objection. The problem is that although James is unthinkable without cricket, cricket is unintelligible to most Americans. Within the United States, cricket is popularly represented as an alien game, aimless, quaintly decadent, and, as a sport, unassimilable. Yet it is not only James's ideas about sport but also his ideas about history, politics, and ideology that bear the decisive imprint of his encounter and lifelong fascination with this game. The conclusion that James is likely to remain a dead letter where American readers are concerned seems inescapable. Thus the celebrated British Marxist historian E. P. Thompson, writes that "I'm afraid that American theorists will not understand this, but the clue to everything [in James] lies in his proper appreciation of the game of cricket."[1] External facts would seem to support this conclusion: when James's classic autobiography *Beyond a Boundary* (1963) was issued in an American edition in 1986, for instance, it failed miserably despite the positive reviews that attended its publication. American readers were evidently unable or unwilling to appreciate a book that, in its author's own words, "is neither cricket reminiscences nor autobiography [but] . . . poses the question *What do they know of cricket who only cricket know?*"[2]

This problem of access to James's thought is doubtless a substantial one. It would be regrettable, however, were it to be viewed as grounds for American readers not to grapple with James's work. The claims that one would like to make for James are not modest. Hazel Carby has written that *Beyond a Boundary* is "one of the most outstanding works of cultural studies ever produced."[3] In this chapter I would like to build upon this proposition. It will be my argument that in his writings about cricket, James reveals himself to be one of the truly decisive Marxist cultural theorists of our century. To neglect these writings would therefore be to neglect a body of work of the stature of those of Georg Lukács, Mikhail Bakhtin, or Stuart Hall.

One's first encounter with James's writing about cricket is likely to induce a sense of shock or displacement. It is not that one will not have come across such prose before; rather, it is that one will not have seen it deployed with reference to sport. Consider the following passages for instance—chosen not, of course, at random, but representing nevertheless only three of literally hundreds of passages that might have been cited:

> There is nothing of the panther in the batting of Sobers. He is the most orthodox of great batsmen. The only stroke he makes in a manner peculiar to himself is the hook. Where George Headley used to face the ball square and hit across it, Denis Compton placed himself well outside it on the off-side, and Walcott compromised by stepping backwards but not fully across and hitting, usually well in front of and not behind square leg, Sobers seems to stand where he is and depend upon wrist and eyesight to swish the short fast ball square to the boundary. Apart from that, his method, his technique is carried to an extreme where it is indistinguishable from nature.[4]

> A great West Indies cricketer in his play should embody some essence of that crowded vagueness which passes for the history of the West Indies. If, like Kanhai, he is one of the most remarkable and individual of contemporary batsmen, then that should not make him less but more West Indian. You see what you are looking for, and in Kanhai's batting what I have found is a unique pointer of the West Indian quest for identity, for ways of expressing our potential bursting at every seam.[5]

> I haven't the slightest doubt that the clash of race, caste and class did not retard but stimulated West Indian cricket. I am equally certain that in those years social and political passions, denied normal outlets, expressed themselves so fiercely in cricket (and other games)

precisely because they were games. Here began my personal calvary. The British tradition soaked deep into me was that when you entered the sporting arena you left behind you the sordid compromises of everyday existence. Yet for us to do that we would have had to divest ourselves of our skins. From the moment I had to decide which club I would join the contrast between the ideal and the real fascinated me and tore at my insides. Nor could the local population see it otherwise. The class and racial rivalries were too intense. They could be fought out without violence or much lost except pride and honour. Thus the cricket field was a stage on which selected individuals played representative roles which were charged with social significance. (B.B., 72)

In the third passage, James identifies cricket as a privileged site for the playing out and imaginary resolution of social antagonisms in the colonial and postcolonial West Indies. In the second passage, he suggests that only a sociopoetics of cricket will be able to do justice to its complexity and ideological resonance. Cricket, he writes in *Beyond a Boundary*, "is a game of high and difficult technique. If it were not it could not carry the load of social response and implications which it carries" (43). We will return to these formulations in due course. First, however, it is necessary to reflect on the first of the passages cited above. In this passage, crafted in the rhetoric of esthetics and taking as its object the question of form—of cricketing *style*—James situates cricket unambiguously and unhesitatingly as art. The register of his descriptions of Garfield Sobers at bat, or of the technique of fast bowler Wesley Hall, derives unmistakably from the universe of high cultural criticism. What James writes about a glorious drive past point by Learie Constantine, off the bowling of Walter Hammond in 1926—that the stroke had never been seen before, but that, having been made, it instantly entered cricket history as defining of the square drive—is reminiscent of, and strictly comparable with, Walter Benjamin's observation that "all great works of literature found a genre or dissolve one."[6]

Nor is this gesture on James's part remotely an accident. Cricket is in his view not an instance of "light" art, which he happens to find stimulating, nor an instance of "popular" culture, although it is certainly popular. On the contrary, James insists that cricket is a form of art to exactly the same degree as drama, opera, or lyric poetry. Attempting to specify the conditions of cricket's estheticism thus, he points first to the extraordinary balance within the game between structure and agency. Each cricket match consists of an indefinite number of discrete events, each with its own resolution, whose objective meaning can only be read at the level of the match as a whole. Yet the logic of the game is such that each and any one of these discrete events bears within itself the potential to shatter the objective pattern of the match as it has unfolded (often over the course of several days) to that point. To win a cricket match, a team needs first to place itself in a position from which victory is possible. Time is involved, and also application; advantages must be consolidated, opportunities seized, mistakes systematically capitalized upon. Yet a cricket match balances upon a hair trigger. A single ball can change its direction and outcome; a single stroke, in anger or defiance or disdain, can shatter and reconstitute the meaning of all that has preceded it. "The total spectacle," James writes,

> consists and must consist of a series of individual, isolated episodes, each in itself completely self-contained. Each has its beginning, the ball bowled; its middle, the stroke played; its end, runs, no runs, dismissal. Within the fluctuating interest of the rise or fall of the game as a whole, there is this unending series of events, each single one fraught with immense possibilities of expectation and realization. . . . In the very finest of soccer matches the ball for long periods is in places where it is impossible to expect any definite alteration in the relative position of the two sides. In lawn tennis the duration of the rally is entirely dependent upon the subjective skill of the players. In baseball alone does the encounter between the two representative protagonists approach the definitiveness of the individual series of episodes in cricket which together constitute the whole. (*B.B.*, 193)

Even baseball, however, cannot quite match the structural complexity of cricket's mode of representation. Like many games, James observes, "[c]ricket is first and foremost a dramatic spectacle. It belongs with the theatre, ballet, opera and the dance" (*B.B.*, 192). Cricket's uniqueness, in these terms, consists not solely in its spectacularity, but in the manner in which its enactment of competition and struggle is conducted at the level of representative individuals—bowler and batsman—whose individual performances emerge sustainedly and uninterruptedly as allegories of the situation of their teams. James distinguishes cricket specifically from baseball in this respect:

the baseball-batter . . . may and often does find himself after a fine
hit standing on one of the bases, where he is now dependent upon
others. The [cricket] batsman facing the ball does not merely represent his side. For that moment, to all intents and purposes, he is
his side. This fundamental relation of the One and the Many, Individual and Social, Individual and Universal, leader and followers,
representative and ranks, the part and the whole, is structurally imposed on the players of cricket. What other sports . . . have to aim
at, [cricket] . . . players are given to start with, they cannot depart
from it. Thus the game is founded upon a dramatic, a human relation
which is universally recognized as the most objectively pervasive
and psychologically stimulating in life and therefore in that artificial
representation of it which is drama. (B.B., 193)

In speaking of cricket as a form of dramatic art, James does not mean
that cricket *resembles* drama. He means that it *is* drama. Indeed, it is
drama of a distinctly orthodox and historic kind. On numerous occasions
throughout *Beyond a Boundary*, he draws an analogy between the spectacle of cricket in the West Indies and the spectacle of drama in classical
Greek society: "Once every year for four days the tens of thousands of
Athenian citizens sat in the open air on the stone seats at the side of the
Acropolis and from sunrise to sunset watched the plays of the competing
dramatists. All that we have to correspond is a Test match" (156).[7]
    The consequences that follow from this association of cricket and clas-
sical Greek drama are significant. Inasmuch as cricket's spectacularity
emerges as an integral aspect of its esthetic being, so, too, does its popularity. The role of the crowd is, in James's view, positively constitutive
of cricket's meaning as a cultural form. In a brilliant passage in *Beyond
a Boundary*, he exposes the elitism of the famous cricket commentator
Neville Cardus, who represented the game as an art form readily enough,
but who insisted at the same time that its meaning as art was unavail-
able to the majority of those who made up its audience. On the one hand,
James notes, "all [Cardus's] work is eloquent with the aesthetic appeal
of cricket" (191).[8] On the other hand, even as Cardus moved to grapple
with this "aesthetic appeal" of cricket, he shied away from its democratic
implications. Although cricket was a form of art to him, he would not
allow that it might be so too for the millions who followed the game
throughout the world. Art was not for the masses: "I do not believe that

anything fine in music or in anything else can be truly understood or truly felt by the crowd." To the extent that cricket was an art, therefore, its true meaning necessarily remained inaccessible to the overwhelming majority of those who watched and played it. James takes strong exception to this sentiment:

> Neville Cardus . . . often introduces music into his cricket writing. Never once has Neville Cardus . . . introduced cricket into his writing on music. He finds this "a curious point." It is much more than a point, it is not curious. Cardus is a victim of that categorization and specialization, that division of the human personality, which is the greatest curse of our time. Cricket has suffered, but not only cricket. The aestheticians have scorned to take notice of popular sports and games—to their own detriment. The aridity and confusion of which they so mournfully complain will continue until they include organized games *and the people who watch them* as an integral part of their data. (*B.B.*, 191–92)[9]

James writes not only against the Neville Carduses of his world, exponents of a frankly confessed conservatism in cultural criticism, but also, implicitly, against such influential Marxist theorists as T. W. Adorno and Herbert Marcuse, who insist upon the "autonomy" of art from life. Adorno, for instance, argues that it is only by virtue of this autonomy (achieved at the price of art's innocence) that art is capable of withstanding the imperatives of commodification in the capitalist era. In his view, only that cultural labor that risks incomprehensibility is today able to resist recuperation by the "culture industry." Sport is specifically listed by Adorno, along with film and mass music, as a wholly fetishistic cultural practice, disclosive only of regressive social values.[10]

James would have refused to concede the validity either of the Adornian principle of art's autonomy, or of the conception that, in Adorno's thought, makes that principle necessary—that life itself has become totalitarian, has been reduced to "the sphere of private existence and now of mere consumption" and, as such, is "dragged along as an appendage of the process of material production, without autonomy or substance of its own."[11] This is not to suggest that James is insensitive to the reified quality of everyday life in the era of multinational capitalism. On the contrary, he both acknowledges "the violence and ferocity of our age" (*B.B.*, 193) and traces the effects of this violence upon the ways in which cricket is played. At no stage, however, does he commit himself to the hypostatized romantic conception of art as that which, in the words of the early Lukács, "always says 'And yet!' to life."[12]

Within the context of twentieth-century esthetic theory, this romantic conception has typically been mobilized in the service of an irreducibly Eurocentric anticapitalism. Even where—as in the problematic of Western Marxism—this anticapitalism has been insistently radical in tendency, it has invariably been sketched against the backdrop of "civilization." While culture has tended to be theorized as that which opposed the consolidation and extension of this civilization (that is, of capitalist hegemony), so, too, and paradoxically, the much heralded "decline of the West" has tended to be theorized not as the death rattle of imperialism but as the end of history. Auschwitz, Adorno has written, "demonstrated irrefutably that culture has failed. . . . All post-Auschwitz culture, including its urgent critique, is garbage."[13]

James is never disposed to think in such terms. Against those conservative cultural critics who complain about "the envy, the hatred, the malice and the uncharitableness" of the modern form of cricket, he points out that it is not in cricket alone that a new ethic has come to prevail, but in "modern society" at large: "Modern society took a turn downwards in 1929 and 'It isn't cricket' is one of the casualties. There is no need to despair of cricket. Much, much more than cricket is at stake, in fact everything is at stake. If and when society regenerates itself, cricket will do the same. . . . The owl of Minerva flies only at dusk. And it cannot get much darker without becoming night impenetrable" (B.B., 190). At first glance this might seem to support the Adornian reading of culture and society, but against such a reading, in turn, James would protest that it is only from a vantage point within "modern society"—that is, from the centers of the capitalist world system—that the darkness seems all-encompassing. In James's view, this darkness is not, in fact, the darkness of "night impenetrable," but rather of a world-historical eclipse signalled, in the world of politics, by the rising tide of anti-imperialism and, more narrowly in one sphere of the world of culture, by the emergence, the sudden explosion in the late 1950s and the 1960s, of West Indian cricket.

Hence the indispensability, for James, of a *sociopoetics* of cricket, an approach to the game that will make neither the mistake of supposing it to be less than a form of art, nor the mistake of supposing it, as a form of art, to be autonomous. In the trenchant "Introduction" to a selection of his writings on cricket that appeared in 1986, he notes that "An artistic, a social event does not reflect the age. It is the age. Cricket, I want to say most clearly, is not an addition or a decoration or some specific unit that one adds to what really constitutes the history of a period. Cricket is as much part of the history as books written are part of the history" (C., xi).

Elsewhere, his tone is even more insistent—as when, in *Beyond a Boundary* (70), he asserts that "cricket and football were the greatest cultural influences in nineteenth century Britain, leaving far behind Tennyson's poems, Beardsley's drawings and concerts of the Philharmonic Society. These filled space in print but not in minds." The point is, however, that as James understands cricket, it is not merely as a form of culture, but concretely and materially as a form of *national* culture. It is for this reason that James can maintain that a biography of Donald Bradman will need, at the same time, to be "a history of Australia in the same period" (*B.B.*, 180). Similarly, no one ignorant of the historical trajectory of West Indian society over the course of the past hundred years will, in his view, be able to grasp the meaning of the play of Wilton St. Hill, Learie Constantine, or Rohan Kanhai.

In order for us to understand why this should be so—to appreciate the extent to which (and the different manners in which) cricket has figured as a constituent of national consciousness in England, Australia, and the West Indies—it is necessary to examine James's social history of the game. He locates its institutionalization in the years between 1780 and 1840. Cricket was created, he writes,

> by the yeoman farmer, the gamekeeper, the potter, the tinker, the Nottingham coal-miner, the Yorkshire factory hand. These artisans made it, men of hand and eye. Rich and idle young noblemen and some substantial city people contributed money, organization and prestige. Between them, by 1837 they had evolved a highly complicated game with all the typical characteristics of a genuinely national art form: founded on elements long present in the nation, profoundly popular in origin, yet attracting to it disinterested elements of the leisured and educated classes. Confined to areas and numbers which were relatively small, it contained all the premises of rapid growth. There was nothing in the slightest degree Victorian about it. At their matches cricketers ate and drank with the gusto of the time, sang songs and played for large sums of money. Bookies sat

before the pavilion at Lord's[14] openly taking bets. The unscrupulous nobleman and the poor but dishonest commoner alike bought and sold matches. (*B.B.*, 158–59)

No sooner had cricket been consolidated in these terms, as a game essentially outside the realm of bourgeois social relations, than it became, during the Victorian era, the site of an ideological struggle. It was not, James writes, that the English national bourgeoisie, the "solid Victorian middle class" (*B.B.*, 159), consciously set out to appropriate the game, to lift it from its artisanal, regional, and predominantly rural roots and to make it over in their own image. Yet it was precisely such an appropriation that was effected, and James describes it as "unerring" (163). Cricket was transformed from a game expressing the social ethos of a residual and increasingly marginal combination of class fractions into a "moral discipline," disseminated above all in such public schools as Thomas Arnold's Rugby and serving the interests of the middle-class rise to hegemony. "The Victorians made it compulsory for their children, and all the evidence points to the fact that they valued competence in it and respect for what it came to signify more than they did intellectual accomplishment of any kind. The only word that I know for this is culture. The proof of its validity is its success, first of all at home and then almost as rapidly abroad, in the most diverse places and among peoples living lives which were poles removed from that whence it originally came. This signifies, as so often in any deeply national movement, that it contained elements of universality that went beyond the bounds of the originating nation." (*B.B.*, 164)

If this transformation of cricket must, retrospectively, be viewed in the light of an ideological struggle, it must be acknowledged that the struggle was not always recognized as such. Indeed, in the person of W. G. Grace, the greatest exponent of cricket in the Victorian era and one of the greatest players who ever lived, James identifies a figure whose astonishing aptitude for the game derived from the seemingly uncomplicated (if compound) presence within him of residual and emergent elements of the national culture. Grace, he writes (and I do not apologize for the length of the quotation, for James's formulation could neither be improved upon nor adequately summarized)

seems to have been one of those men in whom the characteristics of life as lived by many generations seemed to meet for the last, in

a complete and perfectly blended whole. His personality was sufficiently wide and firm to include a strong Victorian streak without
being inhibited. That I would say was his greatest strength. He was
not in any way inhibited. What he lacked he would not need. All
that he had he could use. In tune with his inheritance and his environment, he was not in any way repressed. All his physical and
spiritual force was at his disposal to do what he wanted to do. He is
said on all sides to have been one of the most typical of Englishmen,
to have symbolized John Bull, and so on and so forth. To this, it is
claimed, as well as to his deeds, he owed his enormous popularity.
I take leave to doubt it. The man usually hailed as representative
is never quite typical, is more subtly compounded than the plain
up-and-down figure of the stock characteristics. Looking on from
outside and at a distance it seems to me that Grace gives a more complex impression than is usually attributed to him. He was English
undoubtedly, very much so. But he was typical of an England that
was being superseded. He was the yeoman, the country doctor, the
squire, the England of yesterday. But he was no relic, nor historical
or nostalgic curiosity. He was pre-Victorian in the Victorian age but
a pre-Victorian militant. (*B.B.*, 175–76)

On the domestic stage—and, by osmosis, in Australia—cricket was
refunctioned by the Victorian middle classes as an instrument of moral
discipline. Yet it proved sufficiently pliable as a cultural form to with-
stand several further refunctionings. James offers a sociopoetical analysis
of some of these: the glittering back foot-batting of Kumar Shri Ranjitsin-
hji in England and Victor Trumper in Australia in the Edwardian years,
for example; and the reorganization of batting in the interests of aggres-
sion and efficiency on the part of the Australians, led by Ponsford and
Bradman, in the 1920s and 1930s. Above all, however, he is interested in
chronicling the social history of cricket in the West Indies in the years
before and after decolonization in the 1960s.

Here, a somewhat different canvas must be used. Cricket was not
introduced to the West Indies under the rubric of moral discipline alone.
The social space of the West Indies was marked out as a *colonial* space,
and cricket, imposed there as it never was in Australia, New Zealand,
or South Africa upon a subject people from without, had a specific role
to play in the maintenance of colonial authority. To James, the special
wonder of cricket is that even in the face of these unpromising originary

circumstances, it proved possible to transform the game into "a means of [West Indian] national expression" (C., 171). West Indians have, over the years of this century, been able to pull cricket across the Manichean divide of colonialism; they have been able to force it to carry the weight of *their* social desires and to speak *their* language, whether of emergent anticolonialism, nationalist affirmation, or, since decolonization, of international self-presence. In *Beyond a Boundary*, James remarks on "the grandeur of a game which, in lands far from that which gave it birth, could encompass so much of social reality and still remain a game" (97).

The "indigenization" of cricket in the West Indies could never have taken place beneath the level of popular consciousness as, arguably, its "Victorianization" did in nineteenth-century England. James describes the ideologically resonant but psychologically unproblematical confluence of the old and the new in the person of W. G. Grace. Writing of himself, by contrast, he notes that while he was a colonial subject, "a British intellectual long before I was ten," this subject position contrived to render him "an alien in my own environment among my own people, even my own family" (B.B., 28). Where nativist intellectuals have tended to lament this sort of "alienation," however, regarding it as the ground of a "loss of self" from which they have never been able to recover, James suggests that its ideological implications were not fixed but volatile. Colonial subjection did not always produce obedient colonial subjects: "[I] found [myself] and came to maturity within a system that was the result of centuries of development in another land, was transplanted as a hothouse flower is transplanted and bore some strange fruit" (B.B., 50).

What was true of the "system" was true, too, of at least one of its elements: cricket. Introduced to the West Indies as part and parcel of colonial governance—part and parcel of an ensemble that included "English Puritanism, English literature and cricket"—it was fought for and fought over, made to vibrate with "the realism of West Indian life" (B.B., 30). Because, in order to make cricket their own, the West Indian masses had to prise it loose from British culture; because British culture was precisely what, as a colonized population, they struggled against; and because, by virtue of the specificity of the circumstances of their colonization, they had comparatively few institutionalized forms of cultural practice of their own, they bestowed a privileged position upon cricket. At the risk of oversimplification, one might say that in the West Indies, cricket became culture. Thus, James, citing E. W. Swanton's 1957 observation to the effect that "in the West Indies the cricket ethic has shaped not only the cricketers but social life as a whole," comments that "[i]t is an understatement. There is a whole generation of us, and perhaps two generations, who have been formed by it not only in social attitudes but in our most intimate lives, in fact there more than anywhere else. The social attitudes we could to some degree alter if we wished. For the inner self the die was cast" (*B.B.*, 49).

In the colonial West Indies, cricket emerged as the cultural form most expressive of popular West Indian social aspirations. If, in being introduced to the West Indies, the game had seemed a perfect ideological foil for colonialism, it now began to represent a remarkably different sensibility. This sensibility was not a revolutionary one. It could not have been, in the absence of a revolutionary social movement. The ideological protocols of cricket were refashioned, not overthrown. West Indian cricket emerged entirely within the constraints of the rules of the colonial game. However, where the predominant characteristics of the colonial game had consisted in orderliness, discipline, resolution, and puritanism, the West Indian game reflected a different rationality. The social significance of this rationality was, naturally enough, misrecognized by English commentators. They could see in the emergent West Indian style of play only indiscipline, excess, and irresponsibility. Thus a correspondent for *The Times* reported in 1928 about the West Indian batsman Wilton St. Hill: "W. H. St. Hill . . . can be relied upon to provide the entertainment of the side. He is very supple, has a beautifully erect stance and, having lifted his bat, performs amazing apparently double-jointed tricks with his wrists and arms. Some of those contortions are graceful and remunerative, such as his gliding to leg, but some are unsound and dangerous, such as an exaggerated turn of the wrist in cutting. He will certainly play some big and attractive innings, but some others may be easily curtailed by his exotic fancy in dealing with balls on the off-side" (quoted in *B.B.*, 102–3).[15]

James turns to Wilton St. Hill in discussing the emergence of West Indian cricket because the Trinidadian was one of the truly decisive—and, for James, truly *representative*—figures in the game in the years before 1939. It was on the strength of batting of the quality and style of St. Hill's that cricket in the West Indies was able to shoulder the political burden of its popularity. I have already cited James's comment to the effect that "the cricket field was a stage on which selected individuals played representative roles which were charged with social significance" (*B.B.*, 72). The role St. Hill played, in these terms, was tragic because, as a batsman, he carried all before him except for one season. This one season—with the visiting West Indian side in England in 1928—was historic, however. Not only did it become the yardstick by which the English public measured his play, but it was also read by St. Hill's devoted followers back in Trinidad as a comprehensive setback for the kind of cricket he played, and for the social vision embryonically prefigured in such cricket. For the Trinidadian crowds, James writes, "the unquestioned glory of St. Hill's batting [in the years prior to 1928] conveyed the sensation that here was one of us, performing *in excelsis* in a sphere where competition was open. It was a demonstration that atoned for a pervading humiliation, and nourished pride and hope. Jimmy Durante, the famous American comedian, has popularized a phrase in the United States: 'That's my boy.' I am told that its popularity originates in the heart of the immigrant, struggling with the new language, baffled by the new customs . . . Wilton St. Hill was our boy" (*B.B.*, 99).

For years, St. Hill batted brilliantly against any opposition. He was left out of the West Indian side to England in 1923 solely on racial grounds; he persevered and, in 1926, when the English side visited the West Indies, he was outstanding. When, finally, in 1928, he simply could not be left off the touring West Indian team to England, he left with the expectations of all Trinidad hanging on his performance. "We [were] . . . convinced in our own minds," James writes, "that St. Hill was the greatest of all West Indian batsmen and on English wickets this coloured man would infallibly put all white rivals in the shade" (*B.B.*, 100). The responsibility proved to be too much for St. Hill. Not only did he fail in England, but he failed miserably: "He was a horrible, a disastrous, an incredible, failure, the greatest failure to come out of the West Indies" (101). This collapse must be read in ideological terms: St. Hill failed because no one person could have succeeded, at that time, in doing what he was asked to do. Although he never overcame the blow of this failure, it was not his alone, but that of all Trinidadians whose social desires his batting represented. James concludes that St. Hill's "spirit was untameable, perhaps too much so" (103). Only when it is understood historically is this conclusion fully intelligible. It suggests that St. Hill's tragedy lay in the fact that although he played cricket as it would come to be played, and in such a way as to articulate the aspirations of the masses who adored him, he could not represent himself on the stage of the world when it mattered most.

To raise the issue of self-representation in the colonial context is to raise the issue of nationalism. In the history of West Indian cricket it is to move from Wilton St. Hill to Learie Constantine. James argues that St. Hill's failure was not his alone, but a representative failure reflecting a certain prematurity, a certain lack of cohesion in the social consciousness of the classes whose aspirations were expressed in St. Hill's batting. This argument can be cast counterfactually as a question, What would it have taken for St. Hill to succeed? The question finds its answer, for James, in the career of Constantine, who succeeded—spectacularly—where St. Hill could not. Where St. Hill failed so desperately in 1928, Constantine, his near contemporary and fellow Trinidadian, took England by storm. "He took 100 wickets, made 1000 runs and laid claim to being the finest fieldsman yet known" (*B.B.*, 110).

James locates the difference between St. Hill and Constantine in class terms. St. Hill was born in 1893, into the Trinidadian lower middle class. He worked all his life as a salesman in a department store. His experiences as a cricketer simply underscored his experiences as a "brownish" (*B.B.*, 93) subject of a colonial order. With Constantine, it was different. Born a few years later than St. Hill, he was a member of a cricketing family universally respected in the West Indies: "From the time young Constantine knew himself he knew his father as the most loved and most famous cricketer in the island. His mother's brother, Victor Pascall, was the West Indies slow left-hander, a most charming person and a great popular favourite with all classes. We cannot overestimate the influence of all this on young Constantine. He was born to the purple, and in cricket circles never saw himself as inferior to anyone or dependent for anything on anyone" (107).

Constantine received a good elementary education but found himself incapable of securing a job commensurate with his qualifications. On the cricket field, he was first among equals; off it, and despite his family's reputation, he was black in a colonial society in which a strict color bar reserved preferential jobs for whites. In St. Hill's case, the encounter with discrimination in the social sphere was expected and, partly because of this, met with resignation. In Constantine's case, it was unexpected and bitterly resisted. James reads Constantine's success in England in 1928 in the light of a strike against colonialism: "Constantine, the heir-apparent, the happy warrior, the darling of the crowd, prize pupil of the captain of the West Indies . . . revolted against the revolting contrast between his first-class status as a cricketer and his third-class status as a man" (*B.B.*, 110).

If the tour to England in 1928 was a crushing defeat for St. Hill, it allowed Constantine to emerge as a national hero. In this fact, James locates the fundamental difference between the two players. St. Hill was idolized, revered by his followers, but he could never have been spoken of as a "national hero." The social aspirations to which his batting gave eloquent voice were those of the populace, and they would come in due course to serve centrally as constituents of West Indian national consciousness. They were not—or not yet—*national* in scope or tendency. Constantine, however, was a properly national hero. The irony was that as Trinidad was then constituted it was a colony and not a nation. Constantine's success on the cricket field, James argues, was therefore as instrumental as any other factor in laying the ground for the emergence of a national consciousness in Trinidad and, for that matter, the West Indies.

It is testimony to his extraordinary timeliness that Constantine recognized this. He recognized it, in fact, at a time—the late 1920s—when even James himself did not do so. In *Beyond a Boundary*, James records some of his conversations with Constantine during these years, when both men lived and worked in the north of England, Constantine as a professional cricketer, James as a writer, journalist, and political activist. James recalls Constantine's insistence that despite the fact that West Indian teams seemed invariably to lose important matches to English teams, the standard of West Indian cricket was as high as that of English cricket. Constantine's repeated "They are no better than we" was already a political demand. "It was a slogan and a banner. It was politics, the politics of nationalism" (*B.B.*, 117). It was such because Constantine's proposed solution to the problem was so demonstrably nationalist in tenor: "They are no better than we, he used to say: we can bat and bowl and field as well as any of them. To my—as I thought—devastating query, 'Why do we always lose and make such a poor show?' he would reply: 'We need a black man as captain.' I was stupid enough to believe that he was dealing with the question of race. I should have known that it was not so. . . . What he used to tell me was that the West Indian players were not a team and to become a team they needed a captain who had the respect of the players and was able to get the best out of the team. Not too far from his argument was the sentiment that a good captain would respect all the men" (*C.*, 257).

The fact that this quotation is extracted from a 1970 essay on Sir Frank Worrell points to the direction assumed by James's social history of cricket in the West Indies. If the space between Wilton St. Hill and Learie

Constantine is the space through which the problematic of nationalism entered West Indian cricket, that between Constantine and Worrell
marks the moment of decolonization. What Constantine was prescient
enough to be able to imagine, Worrell was able to make real, but not
before conditions were ripe. Worrell's captaincy of the West Indian team
in the late 1950s and early 1960s—like the play of individuals such as
Garfield Sobers, Rohan Kanhai, Lance Gibbs, and Wesley Hall on this
team—had everything to do with the current of West Indian politics.
James, in a passage I have already cited, speaks of Kanhai's batting at this
time as expressive of the "West Indian quest for identity," after all.

It would be possible to extend James's examination of West Indian
cricket as "national allegory"[16] almost indefinitely. James himself has
written extensively on Worrell, Sobers, and Kanhai. It would not be difficult to apply his analytical methods to the eras of Clive Lloyd and Vivian
Richards—a period of more than a decade in which the West Indies never
came close to losing a test series—although it would be impossible to
match his insights, generated, as he points out, from a lifetime's *study*
of cricket. "I did not merely play cricket. I studied it. I analysed strokes, I
studied types, I read its history, its beginnings, how and when it changed
from period to period, I read about it in Australia and in South Africa. I
read and compared statistics, I made clippings, I talked to all cricketers,
particularly the intercolonial cricketers and those who had gone abroad.
I compared what they told me with what I read in old copies of *Wis-
den*. I looked up the play of the men who had done well or badly against
the West Indies. I read and appreciated the phraseology of laws" (*B.B.*,
41–42).

Two passages, for me at least, represent James's cultural criticism at
its most illuminating and expansive. The first is just two sentences long:
"Garfield Sobers, I shall show, is a West Indian cricketer, not merely a
cricketer from the West Indies. He is the most typical West Indian cricketer that it is possible to imagine" (*F.P.*, 213). In order to understand
this formulation, it is necessary to cite the second passage, drawn from
Beyond a Boundary (225):

What do they know of cricket who only cricket know? West Indians
crowding to Tests bring with them the whole past history and future
hopes of the islands. English people, for example, have a conception of themselves breathed from birth. Drake and mighty Nelson,
Shakespeare, Waterloo, the Charge of the Light Brigade, the few who

did so much for so many, the success of parliamentary democracy, those and such as those constitute a national tradition. Underdeveloped countries have to go back centuries to rebuild one. We of the West Indies have none at all, none that we know of. To such people the three W's, Ram and Val wrecking English batting, help to fill a huge gap in their consciousness and in their needs. In one of the sheds on the Port of Spain wharf is a painted sign: 365 Garfield Sobers.

"365 Garfield Sobers": the reference is to the highest score made by any batsman in a test match and to Sobers, who made it. Two features of these passages seem to me momentous in their implications. First is James's argument, to which I have already alluded, that in the West Indies cricket is not only *also* culture, that is, one cultural form among several, but culture itself. It was not only the rare cricket critic who, watching Sobers send a good length ball skimming to the cover boundary, felt himself to be in the presence of a national cultural treasure. Rather, this was the experience of the West Indian crowd as a whole, as explained by the fact that a popular phrase was coined to describe this very stroke: "Not a man move" (*F.P.*, 215). Could it be that all followers of cricket in the West Indies are then to be understood as intellectuals, the knowing possessors of national culture? The second feature follows from the first, James's restatement of the category of genius. For James, Sobers is unquestionably a genius, where "genius" does not describe an individual who transcends temporal or geographical situation, but one who most succinctly, "unerringly," represents it in its compound and overdetermined tendencies. It is an index of the achievement of James's writing on cricket that he is able, in an entirely compelling way and in a single passage, to cover all the ground between the exceptionality of genius and the typicality of national culture.

Notes

1   E. P. Thompson, "C. L. R. James at 80," *Urgent Tasks*, no. 12 (Summer 1981): back cover.

2   C. L. R. James, *Beyond a Boundary* (London: Hutchinson, 1963), Preface. Further references to this book [*B.B.*] will be given parenthetically.

3   Hazel V. Carby, "Proletarian or Revolutionary Literature: C. L. R. James and the Politics of Trinidadian Renaissance," *South Atlantic Quarterly* 87 (Winter 1988):51.

4   C. L. R. James, "Garfield Sobers," in *The Future in the Present: Selected Writings* (London: Allison and Busby, 1977), 214. Further references to this work [*F.P.*] will be given parenthetically.

5   C. L. R. James, "Kanhai: A Study in Confidence," in *Cricket*, ed. Anna Grimshaw (London: Allison and Busby, 1986), 165–66. Further references to this book [*C.*] will be given parenthetically.

6   Walter Benjamin, "The Image of Proust," in *Illuminations*, trans. Harry Zohn, ed. Hannah Arendt (New York: Schocken, 1969), 201. The more relevant comparison, from James's own point of view, would be to the writings about prize boxing, chess, or the game of fives by the early-nineteenth-century English essayist William Hazlitt. James refers admiringly to Hazlitt on several occasions in *Beyond a Boundary*.

7   A test match is a match between representative teams of two nations. The duration of such a match is five days (occasionally six days are allotted). Test-match cricket is the highest form at which the game is played.

8   James cites with approval the following comment of Cardus: "Why do we deny the art of a cricketer, and rank it lower than a vocalist's or a fiddler's? If anybody tells me that R. H. Spooner did not compel a pleasure as aesthetic as any compelled by the most cultivated Italian tenor that ever lived I will write him down a purist and an ass" (quoted in *B.B.*, 191).

9   James continues, in a move that I confess I have never fully understood, to concede that "Sir Donald Bradman's technical accomplishments are not on the same plane as those of Yehudi Menuhim. Sir John Gielgud in three hours can express adventures and shades in human personality which are not approached in three years of Denis Compton at the wicket" (*B.B.*, 192). It is difficult to know what to make of this concession because James immediately undermines it by his insistence that cricket is "not a bastard or a poor relation, but a full member of the community" of the arts. Certainly, James's point against Cardus is made: cricket is an art, not for the one or two "sensitive" souls among its viewers alone, but in its fundamental reality as it is conventionally played and watched. Beyond this, it seems contradictory to maintain simultaneously that cricket is not a "poor relation" of the other arts and that the technique of Sir Donald Bradman—the most proficient batsman who ever lived—is "not on the same plane" as that of Yehudi Menuhim. The thrust of James's work as a whole is along the lines of the affirmation—that cricket is indeed a fully articulated form of art—rather than of the concession. (See, for instance, his comments in an essay on "The 1963 West Indians," published just one year later than *Beyond a Boundary*, and reprinted in *Cricket*, 134–46.) This, accordingly, is the tendency I have chosen to emphasize.

10 See Theodor W. Adorno, "On the Fetish-Character in Music and the Regression of Listening," in *The Essential Frankfurt School*, ed. Andrew Arato and Eike Gebhardt (Oxford: Basil Blackwell, 1978), 270–99.

11 Theodor Adorno, *Minima Moralia: Reflections from Damaged Life*, trans. E. F. N. Jephcott (London: Verso, 1978), 15.

12 Georg Lukács, *The Theory of the Novel: A Historico-Philosophical Essay on the Forms of Great Epic Literature*, trans. Anna Bostock (Cambridge: MIT Press, 1983), 72.

13   Theodor W. Adorno, *Negative Dialectics*, trans. E. B. Ashton (New York: Continuum, 1973), 366–67.

14   Lord's is a famous cricket ground in London, home of the Marylebone Cricket Club, and headquarters of cricket worldwide.

15   The scarcely disguised racism of this report does not, of course, escape James. Throughout his writings he has attempted to combat the still pervasive stereotypes about "natural" black athleticism. For an extended treatment of this question, see his "Cricket and Race" (1975), reprinted in *Cricket*, 278–79.

16   The term is Fredric Jameson's. See "Third-World Literature in the Era of Multinational Capitalism," *Social Text*, no. 15 (Fall 1986):65–88.

Eight

Caliban as Deconstructionist:
C. L. R. James and Post-Colonial Discourse
Paget Henry and Paul Buhle

▼▼▼▼▼

To establish his own identity, Caliban, after three centuries, must himself pioneer into regions Caesar never knew.—C. L. R. James, Beyond a Boundary

The literatures of colonial societies are marked by a peculiar economy that sustains a high degree of mobilization around certain social issues. Consequently, these literatures have seldom known the luxury of art for art's sake or the difficulties of exploring the more elusive metaphysical foundations of everyday life. Rather, from birth, the production of discourses in colonial societies is deeply enmeshed in a particular social conflict: the attempts of the colonizers to establish and legitimate their rule, and the attempts of the native population to resist and delegitimate this external imposition. In the Caribbean, the founding discourses such as those of Oviedo and Las Casas, along with the unwritten ones of the Caribs and Arawaks, had their roots in this conflict. The later exchanges between Europeans, Africans, and Indians who were brought in to replace the decimated Caribs and Arawaks did also.

From the late thirties to the early seventies, the suppressed conflicts of colonial societies in Asia, Africa, and the Caribbean erupted with unprecedented intensity. Organized and concerted efforts to regain independence were the result. These political drives stimulated and were themselves reinforced by an unparalleled production of delegitimating discourses. These were produced in a variety of signifying systems, which gave rise to choruses of economic, political, ideological, historical, and literary works affirming the goal of national independence or challenging aspects of the colonial order. For many of these writers and speakers, their activities amounted to acts of textual or discursive insurrection. Just as political activists were undoing the physical violence of the colonial state, these writers and speakers were undoing the symbolic violence of the colonial cultural system. In short, they were an integral part of the insurrectionary overturning of social orders and conventions that is decolonization.

In the Caribbean, this intensified anti-colonial critique was clearly observable in the works of writers such as Marcus Garvey, C. L. R. James, Frantz Fanon, Aime Cesaire, George Lamming, Sylvia Wynter, Samuel Selvon, and Vic Reid. These were the master producers of the epistemic and other symbolic explosives that rocked the cultural hegemony of Western imperialism in the region. The nature of the textual challenge posed by the works of these writers is best indicated by their appropriation and reinterpretation of the Shaksperean character Caliban. Whether it is Fanon's, Lamming's, Cesaire's, or Retamar's reworking of this character, the discursive insurrection cannot be missed. Caliban becomes a symbol of the inner resistance of the colonized, their desire to end the pact with Prospero and to expel him. This explosive power, organically linked to the political struggles for decolonization, gave these discourses appeal and effectiveness.

However, by the mid-seventies, many of these countries had regained their independence and were thus deeply engaged with problems of postcolonial transformation. These problems necessitated new discourses that gradually displaced those of the pre-independence period.

In spite of this local eclipsing, the 1980s witnessed a major resurgence of scholarly interest in the field of colonial discourses. This revival has largely been the work of scholars in the field of literary criticism and is closely related to the deconstructive turn that poststructuralism has given to contemporary literary theory. This turn has made possible new ways of posing such questions as, How do imperial discourses construct their objects and legitimate colonial rule? How do anti-colonial discourses deconstruct and delegitimate? How are their strategies related to those of poststructuralism? In short, it is the unusual capacity of colonial discourses for strategic involvement in either the constructing or deconstructing of social realities that is behind the current revival of interest.

Our primary aim in this chapter is to assess the contributions of this literary approach to colonial discourses and to the problem of post-colonial change. This approach rests its analysis on semio-linguistic models of the colonized rather than on more familiar economically and politically oriented ones, hence the shift in focus and the new basis for analysis and criticism. We will examine the special contributions and problems of this semio-linguistic approach and evaluate how they deepen or obscure our understanding of James as an anti-colonial writer. This examination will be done in four steps. First, we will outline the poststructuralist position. Second, we will give a comprehensive sketch of James's anti-colonial discourse. Third, we will focus on James as a deconstructionist. Here we will show that James's discourse includes a major deconstructive undertaking completed without the tools of semio-linguistics and through social, existential, and dialectical ones. Finally, we examine some of the implications of this deconstructive achievement for the claims of poststructuralist critics.

Poststructuralist Theories of Colonial Discourse

One of the distinguishing marks of the poststructuralist approach is its use of semio-linguistic models of the colonized. The latter is conceived as a *homo significans* in contrast to the exploited *animal laborans* implicit in Marxist and Marxist-oriented anti-colonial discourses. As *homo significans,* Caliban's existence is profoundly shaped by its need to represent itself and its world with the aid of signs. Both its identity and its world are constructed symbolically.

In all of this, there is nothing particularly unusual. The peculiarity of Caliban's situation derives from his dependence upon the discourses of Prospero for signs with which to construct his identity and his world. Poststructuralist theories have focused closely on these processes of imperial reconstruction and the discursive techniques by which they are achieved. This emphasis is clear in works such as Edward Said's *Orientalism,* Tzvetan Todorov's, *The Conquest of America: The Question of the Other,* and Peter Hulme's, *Colonial Encounters: Europe and the Native Caribbean, 1492–1797.*

This inscription of Caliban's identity in the discourses of Prospero raises the question of Caliban's ability to project independent self-images and to imagine new social alternatives. This problem is not a new one.

George Lamming's exploration of it in *The Pleasures of Exile* raised many themes that poststructuralists are taking up again. In particular, poststructuralism's semiotic approach to language, in contrast to Lamming's semantic approach, raises anew the question of how effectively will Caliban be able to "curse" Prospero in the latter's language. In the more current language of Gayatry Spivak, "Can the Subaltern Speak?"

As noted earlier, Caliban has been a symbol of both physical and textual resistance. The ability of the colonized to "curse" effectively in the language of the colonizer has been assumed by James, Fanon, Lamming, Cesaire, and many other Caribbean writers. Although they clearly recognized the chains of cultural colonization, the basic thrust of the new poststructuralist theories has been to suggest that many of these writers have not been fully aware of the depths at which these chains were anchored.

From the poststructural point of view, anti-colonial discourses often achieve their deconstructive goals by means that are effective primarily on the semantic level. These include such strategies as (1) the discursive inverting of the colonial order of things; (2) revalorizing pre-colonial traditions; (3) renaming people, places, and events; and (4) delegitimating the arguments for colonial rule. Semantically explosive as these strategies may be, they often leave untouched the semio-linguistic categories of imperial discourses, many of which the colonized will use in their anti-colonial constructions. In other words, anti-colonial discourses are anchored in the "deep structures," codes or grammars of imperial discourses beyond the reach of these strategies. The persistence of such deep structural effects limits the new imaginings of the colonized and is the source of the cultural-intellectual crisis of Third World revolutions.

In contrast to the strategies of anti-colonial discourses, the deconstructive practices of poststructuralism are derived from a micrological or "subatomic" view of discourses. In particular, they are aimed at the syntactical rules of discourse formation rather than at the semantic inversions possible within the framework of a particular set of such rules. From this subtextual perspective, imperial and anti-colonial discourses do not appear as different as they do at the textual level. Both make use of similar rules and forms of epistemic violence. This symbolic violence, it is argued, is native to the discursive form. To achieve it, and particularly a "canonical" discourse, the initial processes of cognition and signification must undergo a series of changes that will stabilize the inherently unstable and figurative nature of the process of symbolic representation. This internal contradiction of the discursive form is usually contained by a variety of "violent" constructive strategies of the following types: (1) centering the new discourse; (2) grounding it by absolutizing or justifying its epistemic claims; (3) transforming analogical and other tropological constructions into more fixed analytical categories; (4) progressively tightening the referents of the discourse; (5) systematizing the discourse by either suppressing difference or converting it into identity; and (6) seeking institutional recognition for the discourse. These and other moves crystalize a discursive infrastructure capable of supporting a variety of semantic inversions and transformations.

The deconstructive practices of poststructuralism are aimed precisely at these founding strategies. Their goal is the exploding or undoing of these constructive practices, while at the same time revealing the suppression of difference and otherness that they conceal. Consequently, the relationship of this type of deconstruction to established discourses is "a little like the anti-matter of the physicist in its relationship to matter."[1] Further, because it operates at this subtextual level, it is able to at least engage the deep structures beyond the reach of the semantically oriented anti-colonial strategies.

Although the preceding orientations are shared by many poststructuralist critics, the differences among them are just as important. For example, Spivak's emphasizes the silencing of the subaltern woman, which has resulted from the epistemic violence of imperial discourses.[2] In contrast to this focus on silencing is Homi Bhabha's theory of ambivalence in colonial discourses.[3] Here, both colonized and colonizer can speak. However, they both speak ambivalently. This ambivalence is the result of elements of hybridity and mimicry that invade the discursive exchange, complicating the authoritative claims of the discourses of the colonizer. In the work of Sylvia Wynter, the focus is on the enmeshment of anti-colonial discourses in the *cultura franca* of the colonizer and the need to get beyond this enmeshment.[4] Finally, we mention the work of Gilles Deleuze and Felix Guattari. These two have attempted to sketch a general theory of the deconstructive practices of "minor literatures" and the factors that constrain the scope of these practices.[5] To develop more concretely these differences within the poststructuralist approach to colonial discourse, we will briefly examine the works of Wynter and Deleuze and Guattari.

Sylvia Wynter

Sylvia Wynter is a Jamaican woman who is a writer and a critic. Her critical works contain one of the most powerful and comprehensive re-castings of the problems of colonial discourses in the light of poststructuralist theory. Wynter's point of departure is the nature of the sign systems that humans use and the behavior-orienting consequences of this semio-linguistic dependence. At a basic level, these systems (language, religion, art and ideology) operate by classifying reality according to the binary opposition of sameness and difference.[6] For example, light is distinguished from darkness and the sacred from the profane. Once such oppositions are established, the grammar of symbolic representation permits generating a series of closely related or homologous oppositions such as order/chaos, good/evil, and clean/unclean. These oppositions can be produced in both horizontal and vertical directions, leading to an expansive and hierarchical system of representation. It is the involuntary operating and stabilizing of these basic processes that constitutes the deep structure of discourses.

From this general characterization, Wynter develops three important behavioral consequences of human dependence on these semio-linguistic systems.[7] First, in putting their signatures on human identities, these systems also impart their binary oppositional nature. In particular, they inscribe desirable modes of the human subject that at the same time require the presence of their opposite. Consequently, this duality becomes a basic feature of the human self.

Second, the particular identity or mode of the subject guaranteed by these systems shapes our knowledge of the world profoundly. A particular identity brings with it a corresponding order of knowledge. Thus, an identity based on the spirit/flesh opposition will generate an order of knowledge different from one based on the reason/emotion opposition. The process of symbolic self-representation is a factor that governs the nature of our consciousness.

Third, this impact of symbolic self-representation on the structure of consciousness is largely unconscious because the identities provided by semio-linguistic systems are "auto-instituted"[8] and not consciously chosen. They are auto-instituted by abductive extensions of the basic self-defining opposition, which elude everyday consciousness. These extensions are the result of processes of semiosis that fill out the homological and other signifying capabilities of the original opposition, thus auto-poetically grounding the new identity.[9]

This particular set of structural and behavioral consequences of human dependence on sign systems is important for Wynter's treatment of the way Europe's imperial bourgeoisie symbolically constructed its colonial other. The basic set of oppositions were derived from a principle of sameness and difference expressed in terms of the possession or nonpossession of reason. This faculty or its absence became the basis for homologous pairs such as head/body, civilized/primitive, order/chaos, parent/child, us/not us, and property/no property. These categories ordered human groups in terms of degrees of possession of reason. Ownership of property became an important indicator of sizeable endowments of reason, whereas nonownership was indicative of small endowments. These differences in endowments in turn became the basis for determining whether groups could govern themselves and were therefore eligible for basic human rights. Consequently, in this system, the bourgeoisie and its life-style became the desired mode of the human subject, while its opposite was represented at home by the poor and the propertyless.

Abroad, the European bourgeoisie applied these categories to the great variety of people they encountered. As a result, Africans came to represent the "zero-term" of the system, the absolute lack of reason, the very embodiment of Caliban. In general, the colonized were assimilated to the primitive/no reason/body/chaos/not us halves of the founding oppositions. Consequently, they could be enslaved and ruled for their own good.

In this way Wynter links this system of symbolic self-representation to the historic series of colonial "internments" that marked European imperial expansion. The first internment was of the New World peoples in the encomienda systems, who were reconstructed as "natural slaves." Second was the internment of Africans, homogenized under the commercial trade name of "Negro." These internments of the encomienda/plantation "archipelagoes" were followed by the internment of the poor and jobless in Europe. Consequently, at the level of semio-linguistic construction, these internments, these instances of apparent "disorder," are linked to the chaos categories of the bourgeois domestic and international order.[10]

What is important is the dependence that Caliban develops upon imperial discourses in the context of these internments. Self-representation with the symbols of these discourses redefines the colonized in terms of their chaos, primitive, body, not us categories at the same time that it establishes the bourgeois life-style as the desired mode of the subject. The auto-instituting of such a self-definition establishes the bases of the self-negating and imitative behavior of the colonized. The question then arises, If the roots of this imprisoning identity are semio-linguistically grounded, what are the conditions for breaking out?

Wynter's argument is that the deconstructive practices that anti-colonial ideologues have employed in the past have not been adequate. They have not succeeded in freeing Caliban from his attachments to the chaos category or from the normative influence of the bourgeois life-style. Without a more radical epistemic break, programs of deconstruction and decolonization will only be partial in nature and given to early exhaustion. These exhaustions in turn leave the global system intact in spite of the attempts at change. This is the crisis that post-colonial regimes and ethnic minorities in the imperial countries are currently facing.

To get beyond this crisis situation, post-colonial societies need to make a more radical intellectual break with the discourses of the central countries. Like the bourgeoisie, they must establish a new mode of the subject, which will bring with it a new order of knowledge. Achieving this will require more than anti-colonial strategies of deconstruction. These must be complemented by a science of human sign systems that will allow Caliban to unearth the codes and layers of semiosis by which his identity remains inscribed in imperial discourses. Only such an archeological rupture would permit the change in identity and the "rewriting" of knowledge necessary for a new world order.[11]

Gilles Deleuze and Felix Guattari

Deleuze and Guattari are two French critics who share with Wynter the goal of radicalizing the deconstructive strategies of "minor literatures." Focusing on the case of Kafka as a Czech Jew writing in German, Deleuze and Guattari are particularly interested in the use of language in these literatures. Like Wynter, they are fascinated by the anti-canonical and deconstructive tendencies of anti-colonial and other minor literatures. In these tendencies, they see the potential "revolutionary conditions for every literature within the heart of what is great (or established) literature."[12] The problem, of course, is to realize this potential. Deleuze and Guattari attribute the failure of minor literatures to achieve this to the use of languages that have been only partially deconstructed or "deterritorialized."

Minor literatures share three basic characteristics: (1) they are constructed in the language of a major literature; (2) they are highly political because of the "cramped space" in which they arise; and (3) in these literatures enunciation tends to be by collective assemblages as opposed to singular subjects. The anti-canonical tendencies of these literatures derive from the fact that their social situations put them in relations "of multiple deterritorialization with language."[13] In the case of Czech Jews, the first of these linguistic deterritorializations was the dropping of the Czech language. This was, of course, followed by a reterritorialization centered on another language. The major options were Hebrew, Yiddish, the German of state administration, or the German of the academy. Each of these possible sites of deterritorialization or reterritorialization has varying consequences for anti-canonical innovation.

This complex linguistic situation provides the writer in a minor tradition with unusual tools for pushing the internal tensions of major languages to their extremes. For example, hybrid languages such as Prague German make possible incorrect use of prepositions, abuse of the pronominal, and multiplication of adverbs. These strange linguistic usages (or "tensors" as Deleuze and Guattari refer to them) open new possibilities for linguistic play that are not available in major languages.

However, in spite of this unusual ability to stretch language, the innovative potential of minor literatures is often restricted by their patterns of linguistic reterritorialization. For example, anti-colonial literatures often reterritorialize language within a nationalistic program. Thus, some may abandon the major language and return to a native tongue. Others may reappropriate the major language as their national language. However, neither of these modes of breaking out of the colonial territorialization of language will maximize the innovative potential of these literatures. To achieve this, it is necessary to go beyond the various geographical referents of deterritorialization and reterritorialization. Language must be further deterritorialized in relation to worlds of meaning. It must be deconstructed in relation to the broader category of "sense" shared by all geographical reterritorializations.

This is the significance of Kafka for Deleuze and Guattari. He does not "opt for a reterritorialization through the Czech language. Nor toward a hypercultural use of German . . . nor toward an oral, popular Yiddish."[14]

Instead, building on the tensors supplied by Yiddish, he proceeds to a radical deconstructing of German in relation to sense. In this process, words are torn from their established meanings, thus neutralizing domains of sense. Objects are no longer designated by proper names. They cease to have their fixed, discrete appearance. They appear as "sequences of intensive states"[15] that move from high to low and vice-versa. Thus, the writer no longer deals with discrete dogs, beetles, or men, but with processes of becoming, the rising and falling of intensities.

This attack on sense is part of a larger strategy of subverting the normal representational use of language within particular geographical reterritorializations. This subversion opens possibilities for stretching language that go beyond those provided by the tensors of hybrid languages. For Deleuze and Guattari, this subversion of sense represents an absolute deterritorialization of language in that it gets to structures of language not touched by nationalist and other reterritorializations. Only minor literatures that employ such radically deconstructed languages will realize their full revolutionary potential. Like Wynter's, this argument suggests that the colonized must acquire more powerful explosives than those produced in the "Third World Zones"[16] of their languages. Only then will they be able to break the chains of cultural colonization and initiate a genuine rewriting of knowledge. But these explosives can only be gained from an unearthing of the deeper structures of semio-linguistic systems.

As we will show shortly, this emphasis on semio-linguistic factors is in a deep tension with the emphasis on social factors in the classic anti-colonial discourses. The semiotic picture of the colonized reveals to Caliban a depth of symbolic entrapment that appears less of an impediment within the perspective of collective action directed at changing socially constructed identities and processes of domination. The former picture calls for a radical shift in the goal and nature of Caliban's insurrectionary activities. These should now be conceived not so much as attempts to overthrow social structures but more as attempts to break semio-linguistic codes. Such ruptures would permit the new order to be written into being. Breaking codes and establishing new orders of knowledge, these are the real revolutions. Further, the insurrectionary activities that topple social structures are ineffective against semio-linguistic codes. Jean Baudrillard, in customary polemical style, puts it this way: "you cannot defend against the code with political economy or 'revolution'. . . . Can we fight DNA? Certainly not with the blows of the class struggle."[17] This tension between semio-linguistic and social models of constructing the colonized will be expanded by our discussion of James as an anti-colonial writer. Once exposed, it will provide an excellent opportunity to evaluate the contributions of poststructuralist theory to an understanding of colonial discourses.

James as Anti-Colonial Writer

James's activities as an anti-colonial writer span most of his long career as a scholar and an activist. Our examination of this aspect of James's writings will be done in three steps. First, we will look at his use of narrative to deconstruct colonial meanings; second, his ideological work on behalf of Caribbean nationalism; and third, we will briefly outline his theoretical contributions to the problems of post-colonial transformation.

Deconstructing colonial meanings

As noted earlier, anti-colonial literatures are deeply enmeshed in the struggle to resist and delegitimate the practice of colonial rule. Thus the critical intellectual traditions of colonial societies are often dominated by discourses of resistance in which a writer stands on the shoulders of preceding ones. To understand James's early anti-colonial writings, we must take note of its roots in the regional tradition of resisting and critiquing colonial rule. Consequently, there is a profound continuity between the critiques of Edward Blyden, J. J. Thomas, Marcus Garvey, T. A. Marryshaw, Sylvester Williams, Arthur Cipriani, and those of the early James. The traces of this heritage will give James his sensitivity to the race question in spite of his later turn to Marxism, and also account for the many parallels between his career and George Padmore's.

James's earliest contributions to this tradition of anti-colonial writing are beautiful and deceptively innocent narrative photographs of Caliban in the cramped spaces of colonial Trinidad. Whether Anita Perez's anxious wait for marriage in the short story "La Divina Pastora," or Turner's dealing with his demanding creditors in "Turner's Prosperity," James captures so well the confining nature of working-class life in Trinidad.[18] The same is true of "The Star That Would Not Shine"; Gonzalez's strategy for escape was an attempt to sell his extremely fat son to Hollywood filmmakers.[19] The close-ups in these stories are always on the creative solutions that characters find to restrictive circumstances, whether or not they work. At the same time, their narrative style successfully integrates the individual and the social, with the latter emerging largely through the biographies of the former. This narrative photography culminated in James's only novel, *Minty Alley*.

For our portrait of James as an anti-colonial writer, these works are important for two reasons. The first is the value and significance this careful artistic representation gave to the lives of working-class Trinidadians. The recastings suggested that these men and women had been victims of strategic devaluations in need of challenging and correcting. This process of revalorization was probably what Lamming had in mind when he asserted that it is "the West Indian novel that has restored the West Indian peasant to his true and original status of personality."[20]

The second importance of these narrative photographs is in their affirmation of the creative self-projections that such individuals established in relation to their world, even though they were often not the normative ones. This affirmation was rooted in James's view of the human self as a creative projection of possibilities—a view that would later link him to the existentialists and to Wilson Harris. As such, the human self is an agency capable of preserving the integrity of its self-projections through executing a number of strategies. The working of these creative activities in the life of Caliban is affirmed and celebrated in James's photographs. These restored images of the descendants of "the new world internments" were later incorporated into his expanding and ongoing critique of colonial rule.

In his fictional narratives, James's emphasis was on individual, not collective, responses to social problems. The major exception was the short story "Revolution," in which he explores the revolutionary alternative through a Venezuelan uprising that occurred when he was a boy.[21] As his writing became more politically engaged, fiction slowly gave way to political critique via biography. In this new narrative style, James continued to reach the social through the life of the individual and to critique the former through the creative projections of the latter. However, the complexities of the social were clearly beginning to burst the biographical framework and would soon have to be addressed in their own right. The major work of this transitional period was, of course, *The Life of Captain Cipriani*. Its subtitle, *An Account of British Government in the West Indies*, indicates the new synthesis between biography and political critique.

Arthur Cipriani was a Trinidadian of Corsican descent who became one of the island's best known activists between 1914 and the 1930s. He was the first of a number of individuals whose biographies would constitute the narrative infrastructures through which James would concretize his political critiques. Others would include Learie Constantine, Matthew Bondsman, Kwame Nkrumah, and, of course, Toussaint L'Ouverture. The account of Cipriani's life is a very public one. Its focus is on three sets of activities: (1) Cipriani's attempt to organize a West Indian contingent to fight in World War I; (2) his attempts to organize workers after the war; and (3) his experiences in the Trinidadian legislative council. The common thread running through all three sets of activities is Cipriani's unrelenting struggle against colonialism, racism, and classism.

In his account of the military undertakings, James's focus is on Cipriani's challenge to the prejudice and skepticism that ridiculed the idea of a West Indian regiment. The captain was determined to show that such judgments were based on false accounts of the abilities of the colonized. The same was true of his attitude toward workers, whose collective organizing he revived by restarting the Trinidad Working Men's Association in the years after the war. In the responses of the masses to this organizing drive, James found confirmation for his positive position on West Indian self-government: "If there is anything which can prove the fitness of the people of Trinidad for self-government it is the progress of this resuscitated Association during the thirteen years since it has been restarted."[22]

However, it is in the analysis of Cipriani's activities in the legislature that the political critique reaches its culmination. James uses the resistance that Cipriani encountered in the council as a point of reference from which to critique the inner workings of crown colony governments. He begins by indicating his objections to the assumption that West Indians cannot govern themselves and to the corresponding notions of trusteeship and civilizing missions by which colonial constitutions were being legitimated. He then proceeds to examine the gap between the paper models of these governments and real colonial states. The results were state apparatuses dominated by a governor and the nonelected members of the executive and legislative councils. Because of racially discriminatory practices, both of these state councils excluded "dark-skinned" West Indians. In the colonial political system the ideological garb of trusteeship concealed the supremacy of the raw imperialist interests upon which the institution was founded. James saw this state as an essentially repressive apparatus that kept the aspirations of the colored middle class and the black working class subject to interests of British imperialism. It was Cipriani's fight against this type of government, and his efforts to expose its demoralizing impact on the colonized, that James affirmed and celebrated.

In short, this political biography contains a delegitimating critique of British colonial government that is filtered through the life of Cipriani. By concluding that the demoralizing effects of this type of government would be around until "these colonies govern themselves,"[23] this anti-colonial text makes more explicit certain implicit themes in the narrative photographs. Here colonial societies are analyzed more directly and the creative responses of the hero are linked to a collective solution: political independence.

In James's next major exploration of the colonial problem, his discursive framework again changes quite sharply. He has become an active Trotskyist, his hero is Toussaint, and the country is Haiti. At the same time, he has now achieved a mastery over the sociopolitical analysis begun in the previous work, without any loss of his finely honed skills in narrative. The result was *The Black Jacobins*, James's unforgettable portrait of the colonized. He was able to catch them in various revolutionary poses, challenging in word and deed the entire edifice of imperial rule. Not until the work of Fanon would such images be drawn. In the words of Lamming, James "shows us Caliban as Prospero had never known him."[24]

The work begins with the violent capturing of Africans to labor as slaves on the sugar plantations of Haiti. By 1789, the number of African slaves approached half a million. In spite of slaves' resistance, the repressive apparatus of the colonial state made it possible for French capitalists to continue this forced appropriating of the labor of these Africans. Underfed, overworked, poorly housed, and terrorized, they were the objects of the most extreme forms of exploitation produced by the labor internments that sustained the colonization of the Americas.

James's primary concern was to show that "though one could trap them (Africans) like animals, . . . they remained, in spite of their black skins and curly hair, quite invincibly human beings." Beneath the "profound fatalism and wooden stupidity" that often marked their adjustment to their horrible conditions, other creative responses were taking place that would later reveal a very different picture of Caliban.[25] It is these deeper creative responses that will subjectively ground "the transformation of slaves, trembling in hundreds before a single white man, into a people able to organize themselves and to defeat the most powerful Europeans of their day."[26]

In addition to these repressive and exploitative conditions of Africans in Haiti, three other factors facilitated the surfacing of this revolutionary response: (1) The revolution in France; (2) the violent conflicts it produced between royalist and republican whites in Haiti; and (3) the violent conflicts it produced as Haitian whites attempted to deny mulattoes "the rights of man." In this setting, which divided whites and legitimated revolutionary violence, Africans in Haiti made the heroic effort to end their enslavement and colonization.

By early 1791, strategic political organizing had begun, along with premature outbursts of insurrectionary violence. Later, these would give way to three major insurrectionary groups lead by Biassau, Jean Francois, and Jeannot. Turning on their masters and burning the plantations that were the source of their oppression, the Africans began their violent attempt at decolonization. "From their masters, they had known rape, torture, degradation and at the slightest provocation, death. [These] they returned in kind."[27] In this account of the "frenzy of the first encounters" James anticipates perfectly Fanon's account of the start of decolonization in revolutionary Algeria.

Like Fanon, James was also well aware of the limitations of such spontaneous outbursts. They are often based on desires for vengeance that are soon appeased. Consequently, for the revolution to succeed, it must move on to a phase of careful organizing motivated by positive freedoms and reinforced by the training of cadre and long-term strategic planning. It was Toussaint's ability to rise to the challenges of this phase of the revolution that made him so important to James.

Throughout the remainder of his life, James would continue to write narrative photographs of the colonized through such heroes as Garfield Sobers, Mighty Sparrow, or Kwame Nkrumah. Through the lives of these men, James returned in kind the epistemic violence that sustained colonial misrepresentations of Caliban. However, none would approach the portrait of Toussaint. His actions, along with those of the Haitian masses, made it especially possible for James to portray Caliban in a fashion that completely exploded imperial definitions and stereotypes. As an anti-colonial text, *The Black Jacobins* is James's most compelling and explosive work. In it he examined the revolutionary response of the colonized in Haiti and predicted further uprisings in the colonial world until self-government was restored.

The ideologue of Caribbean nationalism

An account of James as anti-colonial writer must include his contributions to the debate on the framing of the Caribbean nation. Was the new nation to be framed as a federation of the islands, or as a series of separate units? Most of these contributions were written after James's return to the region between 1957 and 1962. By this time, his discursive framework had again changed. James had broken with his Trotskyist heritage and had worked out a more culturally nuanced form of Marxist analysis. The marriage of this new method of analysis to his life-long mastery of the narrative form reached its peak in the widely acclaimed *Beyond a Boundary*.

A long-time advocate of Caribbean self-government, James also supported the national unification of the region. This work on behalf of the Caribbean nation can be divided into two phases: (1) James's involvement in the 1958–62 attempt at federation among the English-speaking territories; and (2) his repeated call from 1962 on for the national unification of the entire region.

The 1958–62 attempt at federation was not an undertaking to which all the political leaders of the region were committed. On the contrary, they were deeply divided over the project. Among the more important issues behind these divisions were insular political and economic interests, racial tensions between Afro- and Indo-Caribbeans, and the free movement of people between territories. James inveighed strongly against these problems as insurmountable obstacles to the proposed federation. For example, in his 1958 address at Queen's College in then British Guyana James made an impassioned plea to the people of Guyana to join the federation in spite of the racial tensions that had surfaced. He argued that such tensions were inevitable in post-colonial societies, and that only within the framework of a federation could Guyana achieve the national goals to which it aspired.[28] Despite these efforts, the regional attempt collapsed in 1962.

Not discouraged by this failure, James grew even more emphatic on the national unification of the region after 1962. In characteristic fashion, he moved beyond the federating of linguistically similar areas and called for the national unification of the entire region, from Cuba and Belize in the west to Trinidad and the Guyanas in the east. James suggested that this nation was prefigured in the creative activities of people in the region but lacked institutional embodiment. He attributes this lack to the persistence of colonial modes of production in spite of independence. These modes of production continued to link territories more deeply with individual metropolises rather than with each other. As a result, a shared commitment to defend the region with our lives has not developed. To the extent that such a defensive consciousness has emerged, it is confined to individual territories. However, the Caribbean nation will not come into being without the emergence of a similar consciousness about the region as a whole.[29]

Why then, in spite of all these obstacles, does James remain optimistic about the possibilities for a Caribbean nation? Time and time again he suggests that the masses would respond to confinements of the neo-colonial order in the manner that the Haitian slaves or the colonized population throughout the region responded to the confinements of the colonial order. He expected the Caribbean nation to crystalize in the context of such an upsurge.

Post-colonial reconstruction
The problems of post-colonial transformation, or, more generally, what kinds of changes should follow modern revolutionary upheavals, were issues to which James devoted a great deal of attention. This concern with the post-revolutionary period grew out of the fact that revolutions, in spite of lofty aims, often degenerate and become their opposite. Consequently, in this account we will look both at James's vision of the post-colonial order and at some of the internal oppositions and external pressures that may bring on a collapse.

James's view of post-colonial society, although strongly influenced by socialism, was never permanently marked by a fixed ideological content. The narrative aspects of his discursive framework stood in the way of such totalizing constructions because it required filtering these generalities through biographical self-projections. To the extent that his socialism can be characterized, it was marked by a commitment to maximizing the possibilities for working-class participation and self-expression available within a given set of sociohistorical circumstances. An expanding need for such participatory activity continues after independence as post-colonial societies inherit regimes of class domination from the colonial period. Like colonial domination, class domination systematically devalues and dehumanizes its subject groups. It denies and suppresses a broad range of the abilities of workers and reduces them to mere suppliers of labor power. Just as the colonized in Haiti revealed their suppressed abilities to govern that country, so James believes that workers will reveal their suppressed abilities to manage production, to lead themselves as a class, and be more than just workers. Workers must strive toward this goal through practice in self-organizing. In short, James's post-colonial focus is on liberating the human potential of Caliban from the dehumanizing grip of the colonial class compromise. It is a view of post-colonial reconstruction that places its emphasis first on the people and second on the managerial, technical, or instrumental aspects of social transformation.

The importance of self-organized mass activities derives from their educative significance for the participants. It provides non-bookish education through organized communicative action. For James, this educative activity restores the humanity of the working class, just as in Fanon's view revolutionary violence restored the humanity of the colonized. From their mistakes and successes, the masses will learn what is possible and what is not possible, what they like and what they do not like, who they are and who they are not. Such discovery or recovery of self is the education that the post-colonial class compromise must make available to workers in their mass organization and daily work experiences. The growth it produces is the exact opposite of the warping and deforming of consciousness that colonial regimes of class domination produce. Without such growth, James remains skeptical of the elaborate plans of the state and technocratic elites who often guide the process of post-colonial reconstruction.[30]

As noted earlier, James did not see the building of such post-colonial social orders as processes of easy unilinear expansion. On the contrary, he saw them as undertakings that contain internal contradictions capable of defeating the goal. James first confronted the problem of revolutionary collapse in his critiques of the Stalinist phase of the Russian Revolution. His life-long wrestling with this monstrous development continually influenced his views on the problem of post-colonial reconstruction. He located the internal contradictions that have plagued such reconstruction in the structural and cultural dependencies of new nations that continue into the post-colonial period. These dependencies have had profound effects on the nationalist visions of various classes, often limiting their breadth and depth.

Like Fanon, James was particularly interested in how these contradictions would affect the rule of the middle-class elites who often replaced the colonial rulers. It was largely because of their better education that this class inherited the mantle of leadership. However, time and time again this greater exposure to the culture and values of the West proved to be the source of a narrow nationalism that reproduced many of the class, racial, and ethnic prejudices of Western nationalism. As a result, post-colonial reconstruction becomes a project conditioned by the interests and ideas of this ruling middle class. Nationalism is defined largely in terms of their replacement of the colonial elites in such areas as education, the state, and sectors of the economy, rather than a radical restructuring of these institutions to increase working-class participation. Consequently, as they assume power, the middle class inherits the class contradictions of the colonial period. As these erupt, the prejudices, the narrow nationalism, and the persisting but hidden identifications with the imperial powers are all forced into the open. Add to these the continuing strategic and economic interests of these same powers in the region, and the magnitude of the opposing tendencies should become clear.

Whatever fraction of this class James examines, the bourgeois elements, the political elites, or the intelligentsia, they are often caught in this contradiction, particularly as the class struggle becomes more intense. In *The Black Jacobins*, James notes many such instances of contradictory behavior on the part of bourgeois revolutionaries. Thus he looks at the case of the French bourgeoisie fighting for human rights only to deny such rights to mulattoes and slaves in Haiti. Similarly, he examines the case of Haitian mulattoes and free blacks fighting for these rights, also to deny them to the slaves. Consequently, the more openly the slaves demanded their freedom, the more repressive were the responses of mulattoes and Bonaparte. Although less stark, this is the crisis in which most projects of post-colonial reconstruction are caught, with middle-class elites leading counter-revolutions comparable to that of the Haitian mulattoes'.

Not only is the middle class affected by the process of cultural colonization; the working class is also reached with definite effects on its view of the world. The resulting structures of awareness and nonawareness often become sources of internal negation in periods of intense conflict or insurrectionary upsurge. Like Lukács's, James's portrait of the consciousness of workers is thus divided. In *The Black Jacobins*, this consciousness moves from a mask of wooden stupidity and blind fatalism to the heights of revolutionary awareness. This internal division makes the working class vulnerable to the manipulations and machinations of colonizers and middle-class elites. James makes this clear in the case of those slaves who fought on the side of whites and mulattoes. Again, although less stark, the working classes in contemporary post-colonial societies are open to such manipulation from ruling middle-class groups and may thus act in ways that negate their own liberation. In short, constructing a post-colonial order that maximizes the possibilities for worker participation does not follow a smooth path. On the contrary, it takes a path along which difficult contradictions must be encountered and surpassed.

As an anti-colonial writer James produced a complex discourse that engaged the colonial problem on at least three levels. The first level was the thick edifice of symbolic distortions and devaluations that James sought to deconstruct, delegitimate, and topple. To the task of recovering an authentic image of Caliban from amid these colonial meanings, James brought his skills as narrative artist and social analyst. The second level on which James engaged the colonial problem was that of the national question. Here, he used his skills as ideologue and social analyst to make the case for a united, self-governing Caribbean nation. The third level was his tackling of the post-colonial question.

James as deconstructionist
Poststructuralist doubts concerning deconstructive practices such as those James used are connected to strategies of semantic inversion. Such inversions, although they succeed in demystifying and challenging specific colonial claims, often leave intact the deep structures upon which imperial discourses rest. The linguistic polarities (white/black, we/they), the monolithic figures and stereotypes (the white man, the coolie), and the auto-stabilizing strategies (idealization, concealment) that constitute the infrastructure of imperial discourses often remain in spite of the inversions. These critics emphasize disturbing these founding oppositions and structures that sustain everyday meanings.

This semio-linguistic emphasis has lead to a corresponding displacement of social factors such as state or group violence, institutional control, or manipulation of everyday meanings as the practices that maintain colonial situations. The primary conditions for liberation now become discursive insurrections that break the codes or deep structures of imperial discourses. This subtextual level becomes the privileged site upon which the battle is to be waged. Breaking these subtextual codes liberates possibilities for semiotic play, for "difference" that remains imprisoned in the structures of colonial discourses. These new possibilities for difference constitute the semio-linguistic capital for making a radical break in the post-colonial period.

A more familiar way of thinking about the problem is to compare it with our earlier discussion of colonial regimes of class domination that persist into the post-colonial period. Here, we can speak of colonial regimes of discursive domination that persist into the post-colonial period. Just as the former regimes suppressed the human potential of the working class, so the latter impose specific restriction on the semiotic play of difference that is native to language. Undoing these restrictions is the primary aim of the discursive insurrections of poststructuralist critics, hence the shift from the social to the subtextual field as the primary zone of conflict.

This shift in emphasis was clearly reflected in Wynter's conditions for post-colonial transformation. They were the radical deconstructing of the desirability of the bourgeois mode of the subject and the supporting oppositions through which it had been auto-instituted. Similarly, Deleuze and Guattari suggest that failure to deconstruct colonial languages radically will necessarily leave large areas of colonial meanings intact. In his poststructuralist reading of Fanon, Bhabha tries to show that no adequate insurrectionary strategy can be derived from the semantic inversions that Fanon and James use so effectively. Rather, the insurrectionary powers of Fanon's texts are located in their capacity for disturbing underlying polarities.[31] This privileging of the discursive field is also clear in the work of Spivak. She portrays the subaltern woman as unable to answer the epistemic violence of imperial discourses. Yet breaking out of this mute state is the condition for liberation. This poststructuralist relocation of the zone of conflict within the subtextual field raises the issue of the role of culture in the process of change: culture defined in semio-linguistic terms.

Our analysis of James as an anti-colonial writer poses some problems for this new cultural approach. First, within its semio-linguistic parameters, the cultural approach is unable to account for the radical nature of James's discourse, its aggressiveness and comprehensive sweep. The discourse is not muted, nor does it ambivalently reinscribe both colonized and colonizer as discursive constructions. Second, it is instructive at this point to take note of an important limitation of James's thought: the fact that it never included an explicit philosophy of language. This failure to thematize language as a domain or medium of human self-formation eliminated it as a base of deconstruction. Third, three enabling bases provide the deconstructive power of James's anti-colonial discourse, none of which are linguistic. These bases are derived from James's mastery of the practices of social, dialectical, and existential self-reflection. In his works, the constructive activities that establish identities, discourses, and social orders operate on all three levels. Consequently, the deconstructing of these formations will require critical activity on all three levels.

The social basis of James's deconstructive practice rest on the principle that texts and identities are in part the result of creative activities systematically influenced by the interests of particular social projects. In colonial societies, this project is usually one of capital accumulation that subordinates and denationalizes an indigenous population. Integral to this process of subordination is the stereotypical redefining of native identities (e.g., the coolie, the fellah, the Negro) and their grounding in racist ideologies. These discourses include justificatory strategies that deny, minimize, or rationalize the dehumanizing consequences of the colonial project. They are adopted as justifications not because they are true, but because the project requires them, hence the systematic distortions and the epistemic violence characteristic of imperial discourses. Throughout *The Black Jacobins*, James is explicit in linking the animal-like representation of the African to the colonial project: "to cow them into the necessary docility and acceptance, required and necessitated a regime of calculated brutality and terrorism."[32] To the extent that social practices require the use of epistemic violence their symbolic representations can be deconstructed by self-reflective processes that expose determining influences from a larger social project.

Ironically, the best account of the depth and social nature of James's counterdiscourse is that of Sylvia Wynter. Using all of the techniques of poststructuralist analysis, she captures brilliantly James's uprooting of the founding opposition of bourgeois thought, and those of his own thinking. The Jamesian poiesis, says Wynter (chapter 6), "has been a constant and sustained attempt to shift 'the system of abduction' first of colonial liberalism, later of Stalinist and Trotskyist Marxism, and, overall, of the bourgeois cultural model and its underlying head/body, reason/instinct metaphorics."

Unlike Bhabha's reading of Fanon, Wynter locates the basis of this "sustained attempt" in James's self-reflections upon his social status as a "Negro," and not in his deliberate disturbing of underlying linguistic oppositions. This status, she suggests, required that the growth of James's consciousness would be shaped by responses to a number of distorted and contradictory social practices around such issues as race, color, class, levels of education, and culture.

The integrity of Wynter's analysis resides in its clear recognition of this social base empowering James's discourse in spite of her use of semio-linguistic categories. James's deconstructive texts cannot be separated from the struggle against the institutions and social meanings that maintained "the Negro" as a strategic stereotype while inhibiting the emergence of a more authentic Afro-Caribbean identity. Thus, like the discursive field for the poststructuralists, the social field emerges in James as the major domain of human self-formation; an undoing of its structuring activities becomes a major condition for change.

These self-reflections on the Negro as a socially constructed status were later reinforced by reflections that focused upon the discursive aspects of the legitimating and delegitimating ideologies produced by working-class and colonial situations all over the world. However, this discursive analysis used dialectical rather than linguistic techniques. It was an approach to the problem of discursivity that grew out of a major study of Hegel in the early forties and culminated in *Notes on Dialectics*.

The focus of dialectical self-reflection is cognition, the process of thinking. Its key to this process is logic, not the oppositions of poststructuralism. However, logic here means more than the formal processes of induction, deduction, and abduction. Along with these are included the basic categories (time, space, quantity, and quality) used in conceptualization, the processes by which they combine to form complex "thought determinations" and their subsequent deformation. This immanent movement of thought is for James the key to philosophical cognition. It is the activity that insures that "categories of thought are adequate to the object it is thinking about."[33] In his typical anti-elitist fashion, James asserts that the movements of philosophical cognition have "nothing to do with Hegel or Kant" or any particular philosopher.[34] Rather, the accounts of these individuals must be seen as attempts to make more explicit the immanent activities of cognition that occur in everyone.

In analyzing the movement of his own thought and that of Trotskyism, James used the Hegelian distinctions between common-sense thinking, understanding, and reason. Common-sense thinking is rooted in the re-productive activities of everyday life. Therefore, its symbolic construc-tions are limited by concrete and pragmatic concerns. Understanding makes possible the deconstructing and transcending of the constructs of common-sense thinking. It opens possibilities for abstract conceptual-ization that are denied on the common-sense level. Through processes of categorization and subsumption, the understanding can make deter-minations of varying degrees of complexity and generality. These deter-minations may then become parts of embracing symbolic systems such as socialism or capitalism.

The understanding not only makes determinations, but it also has the power to maintain them by imposing the universal form on con-structions that are finite, time-bound, and unstable. Thus the determi-nations of the understanding are often given greater permanence and generality than their actual capacity to represent would warrant. These "fixing" or stabilizing strategies are similar to the epistemic violence of the poststructuralist. Consequently, to the extent that they constitute a discourse, that discourse can be deconstructed by undoing these stabi-lizing effects.

However, in spite of these great powers, the understanding, like common-sense thinking, has its limitations. The one that concerns us is the inability to undo the universalizing "knots" through which it can-onizes its own determinations. Thus it is often stuck with categories that external events have made obsolete. "The enemy," James quotes Hegel, "is thinking in categories which were precise, but acquire inde-pendent life and do not move." Reason, or dialectical thinking, is the activity that has the power to undo these knots of the understanding, get it unstuck, and dismantle its constructions. "Reason is negative and dialectical because it dissolves into nothing the determinations of the understanding."[35] It is also positive because it becomes the source of a new universal, hopefully a more concrete one in which the particular is more adequately comprehended by the understanding.

With these and other tips from Hegel, James integrated this explicit thematizing of the immanent movements of human thought into his cri-tique of imperial discourses and into his own Marxist counterdiscourse. The impact of these developments can be seen in the discursive aspects of his critique of Trotskyism. "As far as thought is concerned," James says, "[Trotskyism] is the use of the categories, etc. of Lenin's practice, 1903–23, preserved in their essential purity, and transferred to the period for which they became day by day more unsuited."[36] Similarly, his critiques of various ideological positions in works such as *Party Politics in the West Indies* reveal the influence of this dialectical awareness of the discursive level. In short, James saw the problems of textuality and discursitivity in dialectical terms, and when necessary pursued their deconstruction in a similar manner.

Given the comparatively late plunge into the intricacies of Hegel's dialectics, this type of deconstructive activity does not account for the explosive power of the early narrative photographs. To grasp the challenge of these narratives, we must see that in addition to James's reflections upon the social status of the Negro they were further empowered by an implicit existential awareness. This awareness was rooted in James's view of the human ego as a dynamic, self-positing agency that established its identity through the projection of possibilities that it would strive to realize, and through withdrawals from old or inadequate projects. These self-projections were in part symbolically mediated reterritorializations around the possibilities and constraints of particular sociohistorical situations. However, the creative dynamism of this ego is not reducible to this dependence on the constitutive abilities of linguistic signs and social institutions. On the contrary, it is, for James, the locus of a relatively autonomous source of constructive activity that goes into the projecting of an identity. Consequently, its own conditions of internal stability may be an additional source of self-misrepresentation and epistemic violence. To the extent that this violence has been egotistically invoked, existential self-reflection can be the base of a deconstructive practice.

Equally—if not more—important for James is the access this type of self-reflection provides to the social element in the ego's identity. This access makes possible the deconstructing of social stereotypes through the reconstructing of the intentional movements that established or disestablished a project. The social nature of these projects, the extent to which they brought individuals alienation or fulfillment, became important prisms through which James viewed societies. Without this dynamic existential link between the biographical self and the social order, we cannot understand the socially explosive aspects of his fiction or his biographical writings.

The best example of James's narrative use of this existential dynamic is his skillful characterization of Haitian slaves before and after the revolution. The identities of wooden stupidity represent necessary but deformative responses that reflect the human costs of the social order of Haitian society. On the other hand, the revolutionary projections contain not only the subjective bases for rejecting the old order, but also the bases for a more human one. Similarly, the implicit but pervasive critique of the Trinidadian social order that emerges from the lives of James's fictional heroes, and the autobiographical parts of *Beyond a Boundary*, rest upon this existential mediating of the social. In all of the narrative works, however, these themes are treated artistically, and thus without explicit theorizing.

It was not until the sixties that this implicit existential consciousness would find explicit thematization. The context for this would be James's encounter with the existentialist philosophers and with Wilson Harris.[37] Thus, in Sartre, he would find confirmation of his view of the human self as the creative projecting of possibilities. From Heidegger, James would adopt the distinction between authentic and inauthentic existences to describe old and new projections. From Jaspers and Harris, he would take the notion of an extreme or boundary situation as the crucial catalyst for the movement from inauthentic to authentic. James also confronted the problem of language, particularly in relation to Harris and Heidegger. Whether implicit or explicit, this existential awareness served James as a deconstructive tool in ways comparable to his use of the social and the dialectical as enabling bases.

In short, at the subtextual level of James's anti-colonial discourse three sets of deconstructive practices can be isolated: the social, the dialectical, and the existential. These practices empower the semantic inversions of the textual level. Unlike Bhabha, we take the position that Fanon made similar use of social, dialectical, and existential modes of self-reflection, and that it was from these bases that his deconstructive practice derived its power. Thus, as deconstructionist, Caliban has been able to reply to Prospero upon the basis of a discursive mobilization that did not explicitly address its own semio-linguistic foundations. James's successful use of such practices without resort to those of semio-linguistics raises additional questions for poststructuralist claims about conditions for change in the post-colonial period.

Post-structuralist Claims and the Jamesian Discourse

James's deconstructive activities, because they were achieved without recourse to semio-linguistics, raise at least two sets of questions for poststructuralist claims regarding the constitutive role of language. The first set deals with the relations between the linguistic and nonlinguistic determinants of texts or discourses. That is, are linguistic factors in any way more basic than nonlinguistic? Or, can the former be given a legitimate priority over the latter consistent with poststructuralism's own deconstructive practices? The second set of questions concern the relationship of the textual or discursive field as a whole to that of the social because of the importance of the latter in James's works. In particular, these questions cluster around the consequence for post-colonial change of giving the textual priority over the social. By raising these questions, we hope to show that in the Jamesian mirror some important difficulties are revealed regarding poststructuralism's claims for language as the primary determinant of discourses, and its claims for the textual field as a more fundamental condition for post-colonial change.

The existence of multiple bases of deconstruction in James's discourse points to a linguistic foundationalism within poststructuralism that contradicts its explicit anti-essentialist stance. Embedded in the constituting claims that poststructuralism makes for language are contradictions that suggest that its thought rests on a resolution of the opposition of essentialism/anti-essentialism that is not consistent with its own deconstructive strictures. This tension emerges whenever poststructuralism ceases being critical and turns constructive. Then it reveals its need for a center and other essentializing procedures. These tend to cluster around the poles of Saussurean/Lévi-Straussian structuralism from which poststructuralism originally sprang. In this constructive stance, societies become ensembles of symbolic/communicative systems, whereas discourses and human egos become semio-linguistic creations. In Derrida's fine phrasing, subjectivity is "an effect inscribed in a system of difference."[38] Thus, in accounting for the orders of societies, discourses, and human subjects, the appeal is to semio-linguistics. This essentializing of language was evident in the discourses of Wynter and Deleuze and Guattari. Our first question then becomes, How do discourses as semio-linguistic creations appear in the Jamesian mirror? Do they have supplementary contributions to make to James's discourse, and vice-versa?

First, in relation to James's and other anti-colonial discourses, the poststructuralist perspective opens new possibilities for critique through the way it exposes and makes available the constitutive capabilities of language. These aspects of language remained largely suppressed within the framework of James's works. The suppression occurred in the context of James's resolution of the opposition between language and thought, a resolution that gave thought real creative and constituting powers. Consequently, language was seen largely as an instrument or medium of communication for the thinking ego.

This restricted view of language has created some problems for James. In his essay "A National Purpose for Caribbean Peoples" he discusses the impact of Caribbean literature on French and English literature as part of a broader analysis of foreign influences on these literatures. His descriptions of the innovative contributions of these Caribbean influences are very close to the position of Deleuze and Guattari on minor literatures. However, James was unable to say what precisely was the source of these innovations in language use. By comparison, the greater success of Deleuze and Guattari in doing so is clearly related to their more explicit thematizing of the dynamics of language. Consequently, in this aspect of language James's discourse could benefit greatly from a poststructuralist supplement.

However, in spite of this distinctive approach to the critique of colonial discourses, the plural nature of the constitutive or subtextual foundation of James's discourse does not support the privileging of linguistic over nonlinguistic factors. Because it is a plurality in which the constituting effects of the social, dialectical, and existential factors are not absolutely hierarchized, it suggests that linguistic factors are no more foundational to discourses than any of the others. Like the others, it represents a specific reterritorialization around a limited domain. In this case, that domain is semio-linguistics. Consequently, it cannot be the basis for an absolute deterritorialization as claimed by Deleuze and Guattari. As a specific reterritorialization, it overlaps the other discourse-constituting factors, although it does not coincide with any of them.

Closely related to these questions of language as a privileged determinant of discourses is a second set of questions: the practical consequences of privileging the textual field over the social in the analysis of post-colonial change. Because of the importance it attaches to the uncovering of the strategies by which texts produce "the effects" we call meaning and truth, poststructuralism has given primary importance to the textual field. As a result, this field has become important in the competition for privileged determinants of human behavior and of social orders. Such claims were clearly reflected in the conditions for post-colonial change laid down by Wynter and by Deleuze and Guattari. What are some of the practical implications of viewing post-colonial change through the prism of the textual field?

By linking deconstruction to the task of uprooting the founding oppositions and codes of the discourses that legitimated capitalism and its global expansion, poststructuralists like Wynter have opened a new window on the problem of post-colonial cultural transformation. They have succeeded in isolating and drawing attention to an area of cultural formation that does not appear to be governed primarily by social or semantic rules. This suggests that areas of colonial cultures will not respond to social and semantic approaches to change. Consequently, if this semio-linguistic area is ignored, programs of cultural transformation may not be as comprehensive or as thorough-going as their proponents would wish. Wynter's position on this is very clear. Without a science of human signifying systems, attempts at cultural change will always tend to be partial and subject to premature exhaustion. This perspective introduces a unique set of conditions for cultural change that are not accessible through other perspectives.

However, the practical consequences of this positive contribution are obscured by the failure to work out its relationship with social and other factors affecting post-colonial cultural transformation. If language is indeed only a partial constituting domain, then it cannot be as absolute or foundational a condition for post-colonial change as Wynter claims. If it were, how are we to explain the new social order imagined in James's discourse and its success in breaking free from its entrapment in imperial discourses? Clearly, these achievements were made possible by the other enabling bases, which in James provided enough intellectual space for the writing of a participatory post-colonial order. The distinctiveness of the textual approach rests on the claim that aspects of cultural and institutional processes escape the reach of social and semantic analyses. The question that James's discourse poses for the privileging of the discursive field is whether the reverse is true. Does the uniqueness of social analysis rest in part on its relative independence of semio-linguistic processes?

Implicit in a large number of poststructuralist analyses is the assumption that semio-linguistic processes represent a higher level of cybernetic coding that inscribes its ordering on social and interactive processes. However, this Lévi-Straussian assumption remains a suggestive but unsubstantiated hypothesis derived from a number of analogical assumptions about the nature of linguistic and social processes. This position becomes more reasonable when the analogical mappings remain explicit and are not hardened into analytic propositions. Ricoeur's use of the model of the text to analyze meaningful social action is a good case in point.[39] However, because of the explicitness of its figurative moves, the essay makes clear the limits of the analogy between texts and social processes. There are points of significant overlap, but the two do not coincide. Social institutions are not exhausted by an analysis that maps their structure to that of a text.

Although they can be viewed as systems of communication and symbolic exchange, it is also necessary at times to view institutions as structures of domination that further the interests of some groups over others. As such, they constitute domains of social practice that are not governed by textual/communicative rules. Rather, they are ruled by interests in efficiency and economic and political accumulation—practices that do not conform to linguistic rules. There must be a limit to the analogy between texts and institutions. The attempt to establish the priority of the textual over the social remains a problematic move on the part of poststructuralist theory.

Finally, in addition to these general theoretical problems, difficult political consequences also follow from the privileging of the textual over the social. The most disturbing is the very long distance between the textual/subtextual field and that of organized political activities. Making the connection between the two is extremely difficult so there is a tendency simply to assume it. Thus, in Wynter's analysis, there is little discussion of the alliances of classes and groups, the relations to political and economic factors that will be necessary for the culturally led transformation she envisions. Once the semio-linguistic conditions have been articulated, it is assumed that the class alliances and the economic and political conditions will follow. This has been a major problem of cultural analyses in the past, and it reappears here in stark form.

Conclusion

The primary focus of this chapter has been the application of poststructuralist theory to the field of colonial discourses. This application has converted these discourses into sites of sharp confrontation between the social and textual fields. The source of this confrontation is the fact that colonial writers have tended to see themselves and their discourses in social terms, whereas poststructuralists have been suggesting a textual/discursive understanding of both self and discourse. We have attempted to demonstrate the richness of James's anti-colonial discourse as a site for exploring the outcomes of this interchange. On the one hand, the confrontation with James's texts suggests that colonial discourses can absorb much about language. On the other, it suggests that the textual field is not likely to replace the social in Caliban's understanding of his identity or his discursive enmeshments—and consequently how they are to be deconstructed.

Notes

1 Rene Girard, "Theory and Its Terrors," in *The Limits of Theory*, ed. T. Kavanagh (Stanford: Stanford University Press, 1989), 236.

2 Gayatri Spivak, "Three Women's Texts and a Critique of Imperialism," *Critical Inquiry* 12 (Autumn 1985):243–61.

3 Homi Bhabha, "Signs Taken for Wonders," *Critical Inquiry* 12 (Autumn 1985): 145–65.

4 Sylvia Wynter, "The Ceremony Must Be Found," *boundary 2* 12 (Spring 1984):19–70.

5 Gilles Deleuze and Felix Guattari, *Kafka: Toward a Minor Literature* (Minneapolis: University of Minnesota Press, 1986).

6 Wynter, "The Ceremony Must Be Found," 22.

7 Ibid., 22–30.

8 Ibid., 44.

9 Ibid., 34.

10 Ibid., 34–35.

11 Ibid., 56–59.

12 Deleuze and Guattari, *Kafka*, 18.

13 Ibid., 19.

14 Ibid., 25.

15 Ibid., 21.

16 Ibid., 27.

17 Mark Poster, ed., *Jean Baudrillard: Selected Writings* (Stanford: Stanford University Press, 1988), 122.

18 C. L. R. James, *Spheres of Existence* (London: Allison and Busby, 1980), 1–9.

19 C. L. R. James, *At the Rendezvous of Victory* (London: Allison and Busby, 1984), 9–12.

20 George Lamming, *The Pleasures of Exile* (London: Allison and Busby, 1984), 39.

21 James, *Rendezvous of Victory*, 108.

22 C. L. R. James, *The Life of Captain Cipriani* (London: Coulton and Co., 1932), 40.

23 James, *The Life of Captain Cipriani*, 39.

24 Lamming, *Pleasures of Exile*, 119.

25 C. L. R. James, *The Black Jacobins* (New York: Vintage, 1963), 11, 15.

26 James, *Black Jacobins*, 46.

27 Ibid., 88.

28   James, *Rendezvous of Victory*, 85–106.

29   C. L. R. James, "Birth of a Nation," in *Contemporary Caribbean*, ed. Susan Craig (Port of Spain: College Press, 1983), 1:3–35.

30   C. L. R. James, *Party Politics in the West Indies* (San Juan: Vedic Enterprises, 1962), 11–33.

31   "Introduction" to Frantz Fanon, *Black Skins, White Masks* (London: Pluto, 1986).

32   James, *Black Jacobins*, 12.

33   C. L. R. James, *Notes on Dialectics* (London: Allison and Busby, 1980), 15.

34   Ibid.

35   Ibid., 82, 38.

36   Ibid., 34.

37   James, *Spheres of Existence*, 157–72.

38   Jacques Derrida, *Positions* (Chicago: University of Chicago Press, 1981), 50.

39   Paul Ricoeur, "The Model of the Text," *Social Research* 38 (1971):529–55.

PART IV
Praxis
▼▼▼▼▼

The last, relatively specialized, set of issues addressed in this volume are intimately linked to the Caribbean and its international marginality. These issues are problems of theory and political praxis in the region. They are considered in light of James's long absence from the region, 1932–58, and also from the point of view of unresolved problems faced by political activists thereafter.

The questions raised by Caribbean praxis can be divided into two groups. The first includes those related to James's own writing, speaking, and organizing during his period of intensive involvement with the People's National Movement in Trinidad. Many of the details of this turbulent period of early independence, and the events that precipitated the dramatic end, have up to now remained virtually unknown. The impossibility of separating internal party conflict from external pressures continues to render most difficult an interpretation of James's political work between 1958 and 1962.

The second set of issues involves problems of groups that have adopted (or adapted) James's ideas, in more or less direct fashion. The most important, Trinidad's New Beginnings Movement and Antigua's Afro-Caribbean Liberation Movement (ACLM), each have their own distinct histories.

Many radical organizations in the region did not, of course, adopt Jamesian perspectives. His conceptions found sharp competition from Black Power and more orthodox Marxist positions. The presence of all three simultaneously, inside the New Jewel Movement in Grenada, and the ways in which the competition between the three contributed to the collapse of the Grenadian Revolution in 1979, provides perhaps the best single indicator of the broad milieu in which Jamesian groups operated. Black Power advocates questioned the Eurocentric aspects of James's Marxism, while the orthodox Marxists concerned themselves with the appropriateness of James's commitment to radical, popular democracy.

In Henry's first paper, James's economic program for the region is rigorously evaluated and contrasted with other programs put forward by Caribbean economists. Look Lai and Worcester explore the difficulties, and the achievements, of James's writing and active politics in Trinidad. Henry's second essay takes up the political experiences of the ACLM as a case study in the practical adjustments that an ongoing Jamesian political organization has made necessarily in response to local conditions.

Nine

C. L. R. James and the
Caribbean Economic Tradition
Paget Henry

▼▼▼▼▼

James's economic writings are marked by a number of peculiarities, two of which are important for this discussion. First, compared to his texts on politics and culture, James's writings on economics are strikingly small. They are also scattered throughout the corpus of his work and were never systematically pulled together. Consequently, *State Capitalism and World Revolution* is the book that comes the closest to being as comprehensive a statement on economics as *Modern Politics* is on politics or *Beyond a Boundary* is on culture. Yet, in spite of the small size and scattered nature of these writings, economics is extremely important to James's *oeuvre*. Without it, there is no understanding of his radicalism, his involvement with labor movements in Trinidad, Britain, and the United States, his ties to Marx and Lenin, or his views on societies and their transformation.

The second peculiarity of James's economic writings is their noticeable distance from the main body of Caribbean economic thought. This distance is such that James's views have seldom been included in analyses or reviews of this tradition.[1] Like Arthur Lewis, the father of modern economic thought in the region, James's interest in economics was closely associated with the regional labor movement of the 1930s. However, after some initial points of correspondence, the basic pattern of their thinking began to diverge. Lewis's thought and the main body of the tradition moved in a technical direction that focused upon the managing of economies. The aim of this management was to increase productivity and profits. These, in the long run, it was assumed would lead to economic development and transformation. On the other hand, James's thought moved in the direction of humanizing the labor processes within economies. Its focus was on various strategies of workers' control over important decision making that would facilitate the larger project of humanization. In short, James focused on the practical, as opposed to the merely technical, activities to be addressed if economies are to be not only productive but also humane institutions.

The two primary issues raised in this chapter are closely related to these features of James's economic texts. The first is the question of the overall pattern of James's economic thought and the problem of economic development in particular. Implicit in the scattered fragments is a coherent labor-theoretic model of economies that constitutes the basis of James's peasant-led strategy for Caribbean economic development. The second issue is that of the relationship between this peasant-led strategy and the tradition of economic thinking in the region. Despite obvious differences, the two supplement one another in important ways.

The Caribbean Economic Tradition

Along with novel writing, economic theorizing has been one of the more remarkably dynamic areas of intellectual life in the contemporary English-speaking Caribbean. Both were greatly influenced by the labor struggles of the thirties, which revived the push for decolonization. If George Lamming, Wilson Harris, and Vidya Naipaul are the great masters of the literary tradition, Arthur Lewis stands unrivaled as the primary architect of the economic tradition. From the mid-forties to the mid-sixties, the works of this Nobel laureate provided the basic framework, and a lot of the substance of regional economic thinking. Although the latter has developed and diversified substantially since the years of Lewis's dominance, it still retains his emphasis on management and productive performance. Thus, in spite of socialist tendencies that developed after the mid-sixties, the question of praxis in the Jamesian sense remains outside of the systematic reach of this tradition. To demonstrate this continuity, I will briefly examine the works of Lewis and Clive Thomas, the most important of the socialist theoreticians.

Arthur Lewis
Among the factors creating distance between James and the regional economic tradition are differences in their conceptions of labor. Is labor a

living commodity to be appropriated by capital in the most cost-effective and technologically efficient manner? Or is it a human activity that should be governed with the consent of the laborers? This underlying tension provides an important clue to the thinking of both James and Lewis. Lewis's *Labor in the West Indies* is most open and sympathetic to the practical, political problems of incorporating labor into economic systems. It was written at a time when he was active in the regional labor movement and shared many of its goals and aspirations. Consequently, the work can be fruitfully compared to James's *The Life of Captain Cipriani*, which was written when James was also a young middle-class intellectual who had thrown his support behind the same movement. Although both works championed the cause of the workers, the distinct political and technical orientations that would develop later on can already be discerned.

In *Labor in the West Indies*, Lewis recognizes clearly the oppressive and dehumanizing conditions under which laborers had been incorporated into plantation economies. He analyzes the poor health, poor housing, low wages, and absence of supportive legislation that followed from this pattern of labor appropriation. These conditions had to be changed, and Lewis supported workers mobilizing in trade unions for this purpose. Within the context of this project, he was sympathetic to the riots and strikes that erupted in the region between 1935 and 1938. He saw them as "the worker's only weapon for calling attention to his conditions." In establishing trade unions, workers would have "constitutional machinery for the redress of grievances."[2] In other words, Lewis saw trade unions as satisfactory solutions to the political domination of labor within the work routines of regional economies. As a result, he did not advocate forms of worker organization that would further challenge the capital–labor relationship.

With this adoption of the trade unionism, Lewis's interest in the political organization of economies reached its peak. It provided him with rather routine responses to problems generated by this aspect of economic organization. The availability of these responses allowed Lewis to focus his attention more exclusively on the technical problems of Caribbean economies: poor competitive position of major agricultural commodities, outdated technology, a crippling shortage of investment capital, and the virtual absence of industrial production. To resolve these problems, Lewis suggested a number of measures: continued imperial protection for Caribbean agriculture, social welfare legislation, exploring the U.S. market, a program of industrialization, and federation of the territories of the English-speaking Caribbean.[3] As Lewis's thinking developed, it moved in the direction of an academic formalizing of this technical side of his early work. On the other hand, James's economic thought developed via the formalization of the practical, political side of his early works. In Lewis, this technical focus changed significantly the nature of his views on the political aspects of economic organization which, in turn, increased his distance from James.

Lewis worked at this project of formalization through a series of papers on Jamaican, Puerto Rican, and British West Indian economic development. His work peaked with two celebrated writings: the classic essay "Economic Development with Unlimited Supplies of Labor" and the comprehensive work *The Theory of Economic Growth*. In these efforts Lewis was concerned with "the growth of output per head of population" in developing countries.[4] From comparisons with more developed societies, he conceptualized this task as one of getting developing countries to save and invest around 12 percent of their national income. Lewis associated such levels of saving with capitalist classes as opposed to aristocracies, peasants, or wage earners. Because one of the major problems of developing societies is the weakness or absence of capitalist classes, the elements of one must be imported until locals acquire corresponding levels of entrepreneurial skill. To initiate this process of transformation, the industrial capitalist sector must be allowed to grow at a higher rate than the agricultural sector. As the former expands, it should be able to draw "surplus labor" from the peasant sector at subsistence costs.[5] Goods produced at these labor rates should be competitive on the world market and thus maintain the growth momentum.

What is significant about this pattern of theoretical formalization is the tension it produced with Lewis's earlier labor commitments. For example, appropriating labor at subsistence costs was at odds with the unionization of agricultural workers. Further, the racial or ethnic difficulties that accompany importing a capitalist class are suppressed by the technical requirements of the model. Thus, it was not surprising that in the pursuit of transformation, Lewis's praxis ceased to be that of labor mobilizing and became the advocating of foreign capitalists as agents of development. This elegantly formulated model, along with its rather problematic praxis, constituted the beginning of the Caribbean economic tradition.

Clive Thomas

By 1965, it had become clear to such economists as Lloyd Best, William Demas, George Beckford, Clive Thomas, and Norman Girvan that the transformation Lewis envisioned was not taking place. Two factors in particular indicated this: the failure of a strong local capitalist class to emerge and the persistence of high levels of unemployment. These and other factors forced Caribbean economists to reevaluate regional economies. A number of new approaches resulted that culminated in a shift to the Latin American dependency conceptual framework. Consequently, these new approaches focused more on the institutional constraints that were retarding the efforts at transformation. Although this institutional focus has given this generation of economic theories a different practical focus, it was quite distinct from James's.

Unlike Lewis, Thomas shares James's view that the needed transformation of Caribbean societies can only take place within a socialist framework. For Thomas, this has meant a political process of transformation within the context of a worker/peasant-controlled state. However, he spends little time developing this aspect of his strategy, and even less on the political aspects of the reorganized labor process. The political aspects of economic transformation are put on hold after their initial formulation. Consequently, the relations of workers to the state and to the labor process are not theorized explicitly. It is also true of Thomas's political work, *The Rise of the Authoritarian State in Peripheral Societies*. This absence of theoretical elaboration constitutes an important difference between Thomas and James despite their socialist orientations. In contrast to these political areas, the productive and technological aspects of economic transformation, their coordination and phasing, are all elaborated rigorously and comprehensively. Thomas's work shares this feature with Lewis's in spite of their different practical and ideological orientations.

Central to Thomas's approach to transformation is his redefinition of the condition of underdevelopment. It is a mode of dependent economic adaptation that is sustained by two sets of "dynamic divergences."[6] The first involves divergences between patterns of resource use and patterns of demand. The second deals with divergences between existing patterns of demand and the basic needs of the masses. These divergences are the results of colonial penetrations that separated the productive forces of Third World societies from their roots in domestic markets. These productive capabilities were then linked to imperial markets, while local demand was forced to adjust its tastes to imperial consumer production. The phenomenon of underdevelopment is constituted by the variety of dependent economic formations that have emerged from the constraints of this separation and externalization of productive and market forces in Third World economies.

Getting beyond such formations would logically require two sets of "dynamic convergences" to reverse these separations.[7] The first would be the relinking of local production and local markets via an indigenous technology. The second would be to bring existing patterns of demand more in line with the basic needs of the population. To secure these convergences, Thomas suggests that underdeveloped economies need to establish a number of basic agricultural and manufacturing industries such as iron, steel, textiles, rubber, paper, fruits and vegetables, and dairy products. These basic goods are important because they permit the production of so many other commodities. The major chapters of Thomas's book are given over to the planning mechanisms, the interconnections and phasings that must accompany establishing this core of basic industries if they are to secure such convergences. Such a strategy would radically change the plantation nature of Caribbean economies. It would sharply reduce their external dependence and orientation, widen their narrow productive bases, and increase their limited capacities to respond innovatively to environmental changes.

This commitment to move beyond both the plantation economy and the capital importing model of industrialization separates this generation of theorists from Lewis and brings them closer to James. But in spite of this shift, the concern with increasing productivity has obscured the ongoing problem of workers' role in the organization and control of the labor process. The way in which increased productivity is pursued still links these theorists to Lewis's tradition, which has brought them into conflict with James.

The tension between James and the tradition as a whole is perhaps best indicated by his comments on Thomas's strategy. James wholeheartedly embraced Thomas's call for a worker/peasant state and dynamic convergences. However, he also asserted that "Thomas does not face the fundamental necessity of unloosing the energy and accumulated knowledge of the mass of agricultural labor."[8] James objected to the small theoretical space that Thomas's model gives to the creative activity of workers as opposed to that of planners, experts, and other economic variables. Too often, says James, planners "are not even aware that they (workers) are missing. For them, the business of workers . . . is to work."[9] The theoretical space that James gives to the problems of incorporating labor in economies sets him apart from the main tradition of Caribbean economic thinking, including its socialist wing. Hence, my next task is an analysis of James's peculiar approach to economic systems and its application to regional economies.

James on Economies: A Labor-theoretic Approach

James's interest in economics was closely related to his involvement with workers' struggles for greater control of their productive activities. It was from the point of view of these struggles that James approached the study of economies, and not from that of the technical conditions necessary to keep highly mechanized and profit-driven systems of production in motion. For James, economies are first and foremost social systems that define and reward in unequal ways the productive activities of their human participants. This organization gives rise to two sets of practical problems: one moral, the other political. I begin with the moral set.

As his work on Cipriani suggests, James's early approach to economies was a narrative one that sought to capture the resistance of workers to the dehumanization of interaction within these systems. He was an artist coming to grips with the human costs of economic production in his society. Similarly, his involvement in the labor movement in Britain produced a narrative work, *World Revolution*. However, this text was not constructed around the biography of a labor leader, but around the history of the Third International and the crises that had overtaken Stalinist leadership. *World Revolution* is an important step in James's economic thinking for several reasons. First, it integrates a more analytic approach to economics within his narrative framework. Second, this analytic approach makes clear the centrality of the labor process in James's thinking at the time. This focus on the labor process is a moral-economic inheritance from Marx that would stay with him. Third, the work reveals Lenin's early influence on James's conception of the capabilities of mobilized workers. Finally, when this conception of workers became reformulated in *State Capitalism and World Revolution* it becomes clear that James's reading of Lenin would become an important factor in the break with Trotskyism. However, before examining the economics of this important work, Marx's influence on James's view of the labor process should be examined.

The influence of Marx on the central role that James accords the labor process can be seen in his introductory essay to Marx's *Economic and Philosophical Manuscripts*. In this essay James sharpens his analysis of the moral problems created by commodification of labor and the dehumanizing manner in which workers are integrated into modern economies. He begins with Marx's claim that private property is a consequence of alienated labor rather than the other way around as suggested by the classical economists. This reversal led Marx to focus on the activity of laboring rather than on such results of this activity as value, goods, and private property. Labor as creative activity and source of all value became the most basic of economic categories. This is the labor-theoretic standpoint that James shares with Marx. "His problem, the Marxian problem," says James, "became the analysis of the labor process."[10] And it was precisely the moral dilemmas of workers and of labor as activity in capitalist economies that James extracts from this Marxian text.

At the center of these dilemmas was the need of capital to appropriate the activity of laboring as a commodity. In this form, labor comes to possess a twofold nature, abstract and concrete. As concrete labor, work is craftlike, creative and expressive. As abstract labor or mere labor power, work becomes mechanical production for an impersonal market. In this abstract form, labor can be alienated from its self-expressiveness, from nature, and from cooperation with other workers through external ownership. The tension between these two modes of laboring creates contradictions that are internal to the labor process. As Marx summarized the moral and practical problems created by the growth of abstract labor: "the worker becomes poorer the more wealth he produces and the more his production increases in power and extent. The worker becomes an ever cheaper commodity the more goods he creates. The *devaluation* of the human world increases in direct relation with the *increase in value* of the world of things. Labor does not only create goods; it also produces itself and the worker as a *commodity*, and indeed in the same proportion as it produces goods."[11]

James agreed with Marx that this dehumanization of work cannot be compensated for by increasing consumption. On the contrary, the problem could only be resolved by a qualitative change in the way workers participated in modern economies. This participation would have to be both educative and expressive so workers could grow as human beings through their work. The deformative consequences of work primarily create the human problems of economic systems. "The laborer," says James, "must become a full-developed individual, freedom is an economic necessity and proletarian democracy an economic category." The key to this economic democracy, and hence to the resolution of the human crises of modern labor processes, is that "the substitution of use value for value must take place in labor itself."[12] In other words, a change must occur so that the modern organization of work becomes a more concrete and humane experience. The need for such a change remains a basic moral dilemma confronting all modern economies.

The second set of practical problems that informs James's approach to the study of economics are political in nature. These problems of worker domination arise from the political conditions necessary to maintain existing patterns of labor organization. Integral to these forms of labor organization are authoritarian regimes of political domination that attempt to keep workers subservient to management and to maintain management's control over the labor process and the collectively produced surplus. As in the case of state systems, workers resist these regimes of domination and sometimes counter them violently by more democratic alternatives. The form of these struggles will vary with such factors as the classes involved, the relative strengths of each, and the nature of the regime and production.

The labor process includes concrete expressions of a class struggle that explicitly raises the issue of worker participation in the ownership and control of productive enterprises. James analyzes these political aspects of modern economic organization in *State Capitalism and World Revolution*. In this text, his focus is on the political regimes that maintain the labor process inside the factories of the United States and the Soviet Union. Drawing upon Lenin, James describes these regimes as state capitalist. They are distinguished by the rise of state or state-supported private bureaucracies that are intermediaries between direct producers and those who appropriate the surplus. These intermediary structures constituted the administrative core of political regimes governing the productive process. In capitalist firms, these bureaucracies emerged as administrative arms of private owners' efforts to control labor and other uncertainties. However, the uncertainties of the productive process gradually forced the bureaucracies into closer relationships with the state. In unions, labor parties, and state-owned economies, bureaucracies often began by playing corresponding administrative roles for a working class not yet capable of complete self-organization. However, like other governing elites, the primary problem with such state capitalist regimes is their tendency to entrench themselves and accumulate power at the expense of subordinate groups. James was particularly interested in this process of accumulation at the expense of workers and in the relations that developed between elites and owners, whether private or state. He pursued this interest through the analysis of the labor process in a number of countries including the United States and the Soviet Union.

James relates the emergence of state capitalist regimes in American factories to the early-twentieth-century economic reorganization that produced large modern corporations. This restructuring included assembly lines that made the productive process a continuous flow, "advanced planning for production, operating and control." In the 1920s, the corporation that best represented these trends was the Ford Motor Company. James described the political regime that managed Ford's new production process: "here production consists of a mass of hounded, sweated labor. . . ; and opposed to it as a class, a management staff which can carry out this production only by means of a hired army (Bennett) of gangsters, thugs, supervisors who run production by terror in the plant, in the lives of workers outside of production, and in the political control of Detroit."[13] Here in graphic language are the political conditions upon which this productive process rested, in particular its use of terror and violence.

James's primary symbol of the resistance of American workers to this new form of corporate domination was the CIO. In its early years, this union embodied both a radical and an appropriate response to the governing strategies of management. However, in spite of the appropriateness of unionization, the conflict with management called for a more radical solution. In James's view, this solution was the self-organization of workers to participate in the organization and control of the productive process. Without such self-organization, conditions are created for the union bureaucracy's takeover of leadership in the struggle after the insurrectionary moments have passed. It is to such a takeover by the labor bureaucracy that James attributes the decline of the CIO in the 1940s. He links the changes in the union's direction and militancy to compromises the bureaucracy made with management. Since these developments, the history of production at Ford saw "the corruption of the bureaucracy and its transformation into an instrument of capitalist production."[14] This transformation of the administrative arm of workers into a stratum that seeks a cooperative alliance with management and the state brings maturation of state capitalist regimes of production.

The distinguishing feature of these regimes is that a strongly entrenched worker-based bureaucratic elite becomes a part of the existing productive order and joins efforts of the governing coalition to suppress worker attempts to move beyond that order. Thus, the primary organization of the workers becomes a fetter on their own political activity. It becomes a major obstacle to further self-organization and aids the premature containing of the class struggle. "Without this mediating role of the bureaucracy," James argued, "production in the United States would be violently and continuously disrupted until one class was undisputed master." In exchange for these compromises, "the bureaucracy must inevitably substitute the struggle over consumption, higher wages, pensions, education, etc., for a struggle in production. This is the basis of the welfare state, the attempt to appease workers with the fruits of labor when they seek satisfaction in the work itself."[15] Thus, the challenge of state capitalist regimes in the United States was whether or not they would be able to contain the class struggle through a shift from terror to seductive consumerism and compromises with labor bureaucracies.

James's analysis of the labor process in Stalinist Russia makes even clearer the political dimensions of economic systems. He saw the Stalinist bureaucracy as the early Fordist bureaucracy "carried to its ultimate and logical conclusion."[16] Here, the workers' own party and state bureaucracies entrenched themselves, increased the extraction of surplus value, and violently suppressed the Soviets through which workers sought to control production and end their domination inside the labor process. In making this argument, James outlines the history of the organization of labor inside Russian factories between 1918 and 1943. The pattern is one of increasing state bureaucratic control, suppression of Soviets, and the intensification of both repressive and scientific methods of increasing the surplus extracted from direct producers. Here the transformation of labor bureaucracies into instruments of state-directed surplus extraction was so complete that no compromises produced reductions in the use of terror and corresponding increases in consumption. Hence the Stalinist bureaucracy remained a violent and terroristic regime of production.

These analyses of labor processes in the United States and the Soviet Union reveal clearly James's view of the practical, political problems

inherent in economic systems. As in the case of the moral problems discussed earlier, these political difficulties are permanent issues that stem
from the internal organization of the modern factory. The moral difficulties derive from the need of these organizations to appropriate labor in
its abstract, alienated form, whereas the political ones are rooted in the
need for repressive or seductive regimes to control workers and facilitate
surplus extraction.

Because of their organizational roots, these problems cannot be solved
through the use of technical economic maneuvers. On the contrary, their
solutions raise the practical problems of freedom and meaningful worker
participation in the labor process. Without such a "transition from social
labor as compulsion . . . to social labor as voluntary association," class
conflicts within economies will continue to resurface.[17] Consequently,
in 1940, James predicted increases in wildcat strikes for the United
States and even more violent forms of protest for the Soviet Union and
other Stalinist countries. The dramatic events in Eastern Europe since
the rise of the Solidarity Movement in Poland and the comprehensive
de-Stalinization of Russia since Mikhail Gorbachev assumed power all
point to the salience of James's predictions.

These moral and political problems of economies are not restricted
to modern corporations with state capitalist regimes of management.
On the contrary, just as these problems have a future, so they have had
a past. They have produced worker insurrections of great intensity in
earlier forms of economic organization. For James, these uprisings were
not mindless outbursts of activity. Beneath the violence, James always
looked for self-organizing activity that often contained alternative institutional solutions to problems that workers experienced. This organi-
zationally creative element always caught James's attention, as it was
his key to the stage workers had reached in relation to the task of collectively controlling production. Depending on the organizational forms
that emerged from these uprisings, some have been of world historical significance in their impact upon workers' struggles. Consequently,
James sees a cumulative aspect to these struggles. They pass on organizational achievements from one generation to the next, thus keeping
alive the class project of progressive self-organization. Consequently, a
particular struggle is important not only for its specific outcomes, but
also for the organizational forms it will bequeath to workers as a class in
formation. These cumulative legacies of the moral and political conflicts

within economies can be ignored only at the peril of an inadequate view of the historical development of modern economic organization.

A sense of the historical perspective within which James saw these struggles can be gleaned from a quick look at some of the insurrections he considered crucial, first those from medieval Europe. In a number of works, James examined the struggles of workers in such towns as Cologne, Lubec, and Barcelona from the point of view of a push for proletarian democracy. These struggles failed primarily because of the low level of production and the isolation of the towns.[18] However, with the rise of capitalism in Europe, important changes took place in these two factors. Communications improved, and production was more centrally organized. Thus, the second explosion of class conflict to note is the "Glorious Revolution" of seventeenth-century Britain. In this revolution yeoman farmers were not only the mass leverage for the overthrow of monarchy, but also the source of the basic forms and principles of British democracy. The third important insurrection is the French Revolution of 1789. Here James saw a further development of workers' ability for self-organization, and thus in their formation as a class capable of managing a modern economy. Not only were workers and peasants crucial to overthrowing the monarchy, but in the process they also produced the communes. These institutions of worker self-organization would later have to be suppressed by the bourgeoisie in the struggle to establish its power as a class. The fourth important uprising is that of the early-twentieth-century struggles of American workers; from a techno-bureaucratic standpoint their production processes were the most advanced.

The final two cases allow the consequences of the rise of socialism in Europe to be taken into account. Thus, the fifth uprising of note is the Russian Revolution of 1917. In the Soviets that emerged amid all the violence, James saw an even more important step in worker self-organization than had occurred in the communes. Sixth, and important for James, was the Hungarian Revolution of 1956. Its significance went beyond that of the Russian Revolution. It provided a concrete instance of self-organized workers gaining control of both economic and political decision making. The Hungarian Revolution showed workers who were closest to taking control of production to be a self-organized class.

Summing up this sweep of working-class history, James in 1980 described the Solidarity Movement in Poland as "a movement which began in the Commune, went on to the Soviets, and now has reached a stage where the whole country has mobilized itself to put an end to government by the few."[19] His historical perspective reveals a creative and cumulative dynamic in the violent responses of workers to their domination inside economies. It shows workers moving toward their own solutions to practical economic problems. However, these solutions are not formulated in books, but in the media of collective action and self-organization.

James's basic approach to the study of economics is thus labor-theoretic, not only in the sense of labor being a creative source of all value but also because the central contradictions of economies are located in their labor relations. It is also a practical approach that focuses on the moral and political problems created by modern forms of labor organization. Consequently, the possible solutions to these problems of dehumanization and political disenfranchisement find theoretical elaboration in James's work, and not solutions to the more technical problems of economics. Thus, in contrast to Lewis, James does not stop his labor analysis with the formation of trade unions. Rather, he intensifies the search for post-union forms of worker organization as a response to the state capitalist tendencies of the modern period. The systematic theorizing of this dynamic pattern in worker organization is the special feature that sets James's labor-theoretic approach apart from the Caribbean economic tradition, including Thomas's work.

Caribbean and Other Peripheral Economies

In his essay "Birth of a Nation," James makes it clear that it was upon the "foundation" provided by these ideas that he renewed his analyses of Caribbean societies just before he returned to the region in 1957.[20] The influence of these ideas is particularly clear in such essays as "The Making of the Caribbean People" and "Peasants and Workers." In the latter essay, James uses the Russian Revolution as the first case of a modern labor revolt in an underdeveloped country. He then analyzes major revolts in China, India, Vietnam, and Ghana from his labor-theoretic perspective. The key point of these analyses is that peripheral economies share the practical problems that arise from modern forms of organizing the labor process.[21]

James made two systematic attempts at applying his general economic ideas to problems of Caribbean economic development. The first attempt was a part of his efforts in support of the 1958–62 federation of the English-speaking territories of the region. Such a federation was basic to the economic position that James was developing. He saw the federation as the West Indian way of taking part in "the general reorganization of industrial production, commercial relations, and political systems which is the outstanding feature of our world."[22] In other words, only as a larger unit could the Caribbean take its place with any meaningful degree of autonomy in the international community of industrialized economies.

Within this regional framework, James outlined a model of change, an untidy mix of Lewis's ideas and some of his own. The key problem to be resolved was the "Russian Question," the task of raising "the level of production and the general standard of life of the peasant, the farmer, and the large number of those who live and work in countryside." James began his outline of a solution by dissociating himself from the watered-down versions of Lewis's model, which he labeled "the philosophy of the industrial development corporation." Essentially, this philosophy was "governed by the fact that the initiative, the actual initiative is left to those entrepreneurs, particularly from the outside, who see the possibility of making some profit by introducing an industry in a particular area."[23] For this, the government would give entrepreneurs what is called pioneer status, a set of perks that should help to make their task easier.

In contrast, James proposed a model of development in which the initiative would come from what he called the "State Plan," to be constructed around an industry-led strategy of development. "It takes an advanced industry," James argued, "to raise substantially a backward agriculture." As in the case of Lewis, the primary aim of this industrial expansion was "to take care of the unemployed, who will be relieved from the agricultural areas." Thus, the challenge to this new industrial sector was "not only to raise the level of life in the agricultural areas, our fundamental problem, but to establish industries to take care of all our needs . . . and the overflow from the agricultural areas."[24] Again, as in Lewis's model, this sector would include industries for export. Thus, James noted that "we need industries which our local markets cannot possibly satisfy. We need industries in other words for export."[25]

Coordination and synchronization of the various initiatives between industry and agriculture are beyond the scope of either the individual entrepreneur or the levels of state planning that existed in the region in the 1960s. Because of the nationwide scope of the institutional changes that must accompany this process of economic transformation, only an agency such as the state possesses the appropriate authority. For example, in planning for the needs of the people, James makes it clear that he does not mean "merely the ordinary economic demands, but the social necessities of population."[26] This gap between existing patterns of economic need and demand is a "dynamic divergence" that can only be corrected by a radical shift in the coordination of supply and demand and a reorientation of local consumer tastes. This level of planning was clearly outside the scope of individual entrepreneurs or existing state mechanisms.

However, in spite of this central role for the state, James is clear "that the state itself will not undertake the organization of industry. That at best is a dangerous business and we are in no position to embark upon any such experiments."[27] Consequently, the industrial aspects of this strategy would be organized by private entrepreneurs (local and foreign) who agreed in advance to work within the overall framework of the plan.

Finally, James raises the question of whether or not his plan would work if it were passed on to politicians, economic experts, and administrators to implement. James, the Leninist, could only answer with a vigorous no: "I cannot see any such plan without the mobilization, the educating of the population as to what is being proposed."[28] With the challenges of federation and economic reorganization before the regional community, James suggested that a stage had been reached where "our political leaders will have to recognize the necessity of making demands upon the people for energy, for concentration for greater effort, and even for tightening up of the belt."[29] Without a greater involvement of the people, the plan was sure to collapse for want of moral support and other energizing input.

This model of economic transformation is a rather peculiar one for James in the sense that it is not particularly consistent with his labor-theoretic approach, yet at the same time important tensions between elements occur. Most striking is the fact that this model is not constructed from inside the dynamics of the regional labor process. Consequently, it is sharply less labor-centric than the more general framework would lead one to expect. In this model of Caribbean economic development, the stress is on the more careful planning of an externally initiated, capital-led process of industrial development. Because of the strong export orientation of this industry and its task of absorbing surplus agricultural labor, the major differences between this and the Lewis model turns out to be more comprehensive planning and the mobilization of the population. It is difficult to see how these differences alone could insulate James's model from the difficulties of intense worker exploitation and capitalist domination that have plagued the various versions of Lewis's model. It is not a worker-led strategy of development based upon an assessment of the organizational forms and capabilities that regional workers have produced or demonstrated in the course of their major insurrectionary activities.

The most basic tension between elements of the model is that between the externally led strategy of industrialization and the program of mobilization and education. On the periphery, such programs of industrialization have usually been accompanied by the systematic demobilizing of the population. We need only to think of Brazil, Mexico, and South Korea in the past two decades. Not only are the problems of worker mobilization and participation downplayed, but their formulation also remains rather abstract, without institutional specificity, and removed from the history of the regional class struggle. Further, there are none of the customary references to Lenin, whom James quoted on matters dealing with worker mobilization and participation.

The peculiarity of this model and the contradictions within it may reflect James's attempts to cooperate and work with the liberal nationalists leading the federal experiment, and hence may not be a correctly balanced presentation of his views. Whatever the reason, the model represents the closest that James came to giving more strictly economic factors priority over the practical issues of a free and humane organization of the labor process.

James's second attempt at outlining a strategy for Caribbean economic development is much more consistent with his labor-theoretic framework. It focuses upon the peasants and makes their mobilization the primary basis of the strategy. This shift may be related to the fact that the attempt was formulated outside of the context of regional party politics, and after James had broken with the liberal middle-class elements replacing the departing colonial elites.

This break with the middle class is extremely important for an understanding of the shift in the class context of the second model. James provides an account of this break in *Party Politics in the West Indies*. This celebrated critique of the West Indian middle class, matched only by Fanon's, exposes the social and historical factors that have made it incapable of successfully executing projects of economic development. Although a formally well-educated group, the West Indian middle class has—for racial, political, and economic reasons—been excluded from the circles that controlled big industry, commerce, finance, and agriculture. For example, because of the racial factor there was little "prospect that by social intermixing, intermarriage, etc. they (would) ever get into these circles." This exclusion restricted the social knowledge of the class to the activities of its professionals, clerical assistants, small businessmen, civil servants, intellectuals, and politicians. Thus, they "have no knowledge or experience of the productive forces of the country."[30] They are in no position to lead the process of economic development.

In this analysis, James included not only the political and economic fractions of the middle class, but also intellectuals and other cultural elites. He repeatedly used the character Aleko from Dostoevsky's *The Possessed* to describe the sociohistorical situation of Caribbean and other Third World intellectuals who became involved in projects of political and economic leadership. "Aleko . . . yearns for nature, cherishes a grudge against the higher classes, yearns too for the truth somehow and somewhere lost, which he can nowhere find. . . . Truth continues external to him, perhaps in some European country with its more stable organization and settled mode of life. Nor can he understand that truth is after all within him. How could he understand this? For a century he has not been himself in his own country. He has no culture of his own."[31] In other words, like their economic counterparts, Caribbean intellectuals have been until recently excluded from the production of the ideas upon which their societies rested. This alienation leaves them in an equally weak position for leadership. James endorses Dostoevsky's solution to the problem: "the saving road of humble identification with the people."[32]

However, in spite of these crucial weaknesses, the West Indian middle class uses its formal education to justify its claims to leadership. In James's view, such formal education is no substitute for an intimate acquaintance with the productive processes of Caribbean societies.

To make up this lack, it is necessary for the West Indian middle class to seek alliances in order to govern effectively. It has two options: it can form alliances with foreign investing classes, or it can form alliances with the West Indian working class. In his first model, James took as givens the alliances with foreign capitalists that the middle class had already made. However, he rested his search for a new strategy on the second option. Consequently, the second model gives priority to alliances between the peasantry and a sociohistorically handicapped middle class.

In this new class setting, James was able to deal more directly and immediately with the practical problems that had always concerned him. In determining workers' roles in this alliance, he drew upon the history of regional peasant struggles: slave rebellions, the Haitian Revolution, and, more recently, the regional labor movement. From the levels of self-organization these struggles revealed, James concluded that the Caribbean peasantry was ready for a greater share in the control of production than they were allowed in the 1960s. This practical economic problem had to be resolved; it was comparable to the people's readiness for the political independence they had long been denied. Thus, at the core of the second model is an attempt to advance the goal of labor's control of the labor process to the point suggested by the self-organizing capabilities of peasants and workers.

In James's view, the Caribbean peasantry was ready for an advance in its project of self-formation as a class. This advance was a process of collective reorganization that would transform it into yeomanry or independent farmers. The degree of autonomy and the productive responsibilities of this formation made it an appropriate step in furthering class development. Thus the first step in the new model was to dismantle the plantation system. "No economic regime," James asserted, "has had so demoralizing an effect on the population as the sugar estates."[33] In learning to both master and resist their routines, Caribbean peasants had matured and were ready for a new economic order. Thus, the land the plantation system monopolized would have to be broken up and distributed to peasants, who would be responsible for the bulk of agricultural production. Such a redistribution would make possible a new class of agricultural producers whose activities should necessitate and produce a population with a "highly developed cultural and scientific outlook."[34] James was confident that the Caribbean peasantry could rise to this economic challenge.

Second, in achieving the productive goals of this class transformation, the new producers would need the support of a reoriented middle-class intelligentsia. This group would have to stop using its education to increase the distance between it and the masses. Rather, in this new agricultural project it must both see and find an outlet and a demand for its technical skills. Such support is necessary if production is to remain scientifically current and economically competitive.

The industrial component of the model is the third step. As in the first model, James welcomes foreign investment in profitable areas such as oil, bauxite, and tourism. However, he is adamant that such private investments cannot be the base of the strategy. They must be situated within a broader framework. Absent from James's analysis of these industries is a dynamic of class formation among their workers, a dynamic comparable to but distinct from that of the peasants.

The fourth step is a broad comprehensive framework provided by state planning. This framework will set the basic priorities between the various components of the strategy, in particular the relations between the new agricultural sector and the foreign capitalist sector. James also stresses the need for entrepreneurs who have been apprised of the plan and have agreed to work within its guidelines. Here again, state planning does not mean state-run industries, but industries that will be primarily in the hands of the new farmers and other producers.

Fifth, James stresses the need to break up what he calls "the old colonial system." There is a strong tendency in Caribbean economies—most clearly articulated by Lloyd Best—for new economic initiatives to be distorted by institutional pressures from old colonial structures and interests. James suggests that establishing a landed peasantry would deal "the Old Colonial System a mortal blow."[35] The basis for the old upper class would be destroyed, and room made for the new yeomanry. Along with reorganized agriculture, new industries must be carefully planned. Otherwise, the yeomanry will create the basis for a new upper class that may keep a modified version of the old system in place. The emergence of such a trend led James to a description of post-colonial Caribbean politics: "This new system of independence is only the old colonial system writ large. Contemporary Caribbean politics consists essentially of the capacity to administer the old colonial system either by means of the brutality of a Trujillo, or the democratic forms of Trinidad or Jamaica, or the skillful balancing on the fence of Munoz Marin."[36]

Sixth, James's second model is also regional in scope. He does not detail the precise nature of the federation. However, it is clear that he holds to his earlier view that the various territories can only make it into the modern world as a larger unit.

Finally, the establishment of a landed peasantry was for James not only an economic but also a social issue. This process of class reorganization would not only advance labor's control, but it would also open new opportunities for the practical education and humanization of Caribbean workers. In particular, James argued that it would increase their sense of social responsibility and give them a genuine sense of being "totally involved in the future of the country."[37] Economic development must include such humanization and not just the ever-increasing output of goods and services.

The Peasant Strategy and the Caribbean Tradition

Given the largely technical orientation of the main body of Caribbean economic thinking, it is not difficult to show that James's labor-theoretic approach and his peasant strategy constitute challenging supplements to this tradition. However, James's approach should be completed by some of the technical achievements of regional economic thought. This critical but supplementary relationship between the two becomes clear as James's model is brought into a concrete and determinate relationship with the problems of Caribbean economic transformation.

The primary contribution of James's overall approach is its systematic treatment of the issues of dehumanization and political disenfranchisement, which are inherent in the modern labor process. Its formulations remain unsurpassed by other attempts to address these problems. James's approach makes the class-based competing strategies for institutional reorganization the moving contradictions of modern economies. In particular, the strategies projected by labor are carefully analyzed as guides for the praxis needed to advance the goal of worker control. This aspect of modern economies has been undertheorized by the main body of the regional tradition.

This theoretical lack exists in part because Caribbean economic thinkers seldom abandon the commodity as a framework for conceptualizing labor. Viewed simply as a factor of production, it is difficult to theorize its owners as a class in formation whose progressive self-organization increasingly challenges their imprisonment. Such a view requires a more systematic formulation of labor both as a commodity and as human activity. Without it, the advantages of the Jamesian approach cannot be appropriated. For example, Thomas repeatedly suggests that "development is about people,"[38] but, this ad hoc claim is never conceptually elaborated or systematically integrated into his theory of economic transformation. As a result, the calls for popular and participatory forms of ownership appear to be external rather than internal to his analysis. A more systematic integration of this popular element would require a notion of labor as a medium of human development linked to the larger strategy of transformation. Without it, Thomas's model will be unable to address as adequately the practical issues James raised. James's labor-theoretic approach constitutes a critical contribution to Caribbean economic thinking. It contains an alternative to the ways in which labor has been conceptualized. At the same time, it opens possibilities that are suppressed within the commodity-theoretic framework.

However, the making of this important contribution does not mean that James's theory is without its problems. Specifically, I will focus on three problems of peasant strategy that reveal some of the limitations of the more general approach: (1) the need for technical elaboration in James's models; (2) ambiguities in the methods James uses to interpret the self-organizing activities of workers; and (3) the impact of the decline of regional agriculture for his peasant-led strategy of development.

From the practical standpoint of guiding processes of post-colonial transformation, the technical aspects of James's peasant-led strategy should be more clearly specified and worked out systematically. This is important because the economic environments, both local and international, in which such a strategy is likely to operate are being progressively organized on technical rather than practical principles. These technical principles are derived from various branches of economics as a science and are only partially realized in the more routine interactions of everyday economic life. Consequently, they cannot be grasped fully from simple observation or participation. In addition, one must also have access to the science from which these principles were taken if modern economies are to be understood. Thus, without a realistic assessment of the technical aspects of the economic environment in which a strategy must operate, the feasibility of a strategy must remain in doubt.

James recognized the need for such technical supplements in his models. Thus, to the question of what industries should state planning encourage, he replied, "if you give me two or three economists and six months and a good bit of money, I would turn up with something after that." Similarly, in regard to landed peasantry, the question of the size of the farms to be given to peasants: "I do not know. . . . The West Indian peasantry and experts from elsewhere can easily work out these problems and settle the question of the land."[39] Here again, James leaves the technical side of an important issue underdeveloped and focuses on the practical problem of the "social forces" that such a change would release in the lives of Caribbean peasants. However, given the technically based opaqueness that surrounds modern economic activity, this exclusive focus on practical aspects becomes unacceptable. The technical linkages with the environments in which the strategy will operate must be worked out in some detail with the aid of economics. It is here that supplementary relations can be established between James's model and the main body of the tradition. Two rather striking examples can be used to develop this point.

The first is the relationship of the work of George Beckford to James's second model. A quick comparison reveals two Caribbean authors—the first from the point of view of productivity concerns and the second from that of the dynamics of the labor process—arriving at peasant-led strategies of post-colonial transformation. However, in developing his strategy, Beckford moves in a more technical direction. He does not systematically consider the economic implications of working-class self-organization over time. Rather, his systematic analyses are focused on the important conditions for technically inserting the strategy into the contemporary economic environments of the region. Consequently, he considers such factors as desirable output mixes for agriculture, the link-ages with industry, changes in patterns of expenditure on food, competitive technologies, and other issues affecting the organization of modern agriculture.[40] This view is short term, and labor's status as commodity is taken as a constant. However, without this type of short-term, technical contextualization, James's model will not be a concrete guide for post-colonial transformation.

This point was clearly brought home by the experience of the Manley regime with the 1977 Peoples Production Plan. The plan worked out in concrete detail Beckford's ideas about agriculture as a basis for economic transformation. Production goals were set, and estimates were made of the jobs that would be created, as well as the costs of the plan and its impact on the industrial sector. When it was mapped onto the specific features of the Jamaican economy, however, a number of important problems surfaced. For example, major gaps occurred between needed imports and foreign exchange reserves, gaps between production capabilities and production targets, and the possibility of the loss of thousands of jobs in the industrial sector. These and other considerations led to the rejection of the plan. In the view of the planners, the primary reason for the rejection was a "lack of confidence in the capacity of the masses of black Jamaican people to assert their productive creativity."[41] Whatever the reason, this experience with a peasant-led strategy points to some of the important technical problems that James's model would have to address.

In contrast to this technical elaboration, the underdevelopment of the practical side of Beckford's original model can be seen clearly against a Jamesian background. Beckford stresses repeatedly the need for a highly motivated population. "The dynamic effects of technological change and capital accumulation," he argues, "can come into play only if certain pre-conditions for agricultural development exist. Among these are a highly motivated population to provide the basic human resources (managerial and technical skills, and adaptable labor power)." How is this motivation to be achieved? Beckford is unsure. He deals with the problem negatively by explaining low motivation in terms of certain patterns of social organization.[42] He has even less to say on the patterns of social organization to motivate Caribbean workers. This is where his model could use a practical supplement from James, who would force him to see the problem of motivation in a wider context. Beckford would be pushed beyond the commodity framework (managerial, technical, labor power) in which his systematic analysis confines the problem. Such a push would extend the framework of his analysis so that he could include labor as a human activity, the need for meaningful participation and control and how they are related to worker motivation. It is only in later works such as *Small Garden . . . Bitter Weed* that the creativity of peasants and workers is freed from economistic confinement and allowed to become a human activity. Here, Beckford comes close to James's position but never attains a comparable level of systematic analysis in such practical matters.

The second example of useful supplements that James's model can derive from the regional economic tradition arises in relation to his call for state planning. This planning would rest upon a distinction between the real needs of the people and those indicated by existing patterns of economic demand. Few concerned with the problems of peripheral economies would deny the importance of this problem. However, nowhere does James indicate the steps by which such a shift could be made. The technical and institutional conditions for its realization in Caribbean society are not explored and linked to the practical analysis of regional economies. Hence, it remains an abstract idea that could easily disappear if the model was used.

The importance of the idea is indicated by its reappearance in the work of Clive Thomas. Here, it is more systematically integrated into the strategy of transformation and brought closer to the technical conditions of its application. For example, Thomas identifies the basic goods to supply the needs of the population and explores appropriate strategies of substitutions. It is questionable whether Thomas's work has made this idea concrete enough to be feasible. However, it points in the direction in which the further specification of James's model needs to go.

This contrast in technical emphasis between James and Thomas is just as evident in Thomas's analysis of the Guyanese peasantry in *Planta-tions, Peasants and State*. In this work, the factors affecting the growth and stagnation of peasant production are subjected to an elegant and sophisticated economic analysis. This includes analyses of the conflicts with the plantation sector, but never in ways that break the technical framework necessitated by the concern with productivity. Here, the con-trast with James is probably at its sharpest as the political dynamism of peasants as a class is subordinated to the more strictly economic factors affecting their productivity. In this framework, peasants appear to be a much weaker class. Thomas is thus significantly more cautious than James in his hopes for a vibrant, independent peasantry.[43]

In sum, much technical refinement remains before James's model could serve as a guide for post-colonial transformation in the Caribbean. This refinement can only be accomplished with the aid of the special-ized science of economics, which has provided the technical principles that have reshaped modern economic environments. Here the regional economic tradition could be of help to the Jamesian model.

The second problem with James's analysis centers around ambigui-ties in his use of instances of insurrectionary activities as indicators of the readiness of Caribbean workers for greater economic control. These ambiguities arise from James's tendency to mix economic and politically oriented insurrectionary activity indiscriminately. Because James was always eager to get beyond rigid institutional separations between eco-nomics and politics, resolutions of this tension were often premature. In relation to the region, this collapsing of economics and politics con-sistently got in the way of a clear and objective assessment of where Caribbean workers were in relation to the class project of greater eco-nomic control. It tended to make them appear further along than they really were.

Throughout his long writing career, James consistently rested his case for Caribbean political independence on the organizing and governing skills that emerged in insurrectionary activities. Thus in "The Making of the Caribbean People," he analyzed, among others, the Haitian Revo-lution and Cipriani's movement as examples of political organizing that clearly indicated the readiness of the masses for self-rule. In establishing the readiness for economic self-rule, however, James often used many of the same examples of revolutionary upsurge. This is quite understandable; these upsurges often had both economic and political roots. However, the implications of such uprisings for economic and political self-rule need to be analyzed separately. The self-organizing produced by these upsurges consistently suggests a greater readiness for political than for economic self-rule. When the two are collapsed, economic self-rule becomes inflated.

James on several occasions used Richard Pares's data on the skilled nature of slave labor in the Caribbean to suggest that the laborers "ran the plantations."[44] He supplemented the data by such major upsurges as the Haitian Revolution in assessing workers' capabilities for economic governance. Such analysis extends the brighter aura of political self-organizing to the lesser achievements in economic self-organizing and makes them appear greater than they really are. A close reading of *The Black Jacobins* reveals this difference in the capacities for political and economic self-rule. The achievements in economics do not match the achievements in politics. This is closely related to greater importance of technical factors in modern economic organization. Thus, any mode of analysis that suppresses or blurs such difference stands in the way of a clear understanding of the economic capabilities of Caribbean workers.

Second, within the context of his model, James does not use equal candor to analyze the impact of colonial exclusion upon the economic capabilities of Caribbean workers, something he did in the case of the middle class. The fact that the working class includes skilled technicians is not an adequate premise from which to conclude that they ran the plantations. As objects of colonial socialization and exclusion, Caribbean workers, too, have major gaps in their knowledge of production processes and have internalized aspirations that are antithetical to their liberation. These contradictory aspects of working-class development, which James stressed in *Notes on Dialectics* and *The Black Jacobins*, are overlooked here. The result is a linear pattern of growth and self-organization, not a more contradictory and spiraling path. A real need exists to analyze the practical economic education of Caribbean workers separately from their political education. Such a separation should provide a more accurate reflection of economic capability.

Third, the question of the impact upon James's peasant-led strategy of the current decline in Caribbean agriculture must be addressed. Since the mid-sixties, foreign investments have produced bauxite, oil, the tourist industry, and light manufacturing in various Caribbean territories. This process of dependent industrialization sponsored in part by "the philosophy of the industrial development corporation" has been accompanied by dramatic declines in export agriculture. Plantations have collapsed and continue to lie fallow while food imports skyrocket. This collapse, rather than leading to the birth of a landed peasantry, has converted large numbers of agricultural workers into industrial workers. The change in the nature and composition of the Caribbean working class requires a reinterpretation of James's analysis.

First, the nature of the struggles inside these industrial centers must become more central to the analysis. In particular, the new capitalist classes involved, the regimes of corporate domination in use, and the role of trade unions and the state all must be reassessed. Second, such a reassessment could make some of James's state capitalist notions relevant to this more contemporary analysis. There is a hint of this in his notion of the old colonial system, but it is never really developed. The changes that Lewis's type of industrialization has produced in the Caribbean working class will have to be conceptualized carefully before any attempt is made to use James's model.

Conclusion

In this chapter, I have tried to show that a consistent and coherent theory of economic life can be pulled from James's widely dispersed writings on economics. The key to this theory is labor, both as a creator of value and as an activity performed by human beings who are coercively integrated into economic systems. It is from this phenomenon of social labor as compulsion that James derived the moral and political problems that comprised his practical approach to the study of economics. These problems give rise to class struggles and to the progressive self-organization of the working class. Further, concern with these practical problems of economies constitute a critical supplement to the regional economic tradition, which is marked by a strong technical orientation. Finally, the strength of James's practical orientation permits theorization of possibilities for working-class transcendence of commodity status within regimes of capitalist production. Its weakness is that it does not theorize the more short-term conditions necessary for working survival and growth under the existing conditions of hegemonic capitalism.

Notes

1   Norman Girvan, "The Development of Dependency Economics in the Caribbean and Latin America: Review and Comparison," *Social and Economic Studies* 22 (March 1973):1–33.
2   Arthur Lewis, *Labor in the West Indies* (London: New Beacon, 1977), 19.
3   Lewis, *Labor in the West Indies*, 44–52.
4   Arthur Lewis, *The Theory of Economic Growth* (New York: Harper and Row, 1970), 9.
5   Arthur Lewis, "Economic Development with Unlimited Supplies of Labor," *Manchester School* (May 1954):139–91.
6   Clive Thomas, *Dependence and Transformation* (New York: Monthly Review Press, 1974), 58–61.
7   Thomas, *Dependence and Transformation*, 123–27.
8   C. L. R. James, "The Birth of a Nation," in *Contemporary Caribbean*, ed. Susan Craig (Caracas: College Press, 1981), 1:18.
9   James, "Birth of a Nation," 1:21.
10   C. L. R. James, *At the Rendezvous of Victory* (London: Allison and Busby, 1983), 65.
11   Erich Fromm, *Marx's Concept of Man* (New York: Frederick Ungar, 1966), 95; emphasis in original.
12   James, *Rendezvous of Victory*, 66.
13   C. L. R. James, *State Capitalism and World Revolution* (Chicago: Charles Kerr, 1986), 39, 40.
14   James, *State Capitalism*, 41.
15   Ibid.
16   Ibid., 43.
17   Ibid., 37.
18   James, "Birth of a Nation," 4–5.
19   C. L. R. James, *80th Birthday Lectures* (London: Race Today, 1981), 16.
20   James, *80th Birthday Lectures*, 5.
21   C. L. R. James, *Spheres of Existence* (London: Allison and Busby, 1980), 191–220.
22   James, *Rendezvous of Victory*, 90.
23   Ibid., 119, 121.
24   Ibid., 119, 120.
25   Ibid.
26   Ibid., 122.
27   Ibid., 123.
28   Ibid., 127.
29   Ibid.
30   C. L. R. James, *Party Politics in the West Indies* (San Juan: Vedic Enterprises, 1962), 150.

31 James, "Birth of a Nation," 1:25.

32 Ibid., 1:26.

33 James, *Rendezvous of Victory*, 154.

34 Ibid., 153.

35 Ibid., 154.

36 James, *Spheres of Existence*, 154.

37 James, *Rendezvous of Victory*, 153.

38 Clive Thomas, *The Poor and the Powerless* (New York: Monthly Review Press, 1988), 352.

39 James, *Rendezvous of Victory*, 122, 153.

40 George Beckford, *Persistent Poverty* (New York: Oxford University Press, 1972), 188–96.

41 George Beckford and M. Witter, *Small Garden . . . Bitter Weed* (Morant Bay: Maroon, 1982), 93.

42 Beckford, *Persistent Poverty*, 194.

43 Clive Thomas, *Plantations, Peasants, and State* (Mona: ISER, 1984), 141.

44 C. L. R. James, "The Making of the Caribbean People," in *Spheres of Existence*, 180.

Ten

C. L. R. James and
Trinidadian Nationalism
Walton Look Lai

▼▼▼▼▼

C. L. R. James first left Trinidad in 1932, to make his way as a writer in England. He did not return to the island again until 1958, during the flowering of Trinidadian nationalism. He was then fifty-seven years old. He had been invited by the new Trinidad and Tobago government of Eric Williams to attend the inauguration of the Federal Parliament on April 22, and was persuaded by Williams to stay on and commit himself to the emerging nationalist movement. Thereafter began a brief immersion into Trinidadian politics and public life that took place in two phases: 1958–62, during the first two years of which James was an ally of Williams's and managing editor of the party newspaper, the *Nation*; and 1965–66, when he was a leading figure in a short-lived and unsuccessful opposition party, the Workers' and Farmers' Party (WFP).

Returning first to Britain and then the United States, he spent the rest of his life as an academic lecturer and "guru" to large numbers of metropolitan-based intellectuals, students, and activists of all races and nationalities (including many West Indian students living abroad), never directly involving himself in island politics again. James's name kept surfacing locally (and indeed regionally) during the period of Caribbean social activism after 1968, as different segments of an amorphous regional left movement tried at various moments to come to terms with some of his ideas and perspectives, as expressed in his writings. After his official retirement in 1981, he lived quietly for one year in Trinidad as a guest of the Oilfields Workers Trade Union before finally returning to Britain, where he died in May 1989. Ironically, his former colleague, Williams, died in office in 1981 while James was retired in Trinidad. Trinidad during the late 1950s and early 1960s, therefore, constituted James's primary encounter with the hurly-burly of local political activism, and until quite recently formed the basis upon which much of his public reputation was based. Unlike most other West Indian islands, and indeed the general metropolitan intellectual environment where James lived most of his life, Trinidad (apart from the small intelligentsia) tended to remember him primarily as a controversial activist of the early nationalist period, and only then as a world-renowned intellectual and writer.

When he first returned to Trinidad in 1958, he was hardly a household name, but his work as a radical theorist and activist in Britain and the United States was nevertheless known to select circles of the local intelligentsia (specifically the black intelligentsia), the foremost of whom was Williams. There was then, as there was to be until the last years of James's life, a deliberate compartmentalization of that respect and admiration.

James was admired as a Caribbean intellectual of great depth and insight who was a pioneer in nationalist historiography and literary endeavor, and as a Third World spokesman-activist of some influence in specific movements. He knew George Padmore, Kwame Nkrumah, and Jomo Kenyatta well, and had worked with them. Of James's specifically Marxian involvements and writings (Trotskyist and post-Trotskyist) there was less active knowledge or interest, and those who did know were indifferent or even dismissive. Thus to the small black intelligentsia of the 1950s, *Black Jacobins, History of the Negro Revolt*, the novel *Minty Alley* (and later on, *Beyond a Boundary*), were better known and appreciated than *World Revolution, State Capitalism and World Revolution, Notes on the Dialectic*, and *Facing Reality*.

James's adulation of Arthur Cipriani and Toussaint L'Ouverture was more comprehensible than his complex and intricate judgments on the relative merits of Lenin, Trotsky, or Stalin in the Russian revolutionary movement, or his theoretical-polemical denunciations of the one-party Stalinist state as the antithesis of Marxist-humanist traditions and visions in the contemporary world. The fact that he was the first translator into English of a major biographical work on Stalin (Boris Souvarine's work), or responsible, in collaboration with others, for the first English translations of Marx's *Economic and Philosophical Manuscripts of 1844* (the cornerstone of the revival of Marxist-humanist thought), or—even before that—the author of one of the earliest definitive left-wing critiques in English of the Stalinist International (*World Revolution*), a kind of Bible of the anti-Stalin left in Britain in the 1930s and 1940s—none of these achievements (remarkable for any intellectual from the Third World in those days) were either known or valued by a colonial intelligentsia preoccupied with its own parochial encounter with British imperialism and with the social challenges of the purely local environment of the 1950s.

The nationalist movement, and the middle-class intellectuals and professionals drawn to it, were a motley collection of individuals representing a variety of different political backgrounds and social tendencies. They were all united by the dynamism, vision, and charisma of the scholar-turned-activist who had founded the Peoples National Movement (PNM). Some had been socialists, but their socialism was of the Fabian variety, like most of the early working-class leaders themselves, including Cipriani. Some, a small minority, who stood slightly outside of the new party but were nevertheless supportive of its general direction and appeal, had been socialists of the Marxian-Stalinist variety or had flirted with its doctrines. These had been associated with earlier formations like the United Front, the West Indian Independence Party, or with the trade union movement proper. Most of the middle-class professionals who crowded into the new party, however, were bourgeois-liberal nationalists (some more conservative than others), opposed to British colonialism but deeply committed to, and ardent admirers of, British political traditions and institutions. They visualized the new political-administrative order as simply one of the succession of a native professional class to a slightly rearranged version of the old colonial order.

To such a group, C. L. R. James's beliefs and metropolitan preoccupations were barely comprehensible in the intellectual environment of colonial Trinidad in the 1950s. To the conservative nationalists inside the party (and indeed the conservative anti-nationalists outside of it) it was enough that he was a Marxist. To his admirers inside and outside the party, it was enough that he was C. L. R. James, a populist-sounding and left-leaning element within the nationalist movement and an intellectual of no mean stature.

James arrived in Trinidad when the PNM had been in government for two years and had been a party for about three. He had not been central to its early gestation tribulations and was not personally close to many of the party's elite.[1] Williams, though, had consulted with James, Pad-more, and Arthur Lewis, the economist, in London in 1955 on the draft party manifesto during a visit to Europe.[2] When James came on the scene in 1958, his sudden dominance and the influence he obviously carried with Williams triggered many personal and ideological rivalries within the party.

Central to the whole scenario was the man responsible for James's entry into Trinidadian political life: Williams. In his person and style of leadership, as was the case in so many other Third World countries of that era, was embodied all the promise and all the frailty of Trinidadian nationalist expectations. The ultimate direction of the variety of social tendencies alive within the party and the society at large (class, race, and ideology) and the complex interaction of leader and mass, and leadership among themselves, all hinged upon the philosophical and personal makeup of the political leader and the nature of the options he would choose to exercise at various stages in the nationalist developmental process. The fate of C. L. R. James from 1958 to 1961, therefore, was both a story of his personal relations with leader and party, and a story of conflicting social tendencies within the broader mass movement at a crucial stage in its early evolution (and Williams's method of handling these tendencies).

Ivar Oxaal has observed that James's sudden entry into PNM politics, and the favored position he held for at least a year and more, was comparable to the sudden rise to prominence within the Russian Bolshevik Party of the maverick intellectual Trotsky, elevated after years of being an outsider to being Lenin's right-hand man just before and after the revolution's triumph. The tensions and personal jealousies that this event set off among the party's old guard were comparable to similar anxieties generated within the elite elements of the PNM. The latter consisted of men who had been instrumental in the formation of a study group, the Political Education Group (PEG), in early 1955, a group that preceded the founding of the PNM.[3] The parallel is apt, but the explanation lay in Eric Williams's own personal history, in his attempt to combine his intellectual associations in the metropolis of the 1930s and 1940s with the new political friendships he would form in Trinidad itself in the 1950s.

James and Williams had known each other even before both men had migrated to Britain in the 1930s, one to pursue a career as a radical writer, the other to tread a more conventional but still pathbreaking road into academia at Oxford. Much later, Williams would recount some of his experiences during those early undergraduate years and reveal how intellectually isolated he felt at first as a brilliant colonial West Indian at Oxford, cut off from serious literature on West Indian life and society, with nothing available at first but James's recently published *Life of Captain Cipriani* and the pamphlet "The Case for West Indian Self-Government" (actually an excerpt from the first work). For serious intellectual stimulation, he had to join the Oxford Indian Students' Union (MAJLISS), where he came into contact with progressive Indian nationalist ideas, and keep in touch with James's and Padmore's Pan-African activism in London.[4]

It is well known too that the germ of the idea that became the basis for Williams's doctoral dissertation (later published as *Capitalism and Slavery*) came from an insight contained within James's own pioneering work *The Black Jacobins*, published in 1938.[5] The friendship and association between the two men continued into the 1940s, when both lived in the United States, James as an influential radical theorist-activist in the American left, Williams as a scholar and professor at Howard University, the nation's premier black university. Although the personal bonds and the mutual respect were there, it was obvious from very early that Williams's philosophical temperament, although militantly anti-imperialist and anti-colonialist in its direction, did not extend to the wider visionary preoccupations of James and his Marxist friends (and enemies). Not an activist or a radical theorist, as James was, but essentially a liberal scholar (and a highly trained one at that) with a liberal's ambivalence about the complexities of history and the historical process, Williams tended to draw the line between the militant demystification of colonialism and the imperial political-intellectual tradition, on the one hand, and the vision of possibilities open to small Third World countries attempting to move beyond that tradition, on the other. He was never (as some of his later critics, including James, would claim) a radical who went sour halfway in the nationalist struggle, but rather a complex liberal nationalist, torn often between the militancy of his anti-colonial sentiments and a liberal's pragmatic realism about Third World potentialities.

Williams often vacillated between an inspirational identification with the spirit of solidarity generated by the Afro-Asian Bandung Conference of 1955, and a fatalistic recognition of the Caribbean island's irrelevance in the larger arena of international politics.[6] Kwame Nkrumah's anguished cry in Ghana in the mid-1960s—"You cannot build socialism without socialists"—as his own explanation of what went wrong with Ghana's nationalist movement never would become an issue in Williams's Trinidad. Williams's liberal vision never allowed him to formulate social goals and aspirations for Trinidad, the implementation of which he would find impossible either structurally or because of the personnel at his disposal. Williams never even attempted to ally the PNM formally with the trade union movement, Fabian-style, like most of his West Indian nationalist counterparts, and he did not like the label *socialism*, even the British Labour Party version.

Yet there was a bond between the two men, Williams and James, one that allowed Williams to ignore James's broader visionary preoccupations and to see the value of his Caribbean nationalism; one that valued the philosophical intelligence of veteran Pan-Africanists like James and Padmore but nevertheless sought to distinguish between "Pan-Africanism" and "Communism." James himself had his own unique view of Trinidad and its requirements, a view that was far removed from the vision of a deterministic Marxist mind or "knee-jerk radical." This view allowed him to accommodate himself to the Trinidadian situation and to commit himself to working within it. Ironically, although his critics and opponents inside and outside the party stressed his "communistic" proclivities, James's own perception of what was to be done reflected how far he was from "Stalinist" figures both inside Trinidad and outside (e.g., Cheddi Jagan in British Guyana).

These views were articulated sporadically from 1958 to 1960 within the pages of the *Nation*, while James was editor and subsequently in many articles and speeches, as well as in *Party Politics in the West Indies*, published just after the split with Williams and the PNM. James's famous pronouncement, that during his stay in Trinidad he had never discussed "socialism" with Williams for more than three minutes, indicates what he thought should have been the priorities of the nationalist movement.[7]

C. L. R. James belonged to a marginal tradition broadly defined in the late 1960s as New Left Marxism. He brought the biases derived from his metropolitan battles with pro-Stalinists and pro-Trotskyists back to Trinidad, but he did so in a peculiar manner. He did not believe these schisms (not even his own New Left perspectives) to be relevant to the needs of Trinidad in the 1950s and early 1960s, except in a very indirect manner. Any connection between these positions lay in the notion that empowerment of the masses through the appropriate institutional practices, in an authentically humanist way, is the central challenge of modern politics. But what that meant in the industrial metropolis or communist Russia and in the vastly different environments of the Third World was another matter. In Trinidad (and the Caribbean) James was often impatient with, and dismissive of, all those fledgling formations that saw themselves within the perspectives of prevailing Marxist orthodoxies. Moreover, his unique view of West Indian society and the West Indian people, and the history from which they came, led him to emphasize certain nationalist priorities over others. These attitudes (one derived from his metropolitan left experience, one derived from his view of West Indian society) found expression in James's work. Always, these ideas would be expressed in a somewhat polemical style, with the populist's romantic-activist fervor that many Caribbean academics often found irritating, but which endeared James to the youthful and idealistic.[8]

There were several strands to James's vision of West Indian society, and I will attempt to outline some of the main ones. First, there was the notion that of all Third World people, West Indians were the most modernized because of their long relationship with Western traditions and the loss of classic traditional ancestral ways of seeing. As he expressed it in his own inimitable fashion: "The populations in the British West Indies have no native civilization at all. People dance Bongo and Shango and all this is very artistic and very good. But these have no serious effects upon their general attitude to the world. These populations are essentially Westernized and they have been Westernized for centuries."[9] Thus what an increasing number of Afro-Caribbean intellectuals in the late 1960s saw as a source of alienation (the absence of living ancestral traditions) and writers like V. S. Naipaul saw as a source of weakness (bastard Western imitations), C. L. R. James saw as a source of social strength.

It was not that James was a nonbeliever in African traditional values, but that he did not think these traditions had any socially operative meaning for development in the West Indies. Certainly, the challenge in modern Africa (as in most of the Third World) lay in finding the fusion between modern development institutions and indigenous traditions. But the challenge in the West Indies was to make use of the historical experience of close and long contact with Western traditions and move forward. What this often meant in practice was that Western liberal-democratic institutions should not be jettisoned, but built upon creatively in conformity with the social aspirations of the population. Africa had been, and would continue to be, important, but in a way that had more implications for cultural self-confidence than for concrete institutional developmental solutions. Many Afro-West Indians had to pass through an African phase of interest before making their Caribbean focus concrete because the circumstances of Caribbean history, as well as that of the African diasporal condition, compelled them to discover their existential solidity via this route. But they did so with their Western training and skills and, ironically in the process, often acted as pioneers of nationalist movements—political and literary—in Africa itself:

> The recognition of Africanism, the agitation for the recognition of Africa, the literary creation of an African ideology, one powerful sphere of African Independence, all were directly the creation of West Indians (Garvey, Padmore, Cesaire, among others). The exact proportion of their contribution need not be estimated. The indisputable fact is that able and powerful West Indians concentrated their exceptional familiarity with Western thought, expression and organization on Africa and Africans when these qualities were urgently needed both in Africa and elsewhere.[10]

James's insistence on this Western source of strength of the West Indian people often prompted nationalist intellectuals to wonder whether his attitudes were contradictory, whether this was not evidence of an ingrained colonial mentality in his approach to the challenges of nationalism, a refusal to recognize the inner, self-justifying legitimacy of Caribbean creativity. The Jamaican novelist Andrew Salkey noted from an observer: "Take a man like James. That's another one who'd fool you. Full of contradictions. This colonial mentality is a thing that breaks out, like an embarrassing pimple, when you least expect. Right in the middle of teaching people something new, and out comes a piece of staleness that you yourself really never knew was there, or, if you did, you ignored it and didn't dig it out."[11]

But to James there was no contradiction. His points about Westernization were made with emphasis on Caribbean creativity, especially folk creativity, and his rejection of the contradiction would have been just as firm as his rejection of any notion in metropolitan socialist thinking that would posit a "proletarian" culture as diametrically opposed to a "bourgeois" culture and owing no allegiance to it. The culture that knew Sparrow and Shakespeare was not schizophrenic, but strong. If a duality in traditions existed in the society, the relationship was to be seen as a source of strength not alienation. In one of his exhortatory statements, James phrased the point:

People of the West Indies, you do not know your own power. No
one dares to tell you. You are a strange, a unique combination of
the greatest driving force in the world today, the underdeveloped,
formerly colonial coloured peoples; and more than any of them, by
education, way of life and language, you are completely a part of
Western civilization. . . . All that these underdeveloped countries
are striving for is at your feet. You have to know what you are, and
what you can do. And this nobody can teach you except yourselves,
by your own activities and the lessons that you draw from them. . . .
   All those who say or imply that you are in any way backward and
therefore cannot in a few years become a modern advanced people
are your enemies, satisfied with the positions that they hold and
ready to keep you where you are forever. They still bear in their souls
the shackles of slavery and the demoralization of colonialism which
you, the people, have broken and are ready to cast aside forever.[12]

A corollary to this insistence on the basically Westernized cultural
frame of being of Caribbean people was James's view that West Indians
(of all races) had made such outstanding contributions to the Western
tradition itself that it would be impossible to ignore these contributions
in discussing that tradition. A list of intellectual notables was always
on his lips as examples of people who were not only major achievers in
the Western tradition, but also people whose very background helped to
enrich the nature of the achievement and the contribution. To an objective observer, the list often seemed random and not really proof of much
else than the obvious: Caribbean people are just as talented as any other
within the grand metropolitan tradition, and some are major achievers.
But the listing often served the social purpose of stimulating national
pride and a positive self-image in a region always conscious of its diminu-
tive size and influence. The list included famous white West Indians
like Alexander Hamilton; the French artists Alexander Dumas, Leconte
de Lisle, Jose Maria de Heredia, and St. John Perse; the Cuban Alejo
Carpentier; and such world-famous black historical figures as Toussaint
L'Ouverture, Marcus Garvey, George Padmore, Aime Cesaire, and Frantz
Fanon. Others would from time to time be added, but the basic point
would remain the same: these were not just regional Caribbean figures,
but talented achievers whose creativity had enriched the grand metropolitan tradition.[13] James himself, of course, was an outstanding example
of this trend, being a major early New Left theorist and indeed the only

black or Third World thinker of importance in the tradition of avant-garde Marxism.

In only one respect did James's New Left Marxian visions sometimes (but only sometimes) encroach upon his view of West Indian society. Marxist-humanists of different hues all shared a general revulsion toward the one-party authoritarianism that had become the embodiment of "working-class" political power in the modern communist states and, in various ways, all looked forward to some form of authentic mass participatory form that would be more fully democratic and reflective of true mass power than either Western liberal-democratic institutions or communist authoritarian states. The solutions were not always consistent, but the visions always harked toward some form of mass-inspired "direct democracy," or something approximating it at any rate. Consistent with this preoccupation, James was enamoured of the direct democracy that the ancient Greek city-states represented, and he often wrote and lectured on them.[14] Although he never attempted to suggest that West Indian society should evolve pure direct democratic forms in the way he thought possible for advanced industrial societies (a government of workers' councils), he was often close to suggesting that the social intimacy and small size of the West Indian islands were approximations of that closeness and humanism that characterized the ancient city-states.[15] These points were always present in the form of passing visionary notions, but James's concrete suggestions for institutionalizing mass involvement were somewhat more conventional and more liberal-democratic than social-revolutionary.

The main participatory social instrument in the West Indies should be the mass party, the organized expression of a self-mobilized people, a social as well as a political movement. Unfortunately, there were inconsistencies in this notion. James sometimes made it sound as if he were proposing a totally new form of political party, while sometimes it sounded in its specifics more like a conventional mass-based party. Nor did he ever discuss in this context the question of the relationship between other mass organizations like trade unions and his notion of a mass party, so some of the crucial issues involved in the "massification" of the party structure were avoided.

Nevertheless, the vision of the party as an expression of the self-mobilized people remains relevant, although there is the question of how really new this notion was in 1958. That there were severe deficiencies in the structure and practices of the Peoples National Movement

goes without saying. But how much of this was due to day-to-day transitional exigencies and how much to fundamental philosophical conflicts
about party organizational methods remains somewhat nebulous, especially as the Jamesian notion of a mass party was never fully elaborated
in structural terms. Was the PNM just a badly organized mass party,
or was it a totally different kind of party altogether, conflicting with
Jamesian notions of organization? This never became completely clear
from *Party Politics in the West Indies*. To contrast the idea of the mass
party with that of the vanguard party (the Leninist notion) and to suggest that James's views were new in this respect, as some analysts have
done, is to miss the point that no one in Trinidad in the 1950s proposed
establishing such a formation, certainly not the PNM, and that we are
in danger of transposing the dilemmas of one environment to another
without any basis in social reality. To suggest, moreover, that the PNM
was no more than a mere electoral machine, and that the mass party
notion was contrasted with this view of PNM, might be closer to the
criticism contained in *Party Politics in the West Indies*. However, it is
debatable whether this was either philosophically accurate as a description of how the PNM leadership saw the party, or even accurate as a fair
overall description of how the PNM functioned despite its clearly oligarchical tendencies. Much about the notion of the mass party outlined in
Party Politics in the West Indies remains to be resolved.

One of James's original insights into the nature of British West Indian
political culture was its underlying social trend toward brutality and
tyranny, no different than the norm in places like Haiti, Trujillo's
Dominican Republic, and Batista's Cuba despite the historical exposure
to British democratic traditions.

I have repudiated in unambiguous terms the false and dangerous
conception that we have been so educated by the British that the
instinct for democracy is established among us. . . . I see every sign
that the tendency to naked power and brutality, the result of West
Indian historical development, is here all around us. . . . Has democracy sunk ineradicable roots in us? I say that I see no sign of it and
many signs to the contrary. . . .

Democratic government does not create democracy. Democracy
creates democratic government. Were it not for what the British
people are and do, British democratic government would collapse
tomorrow: It is not held together by government action. It is held

together by the habits and practices and expectations of the British people. . . .

I have never known a population claiming to be democratic where so many people (both Negroes and Indians) live in such fear of the whole apparatus of government. . . .[16]

Clearly, this judgment was derived not simply from the fact that the British West Indies had become accustomed to crown colony government or autocratic rule by the British governor. It was also a statement on a perceived fragility in the social traditions of the island populations themselves, a tendency that to James was not far below the surface of official institutional life and practice. For this reason, he insisted, the active involvement of the masses in a process of thoroughgoing democratization was necessary for the nationalist movement. Historical tendencies could be reversed, but conscious leadership initiatives were required, particularly as the masses were ready and willing to undergo such a deepening process and had demonstrated this collective readiness to move forward many times in the past. The fine dialectical tension in James's vision of the West Indies—between a potential for a humanist city-state development and a simultaneous potential for a gangster-type authoritarianism—is reminiscent of the stark Marxian vision of modern society's only two options: socialism or barbarism.

Closely allied to this social observation about latent gangsterism in the political culture was a penetrating analysis of the fundamental weaknesses of the black middle class, the new professionals who had just inherited power in the late 1950s and sought to take over from the British. The analysis made in *Party Politics in the West Indies* was a development on similar insights James had made since the 1930s, when he wrote *The Life of Captain Cipriani*. The new black middle class was excluded not just from political power, but from the centers of productive life in the society. Social mobility so far had been restricted to the independent professions and to the middle and lower rungs of the colonial bureaucracy. Their perspectives for the new society had been severely limited by their intellectual and social lack of familiarity with the life of the productive private sector, foreign or local. Hence their narrow expectations and preoccupations in the field of economic planning, their sole preoccupation with, as James stated, "income, revenue, expenditure, how this money is to be got and how shared out."

Of the fundamentals of economic development, which necessitated widespread mass mobilization, education, and involvement, the black middle class was innocent because they did not think in that way. Hence also their overwhelming unconcern for the larger challenges and visions that might inspire the new order, their intellectual emptiness, and their individualist preoccupations with office-holding and their opportunistic mobility toward openings within the bureaucracy. Hence also the inherent political instability among a restless minority, as they toyed superficially and ahistorically with different notions of what was to be done with the structures of the old colonial order, and indeed with the masses. A nationalist movement dominated by such perspectives would inevitably corrode the quality of public life as well as the organic institutions of the movement itself, for example, the party. James's bold critique of the Afro-Trinidadian middle class of the early 1960s was outspoken and original in the West Indies of that era. He dared to say at home what other Third World socialist thinkers were also saying about their own growing "neocolonial bourgeoisie," and his critique is eminently comparable with fellow West Indian Frantz Fanon's classic condemnation of the middle classes of post-colonial Africa of the same era (the essay "Pitfalls of National Consciousness" in *The Wretched of the Earth*).[17]

All was not hopeless or backward among the middle classes, however. The authentic creative voices of the nationalist movement could still be heard within the society, and indeed the party itself, and it was the duty of the leadership to so organize the party and the movement that these voices had greater freedom and social meaning. The lower echelons of the party in particular, and the mass movement in general, were ready for such advances and for bold initiatives from above. But to make this possible, the party had to be properly converted into a mass party and divorced from the business of government and pure administration. The political leader had to stop trying to be all things to all people, otherwise the cycle of patronage and dependency connected with British colonial autocracy would only entrench itself further. By 1960–61 a turning point had already been reached in this degenerative process. "Organize your party, Bill, organize your party" was James's well-known injunction to his colleague of thirty years.

On the broader Caribbean scene, the authentic nationalist impulse was clearly visible in the writings of the new novelists, most of whom, because of the philistinism and backwardness of the old colonial order, lived abroad, usually in Britain, and wrote about the West Indies for a mainly metropolitan readership. This social displacement of the artist in exile, nationalist voices without a home, was comparable in James's view to the alienation of the great nineteenth-century Russian writers in relation to tsarist Russia. Somewhat exaggeratedly, he sometimes also suggested that the West Indian writers had collectively produced a body of literature comparable to the Russian greats. A thoroughgoing and deeprooted nationalism would find a proper place at home, in the islands, for these creative elements to thrive and commune organically with the audience they truly sought, the West Indian popular audience. "When our local artists can evoke the popular response of a Sparrow, the artist in the Caribbean will have arrived."[18]

Much of this kind of critique was similar to socialist-populist critiques found elsewhere in the neocolonial Third World. Again, Fanon comes to mind; see the essay "National Culture" in *Wretched of the Earth*. James always hesitated, however, to enter into any recommendation of his own about the actual direction that artistic creativity should take, unlike Fanon and others. In this respect his was a more authentic humanist's vision of the role of the artist in society. What was important was not preferring, say, a Lamming over a Naipaul, but creating the internal social conditions in which both kinds of creative direction could be allowed to flower authentically.

James also had, like the PNM leadership (especially Williams), clearcut views on race and ethnicity in multiracial Trinidad. Before outlining these, some background on race relations in Trinidad in the early 1960s is necessary. The PNM, and much of Trinidadian nationalism in the 1960s, remained a purely Afro-Trinidadian phenomenon despite the multiracial appeals of Williams and the presence of prominent figures from other racial groups in his cabinet and in top echelons of the party. This was because of the fledgling state of the island colony's development. The growth of a sense of shared loyalty to the island's future and a feeling of Trinidadian identity was a challenge for the future rather than an actual reality. The island's anarchic cosmopolitanism, held together by nothing but a somewhat insecure sense of place at the mass level and by British colonialism at the top, was a Caribbean version of the loose multiracialism and multiethnicity of many American communities.

However, the intellectual development of the society within the British colonial mold often prevented many local analysts and social observers (then as well as now) from recognizing its social nature within this comparative framework. Compared with older, more stable, nation-states (even multiracial and multiethnic states in the Old World) Trinidadian society often appeared to be artificial, an anarchic detribalized hodgepodge of Africans, Asian Indians, and white Creoles of French, English, and Spanish descent (many of mixed blood themselves), with a few newly arrived immigrants from China, the Middle East, Portugal, and Venezuela thrown in for added confusion. It was, as one character in a novel described it, a place where people lived, not a place to which people belonged and, according to one writer, a nation of transients. This was the fledgling, unformed island version of Americana that Oxford-educated V. S. Naipaul dismissed as uncreative and unimportant, and which the new leadership of the Peoples National Movement was attempting to transform into an independent nation-state, with its own sense of authentic centrality and distinctiveness. If any incipient nationalist sentiment was to be found in this cosmopolitan amalgam, it was obviously in the Afro-Trinidadian community, and in particular the masses. They alone had nudged the nation forward in earlier periods through worker self-mobilizations and spontaneous rebellions. In them alone resided the germs of any uniquely local creativity, the heartbeat of Trinidadian popular culture.

C. L. R. James, like most responsible elements in the predominantly Afro-nationalist movement, clearly saw the nation's future hope in a larger multiracial solidarity, and he like others—especially Williams— wrote and lectured as much. The whites and the Indians were his main concern, both groups being obviously more important than the fringe minorities. In *Party Politics in the West Indies* a slight shade of individuality in James's own perceptions is discernible. Bearing in mind that he was discussing a theme on which all the leadership were agreed, at least in theory, I shall try to identify it. His main observation about the whites' group political attitudes was that they were basically on the defensive, on the outside looking in, and that it was the duty of a responsible nationalist leadership to woo them into feeling themselves an integral part of the new social movement. The initiative rested with the nationalist leadership and not the other way around. This seemed to contrast with Williams's own political style, a mixture of militant public hostility to vested historical interests ("Massa Day Done") and a policy of quietly relying upon key business figures (mainly white), using the influence of those members of his cabinet who came from that community or had access to them.

The public image of militancy pleased the black masses. The private policy of collaboration and appeasement worked with many specific businessmen but was never really successful in winning that basically conservative community over to the support of the PNM. James's own approach, seemingly more conciliatory than Williams's contradictory signals, in fact never worked either, even when he was on his own (as he was later).[19] Regardless of his own somewhat liberal-democratic perception of what needed to be done, James's image remained that of a "communist," much to the left of Williams and consequently to be less trusted. The Venezuelan Catholic conservative newspaper *La Religion* carried a revealing article in November 1959. A visiting Venezuelan journalist of conservative persuasion wrote of the PNM, and of James's role in it, and provided a fairly accurate view of how the basically conservative white community saw the early Afro-nationalist movement. James even suggested in an editorial in the *Nation* that he got most of his information from Albert Gomes, a conservative Portuguese politician and the main public spokesman for this community in the 1950s and early 1960s.[20]

The article in *La Religion* described the party as having two tendencies, a democratic one under Williams and a leftist one under James, but Williams was described as someone who "encouraged leftism" and "facilitated the spread of Red doctrines." On the issue of race relations, the article stated: "The stimulating of hatred among the White, Hindu and Colored People is the strongest weapon of the PNM. This worries the population and causes unrest in their minds, forcing them to wonder what will happen in the future." Clearly there was a contradiction between the signals that the nationalist leadership felt itself to be sending out on the issue of racial harmony and the signals that different groups were receiving. Much of this miscommunication continued well into the late nationalist period and was directly traceable to three causes. First, Williams often sent violently mixed signals; James was, ironically, despite his "leftist" image always more diplomatic and sensitive in his writings to the anxieties of others. Second, the basically conservative reflexes of the other groups were derived from their upper-middle-class status (in the case of the Indians, their rural-isolationist conservativism) and from the fledgling state of the colony's development (the anarchic juxtaposition of detribalized groups, American-style). Third, among the non-African groups there was a lack of significant influence on the part of those leaders who did identify with the Afro-nationalist movement.

James's views on the Indians were uttered more frequently, in several speeches, articles, and pamphlets, and over an extended period long after his departure from Trinidadian politics. In 1965 and 1966 within the opposition WFP he also attempted to bridge the racial divide on the basis of class politics. Although he was unsuccessful in an electoral sense, he managed to initiate a trend in Trinidad's Afro-Indian politics (racial unity conceived in class terms) that still continues, although with problematic ups and downs and not always among the established politicians.[21] During his PNM period, James clearly expressed sympathy with the cultural-religious pluralism of the society, even expressing a personal wish to learn Hindi and to pay homage to the world importance of Islam.[22] This was an advance on popular nationalist thinking at the time, which was that anything short of a "Trinidadian" cultural loyalty (meaning Afro-Trinidad) was divisive (a view Williams never shared, as distinct from his overzealous followers).[23] At the same time, James often remarked approvingly on the increasingly urban-Westernized appearance of most younger Indians. He was also less disturbed by the persistence of racially based political constituencies, believing that time and the development of society would make their own differentiations.

Citing the United States as an example, James suggested that ethnic-based politics was an expression of community evolution in a multi-racial society, that it was not an "Indian" trait, and that racial frictions in Trinidad were not deep-rooted. He also remarked upon the important role played historically by the Indian (and Chinese) small business sector and the inroads it had made into the white-dominated mercantile class, thereby helping to alter somewhat a traditional monopoly in Trinidad's economic life. He saw this development as progressive and not—as many blacks in the nationalist movement did and still do—as a potentially threatening form of racial dominance no different to the classical colonial pattern.

During the PNM period, James shared Williams's larger views on racial unity, but the men's writings and speeches revealed a marked difference in political temperament and human response to group behavior in a young, multiracial society. James has confessed that Williams's rhetorical vehemence against all those who opposed the party, which often included racial insinuations, often unnerved him. Williams's most famous diatribe was the one in 1958, just after he lost the federal election to the conservative ethnic-based Democratic Labor Party. He called the Indians, especially the Hindus, a "recalcitrant and hostile minority masquerading as the Indian nation" and compared them unfavorably with their progressive nationalist counterparts in India itself.[24] The rank-and-file supporters of both parties could not be expected to understand subtle comparisons between the "good" Indians in India and the "bad" Indians in Trinidad. In the course of his speech, Williams also told the crowd that he was not referring to his own Indian cabinet ministers, who were "good guys," much to their personal embarassment.[25] Williams pragmatically (and often ruthlessly) allied himself with both white and Indian elements outside of his party to achieve specific aims, whether about economic development projects or political battles (e.g., against militant Indian union elements or political opponents on the left, including James himself).

Thus, the racial question in Trinidad was never totally cut-and-dried, but rather complex and always fluid, although neither the PNM nor James's later short-lived WFP ever acquired a significant electoral following among either conservative whites or the mass of the Indian community, whether small businessmen, professionals, workers, or farmers. James's efforts in one short year may be judged in relation to his visions and hopes. For the PNM, which remained in power from 1956 to 1986, a thirty-year failure to build an electoral base among the non-Africans must be seen as a devastating indictment on Williams's brand of interracial leadership.

Such ideas were some of James's major themes between 1958 and 1962. There were, of course, many more topical and immediate issues discussed in the pages of the *Nation* while he was managing editor.[26] Some of the more interesting dealt with James's views on federation, the conservative daily newspapers and their links with the upper classes, Caribbean unity, tributes to working-class heroes like Cipriani, supportive analyses of Williams's politics and personality,[27] the campaign to make Frank Worrell the first black captain of the West Indies cricket team, the background to the battle to regain the Chaguaramas naval and military base from the Americans, commentaries from Ghana on the occasion of its independence celebrations, numerous articles on cricket, and biographical sketches of the James family.

During 1959 the world-famous Pan-Africanist and Trinidad-born leader George Padmore (née Malcolm Nurse) died in Ghana. The *Nation* carried a special supplement on Padmore's international achievements, calling for Trinidadian recognition of a man James considered to be the most influential early-twentieth-century black figure after Garvey. Between October 1959 and January 1960, James wrote a lengthy series of articles on Padmore, articles filled with extraordinary biographical detail and insight on this important figure as well as on James's friendship and work with Padmore in London during the 1930s.[28] The articles were also rich in anecdotal references to key black leaders as James knew them in the 1930s and 1940s, among them Jomo Kenyatta, Marcus Garvey, and Kwame Nkrumah:

What Padmore did between 1930 and 1935 was to organize and edu-
cate the Negro masses on a world scale in the theory and practice of modern political parties and modern trade unionism. Up to 1945, the end of the War, there was hardly a single African leader still active who had not passed through the school of thought and organization which George directed from Moscow. Tens of thousands of Negro workers in various parts of the world received their first political education from the paper he edited, *The Negro Worker*. I have heard from others and Uriah Butler has confirmed it to me that in the thirties Trinidad workers were getting the *Negro Worker*. . . .
One of the reasons why Garvey was so unceremoniously bundled out of the United States in 1926 was the fact that the Japanese Government had been trying to make arrangements to finance (and doubtless to control) his Back-to-Africa movement. They wanted to embarrass and disrupt the imperialist empires in Africa. In 1935 when Anthony Eden visited Moscow to discuss a rapprochement between Great Britain and Russia, we were reliably informed that one of the conditions he laid down was the cessation of anti-imperialist propaganda in Africa. That was the work of George.

James's militant and educated journalism in 1959 and 1960 earned him friends and enemies not only in the wider society but also inside the ruling party. His close association with Williams and the general recogni-
tion of his own independent stature as an intellectual activist generated many anxieties among higher-echelon party figures. The human side to this anxiety is best illustrated by a remark attributed to an influential party figure: "For a year Nello [C.L.R.] was number two in the Party. In fact, there were times when we thought he might be number one."[29]
James himself was not modest about the nature of the close relation-
ship he shared with Williams and their long friendship.

I have known Dr. Williams since he was about ten or eleven years old. I taught him. We played cricket and football on Q.R.C. teams. He followed me as a lecturer in English and History at the Government

[Teachers'] Training College. He spent his holidays from Oxford in London with me. I read with him Aristotle, Hobbes and Rousseau. He, Halsey McShine and I spent a fabulous holiday at Nelson in Lancashire with Learie and Norma Constantine. He spent days in Paris with me working at the Black Jacobins. We spent countless hours discussing West Indian history and history in general. I read various drafts of the thesis which became *Capitalism and Slavery*. It so happened that he came to America a year after I did. He used to come to New York and stay with me. I used to go to Washington and stay with him. We constantly exchanged facts and ideas about all sorts of intellectual subjects. When distance separated us, we arranged to meet once for a few hours in Paris, once in Salt Lake city for two days. Because of this common background, I talk to him more easily and with quicker mutual understanding than with anybody I know.[30]

The details of the story of James's fall from grace and eventual expulsion from the PNM have been told in standard accounts like Ivar Oxaal's *Black Intellectuals Come to Power* and Selwyn Ryan's *Race and Nationalism in Trinidad and Tobago*. James's own *Party Politics in the West Indies* documented his side of the issues and the sequence of events leading to his expulsion from the party in 1961. The broad scenario is clear. It involved disgruntled conservative elements within the party elite (also rank-and-file) concerned about James's undue influence, his leftism, and his personal style, and it climaxed with an attempt to embarrass him at the Fourth Party Convention in March 1960, by launching an investigation into the *Nation* and its management. Matters came to a head with an unfavorable report that hinted at mismanagement of funds. The real crisis, however, resulted from Williams's refusal to intervene decisively to protect James from this political intrigue.

Several factors may have led to this personal estrangement: sympathy with the anxieties expressed by other influential party figures; growing disagreements between the two men on such issues as the state of party organization and the handling of the Chaguaramas base handover talks with the Americans; and Williams's opinions on James's own handling of the responsibilities that had been entrusted to him on the *Nation*. In 1960, during the party crisis, Williams proposed to James that he become editor of an independent daily newspaper that Williams was thinking of establishing to counter the monopoly of the conservative press. James, however, declined that offer. Many years afterward, in his own autobiography *Inward Hunger*, Williams would record some acid (and somewhat dishonest) reflections on the whole episode:

[James] had stayed on [in 1958] but many of our good party members on the General Council objected to his admittance into the Party on the ground of his notorious political record. The *Nation* got into serious difficulties with the Party. . . . [James's] comments before [colonial secretary] MacLeod's arrival were deprecated by the General Council which had been summoned to decide on the line to take. He used the Party Paper to build up himself and his family, and his personal articles on George Padmore and the James family were widely resented. Whilst Party members generally supported his stand that Frank Worrell be made captain of the West Indies cricket team, more than one looked askance at his methods. The Fourth Annual Convention appointed a Committee to examine the relationship between the Party and the Publishing Company, and to ascertain the financial position of the Publishing Company. The Committee's report revealed a situation that bordered on chaos. It condemned administrative confusion, and disclosed a very real absence of liaison between Paper and Party. On October 2nd 1960, the General Council appointed its own Committee to report on the p.n.m. Publishing Co. Ltd. The report stated: "The whole question of management during Mr. James' term of office could be written off quite briefly as a period of mismanagement. Given a free hand, he appeared to use it freely without regard to his own or the Company's responsibilities."

James was placed before the Disciplinary Committee on two charges. He refused to appear to answer the charges, was found guilty and was expelled from the movement. His answer was published in a document entitled pnm *Go Forward* which subsequently formed the basis of a study by him of party politics in Trinidad and Tobago. In it he claimed that the attack by the Convention on him was a political attack on me, that he should have "taken" the post of General Secretary of the Party, instead of Editor of the Party Organ, that the entire General Council should be made to read some study of his, that I was a "gangster" for refusing to discuss the Convention action with him (I refused to be any party to by-passing the action of the Convention), and that I had sold out to the Americans at the Tobago Conference.[31]

Williams conveniently neglected to mention that the Fifth Annual Convention in October 1960 saw a resolution from the floor calling for James's reinstatement as editor of the *Nation* (he had resigned earlier), a resolution that was overwhelmingly endorsed by the convention but totally ignored by Williams and the rest of the leadership.[32]

It would be well to record that the fate of James inside the PNM was, at one level, just a Trinidadian version of a pattern that overtook many nationalist movements in this period, one in which overall unity against colonialism began to founder upon the challenges posed by impending or actual political independence. Conservative, liberal, and leftist agendas often surfaced soon after the transition questions had been resolved; such agendas were expressed in the rise of individual leaders of varying importance within the party and the mass movement. How these agenda conflicts (and personality conflicts) were resolved, whether there was compromise or confrontation, varied widely with each specific set of circumstances. James was clearly an early casualty of this larger drama as it worked out its own logic on Trinidadian soil. That these factors were compounded by the human element, the actual personality interactions between James and all those involved, is obvious. But as important as the human interactions were, they should not be allowed to obscure the fundamental issues involved. Winston Mahabir, a Christian Indian who was a minister in Williams's first cabinet of 1956–61, was not inclined to be so philosophical about the whole episode, however.

Williams apparently disowned James when he became convinced that James' ideology was unsuited to the temper and needs of the West Indian times. But James' ideology was no secret. He had always been forthright and even boastful about it. Williams had sustained an active and passive association with this ideology for thirty years. Williams had kept in active touch with James throughout the years. He had consulted him on the first P.N.M. Manifesto. It was Williams who brought James back to Trinidad. James was lionized by Williams who commandeered his services for the Party newspaper which James rescued partially from its increasing insipidity. It was James who helped to develop the case for Chaguaramas. The catalogue is long and I am familiar with but fragments of it. Not being a close friend of James I can say little more. And James is perfectly capable of defending himself. But the unceremonious ditching of James by Williams posed the question in my mind: does Williams

care at all about people apart from their value as manipulable political objects? To retain power, would Williams not continue to be
completely ruthless to the point of being unresponsive to the chords
of thirty years of friendship? These are some of the questions that
caused shudders in some who, even while they were the objects of
current favours, feared the unpredictable day of doom.[33]

One curious fact that analysts have often overlooked (and all of whom
may wish to agree about James's "leftism" and Williams's "liberalism" as
causes of the conflict) is the surprisingly mild nature of James's own left-
leaning agenda for Trinidad, compared with his bold New Left visions
for the advanced industrial world (capitalist or communist), or even with
traditional left social programs in the Third World. There was nothing
exclusively leftist about most of his key ideas on West Indian society,
nothing that any progressive nationalist could not champion with equal
enthusiasm, nothing indeed that even Williams and the PNM, with a little
more political generosity, could not have accommodated (and indeed,
Williams did accommodate, for just over a year).

The sticking point was more about method, and most important, the
issue of mass mobilization and involvement in the whole process. For
James, this issue was always the cornerstone of all authentic social development, whether in the metropolis or in the Third World. As he himself
stated in *Party Politics in the West Indies*: "Squabbling with Dr. Williams about neutralism or socialism was and remains quite remote from
me. I was concerned with something else."[34] The nature of his priorities
becomes clearer when we study his economic agenda, his views on the
economics of transformation. As these evolved and found more concrete
formulation in the second period of involvement in 1965–66 in the WFP,
an economic agenda emerged that was somewhere between Williams's
early positions (i.e., pre-1970) and the classical social programs of typical
Third World leftists. Before this aspect of James's West Indian vision is
discussed, however, a brief history of the process that led to his attempt
at opposition politics in Trinidad is necessary.

As a strict political venture, James's involvement in the short-lived
WFP was probably ill-advised. Indeed, many of his wellwishers and associates in the metropolis (and even in Trinidad itself) did not give the
venture their wholehearted support, concerned as they were at the time
that someone of James's stature as an independent intellectual and writer
should not attempt to get burned a second time in the fickle heat of

Trinidad's politics. James had lived in London since his return in 1962, a few days before the island's independence celebrations. The scandal of his break with Williams and the PNM, and the vindictive treatment by his enemies within the party, had reverberated far beyond the shores of little Trinidad.

When James returned to the island in March 1965, as a cricket correspondent for two major English newspapers, the *Observer* and the *Times*, he probably had no intention of directly involving himself in the island's politics because he had never attempted to do so after his expulsion from the party in 1961. Unfortunately for him, he arrived right in the middle of a major strike among the sugar workers, a few days after a state of emergency had actually been declared in the sugar belt, and troops were stationed in the trouble spots. It happened to be the country's most severe labor disturbance to date. There was also a hint of active political leftism in the air, with the radical George Weekes, recently emerged as the president-general of the Oilfields Workers Trade Union, extending overt support for the striking Indian sugar workers as they rebelled against their formal conservative and traditionalist leadership and sought new leaders.

Eighteen hours after James's arrival, Trinidad's government promptly extended the state of emergency to apply to the non-sugar district of Barataria, where he was staying with his sister, and placed James under house arrest. During the entire period of the emergency, which lasted until the end of the month (during which the government rushed through Parliament the controversial Industrial Stabilization Act banning unregulated strike activity), James remained confined to his sister's home, unable to perform his journalistic functions for the London newspapers. He was never given any official explanation for the treatment extended to him. It may have been coincidental that on the day the emergency was lifted a major protest delegation of influential West Indian intellectuals and political leaders in London was scheduled to appear at the Office of the Trinidad High Commissioner there. They included George Lamming, Andrew Salkey, Wilson Harris, Jan Carew, Samuel Selvon, Learie Constantine, and David Pitt.[35]

To add insult to injury, an official investigation into subversive activities in Trinidad and Tobago released a report in April after a year's delay (the Mbafeno Report, 1965). In a section entitled "Trade Union and Other Personalities," James was described as "a demagogue who would not hesitate, if he had the power, to destroy that which does not suit him," and as "having the intellectual capacity and power of expression which might appeal to intelligent and exuberant youth." The report based its findings purely on a study of his writings. It went on to state that "we had no evidence from other sources to support the view that a revolution was in fact planned at this time by Mr. James or anyone connected with him, although it does seem that he would like to see one started."[36] Various public figures condemned the report as an exercise in witchhunting and slander against public figures and called it a waste of public funds.

After his journalistic duties as a cricket reporter had been completed, James decided to stay on in Trinidad and plunge himself into opposition politics. His decisions at this point seemed to have been spontaneous and individualistic. He developed a close relationship with Stephen Maharaj, leader of the opposition Indian-based Democratic Labor Party, who was deputizing for the official leader Rudranath Capildeo, a London University lecturer. Maharaj himself was an old worker-activist, a former deputy of the veteran labor leader Uriah Butler, hero of the 1937–38 disturbances in the oil belt. He represented a labor-oriented tendency within a party that had become notorious in Trinidadian politics for its political instability and conservative ethnic-chauvinist opposition to the Afro-dominated progressive PNM. The passing of the Industrial Stabilization Act (ISA) had polarized society and even the labor movement itself; many pro-PNM workers supported it, in fact. Within the ranks of the conservative DLP, the Deputy Leader Maharaj was virtually alone in his vigorous opposition to this repressive piece of anti-worker legislation. Key DLP parliamentarians and senators supported the PNM-inspired act, providing a rare early instance of interracial middle-class collaboration on a matter that threatened interracial worker alliances (African oil workers and Indian sugar workers).

The incident gave the lie to those Afro-chauvinists who saw the Indian community as an intransigent and monolithic conservative ethnic bloc. It also indicated how far rightward the PNM had shifted in a few years. C. L. R. James, for whatever reasons of his own (some said opportunism, some said personal hurt at Williams's callous treatment of him, some said idealism over the prospect of an interracial labor collaboration, something the Machiavellian Williams had killed earlier and continued to discourage), decided to join forces with Stephen Maharaj in his own battles against the pro-ISA elements within the DLP. He allowed himself to be named by Maharaj as a substitute senator for one of the sacked DLP senators, as Maharaj attempted to replace four senators with prolabor figures, one of whom was Adrian Cola Rienzi, the veteran Indian labor leader.[37] The move was not successful. Capildeo returned from London, announced that "the DLP has no place for people like Mr. James," endorsed the pro-ISA party position, and secured the ouster of Maharaj.[38]

These developments set the stage for an alternative formation, and the Political Action Committee, later the Workers' and Farmers' Party, was formed in late 1965, with Stephen Maharaj its chair, and C. L. R. James its general secretary and editor of its paper, *We the People*. Its self-proclaimed mission was to create a proper labor party uniting workers and farmers of both races in a new progressive coalition. The WFP, however, never managed to develop truly organic links with either ethnic section of Trinidad's working class. Nor, ironically, did it draw the large body of James's supporters who undoubtedly existed in the Afro-nationalist movement, and who had earlier been extremely upset by the shabby manner in which he had been treated by the PNM and by Williams. The reasons may have been complex, but there is no question that the public did not perceive the WFP as a stable political formation, but rather as an ad hoc opposition party with leftist leanings, thrown up with no organic ties to the working communities on whose behalf it claimed to speak. Not even James's reputation could alter the public's view of Maharaj as a weak and somewhat dull figure, someone who moreover had been tainted with the opportunism and ethnic conservativism of the DLP despite his past as a labor leader.

James's own image was somewhat damaged by this hurried venture into left politics, even among his previously ardent admirers. Gordon Lewis declared that "the passion for power can bring together strange bedfellows."[39] The *Nation* lamented, "How are the mighty fallen!"[40] Indian sugar workers, restless under their traditionalist leadership, nevertheless did not flock to the new party, or to Maharaj's leadership. African workers, still largely under the charismatic spell of Williams, continued to support the PNM. Even the radical young leader of the oil workers' union, George Weekes, who was an active member of the WFP and who became James's life-long friend after this experience, could not persuade the rank-and-file oil workers who adored him to transfer their loyalties into the electoral arena. During the election campaign of 1966, the PNM tried to smear the WFP and its members with the "communist" taint, calling them "Castro's stooges,"[41] and "Marxism dressed up in the white robes of purity."[42] The WFP did very badly in the election, failing not only to win a single seat with just about 3 percent of the popular vote, but also actually losing all their candidates' deposits in the process. This included James himself, who managed to win just 2.8 percent of the votes cast in his own home constituency of Tunapuna, where he was born. It included also such well-known left figures as Jack Kelshall, Lennox Pierre, Max Ifill, Walter Annamunthodo, George Weekes, Clive Phill, George Bowrin, and the young Basdeo Panday. Stephen Maharaj got 5.5 percent of the votes cast in his constituency of Princes Town. The PNM won twenty-four seats, the DLP twelve, and the effort to create a multiracial labor party was stillborn. Not long thereafter, James returned to his London base, and the WFP folded quietly soon after that.

Nevertheless, the WFP's election manifesto provides a concrete view of James's economic agenda for Trinidad. It was an agenda that evolved through interaction with others in the party because James, like most radical theorists, was always more preoccupied with the philosophical and political parameters of change: the issues of power versus powerlessness and the empowerment of the masses through collective social experience and self-discovery, collective trial and error. More important than the specific content of an economic agenda was always the visionary and collective-motivational aspects of the transformation process, the sense of moving collectively from one stage to another. As one of his former WFP colleagues recently described him, James was not a politician in the true sense. He was always more preoccupied with the macrohistorical picture and not with the smaller details of policy.[43] Despite his leftist image and orientation, James's attitudes toward standard radical economic prescriptions during the PNM period and after had been surprisingly hostile. He had warned against "irresponsible" talk about nationalization of the commanding heights of the economy.

> Young West Indians talk of nationalization, even of revolution. They are either ignorant or crazy. Nationalize what? Oil? That is insanity. We should leave the sugar factories just where they are. To talk nationalization is to start a fight you are bound to lose: you thereby advertise your immaturity. Little countries must know their limitations, how and when to fight. We clarify the national purpose by discouraging any belief in nationalization as a panacea.[44]

In a 1961 analysis on the failure of the federation, however, he saw an active role for the state in the process of transformation:

> If we had 150 years . . . there would be no need for this telescop-

ing of economic developments. But I see no possibility of individual entrepreneurs, either inside the West Indies or from outside the West Indies, developing the economy to a pitch at which it will be possible for us to feel that the economy is now a going concern and sure to move forward, taking up the increases in population as time goes on. I cannot see it being done by private enterprise in the old sense of the term. There has to be a set plan, in which the State, taking all needs into consideration, not merely the ordinary economic demands but the social necessities of the population, will decide on a programme. . . . to satisfy the urgent needs of the people, and, this is very important, because this is the political issue, to make an impatient people understand that some serious, tremendous, new and sustained effort is being made to satisfy the demands which are increasing every day.[45]

By 1965–66, his views on the question had shifted somewhat. The WFP manifesto advocated state purchase of the large sugar plantations in order to break them up and redistribute the land to tens of thousands of small farmers; it claimed to be following the recommendation of the 1897 Royal Commission on the Sugar Industry. The manifesto advocated some form of state involvement in the oil industry and the formation of a national oil company, but was not specific and did not advocate nationalization of foreign oil companies. It hinted at the need to do something about the banks, almost all of which were foreign in 1965 and, which typically diverted local capital out of the island for developmental uses elsewhere. It also advocated encouraging the growth of the local private sector (commerce and industry) to reduce dependence upon foreign private capital. Thus the WFP advocated some form of mixed economy, with state and local capital combining to lessen the dependence on foreign capital, and banks reorganized so that nationally generated capital resources would remain at home for use locally. The breakup of the plantation sector was seen as key to liberating the energies of thousands of people tied to the plantations, and to creating a viable authentic community of small farmers motivated by their own collective agenda rather than the agenda of the foreign sugar companies.

Surprisingly, the manifesto was not specific on a proposed state productive sector, but concentrated more on the issue of using the state to loosen key bottlenecks in the economy, for example, banks and sugar plantations. It also committed itself to making existing and future in-

vestments more beneficial to the national community and did not advocate state takeovers of any part of the new small industrial sector. Nowhere, not even with the banks and the sugar plantations, did the WFP
advocate nationalization without compensation. Whatever nationaliza-
tions were contemplated were strictly orthodox and definitely not revolutionary.

Leaving aside the issue of the electorate's own judgment on the mes-
sengers and concentrating for the moment solely on the message of the
WFP, it is clear that the outline of economic policy laid down in the
manifesto was bold in relation to the standard PNM policies of the 1960s.
Despite all his militant rhetoric, Williams had studiously avoided any
attempt to touch the traditional economic arrangements inherited from
the colonial order. The Afro-nationalist movement had made gains in the
public service and all governmental institutions traditionally dominated
at the top by British personnel; it had advanced in sectors like education.
But the productive organization of the society remained untouched.

The oil industry, the sugar plantations, the banks, and the new small
industries were all dominated by foreign capitalist concerns, while the
large commercial-mercantile sector was controlled by local white Creoles, with a host of small business enterprises operated by the small
immigrant groups and a number of Indians. The PNM's economic policies,
relying on a modified Operation Bootstrap strategy (the Puerto Rican
model), philosophically reinforced this reliance upon foreign investment
but were not as concretely successful as the Puerto Rican experiment in
attracting foreign capital to nontraditional areas for import-substitution
purposes. In that context, it was certainly accurate to accuse Williams's
regime of imposing a neocolonial arrangement on the society, and certainly quite bold to suggest an intervention by the state to minimize
(if not eliminate) this foreign domination and redirect economic planning priorities inward. Williams himself would move in that very direction, evolving a mixed economy and an inward-looking strategy much
later in the 1970s. But in 1966, the WFP economic outline was forward-
looking and progressive, and the party is to be credited with articulating
economic sentiments that would only find their fullest expression and
widespread acceptance at all levels of the society after 1970.

The year 1966 marked the formal end of James's involvement with
local politics in Trinidad. He would not return to the island again until
1980, when he was in official retirement from Federal City College in
Washington, D.C. Even then, he stayed for just about a year, working on

his autobiography (never completed), as a guest of George Weekes and the Oilfields Workers Trade Union. However, from his academic perch in the metropolis, he remained the ever-resourceful commentator on Trinidad and its political developments to those of his listeners and aficionados who were interested in Caribbean events. He followed the Black Power revolts of the early 1970s with keen interest and propounded the view that Williams was politically dead by 1973, but had been "saved" by the oil boom, a totally external development in the global economy.

James himself remained personally distanced from events after 1966, but his influence continued to surface (again controversially) in an indirect manner after 1968, as youthful radicalism swept through the region. The late 1960s saw a new generation of West Indians come to political maturity and consciousness, inspired partly by such major radical events of the decade as Black Power, the Cuban Revolution, metropolitan socialist and counter-culture trends, and New Leftism, and partly by a Fanonist knowledge that the nationalist agenda of the previous era had been left incomplete. The WFP had, ironically, been simultaneously a part of that first generation of nationalists and an early, unsuccessful premonition of the second.

The year 1968, rather than 1966, was the signal for a new birth of social consciousness and activism region-wide. This was the year that the Guyanese historian Walter Rodney, perhaps the finest product of the new generation, was expelled from Jamaica (and his university job) for daring, with others, to make the transition from campus elitism to community involvement and black popular consciousness-raising. His expulsion sparked a week of mass riots in Kingston and set off a wave of social idealism that surfaced everywhere in the region, with varying degrees of intensity and sophistication. Subsequently, there was the Black Power revolt in Trinidad in 1970, the emergence of Michael Manley in Jamaica in 1972, the conflict between the left authoritarianism of Burnham and the New Left of Rodney's Working People's Alliance (WPA) in Guyana, the Grenada revolution of Maurice Bishop's New Jewel Movement (NJM) in 1979, and the rise of a multiplicity of small Black Power and socialist groups on almost every island. These were the symptoms of a whole new generation rising, somewhat disjointedly, to nationalist consciousness and commitment and severely testing the authority and stability of existing liberal-nationalist regimes. The mood was Fanonist and often insurrectionary, the target the neocolonial social order, which had seen the transition from colonialism on the political but not on the economic front. Everywhere, the symbols of the new consciousness battered on the doors of the old, and the issue was as much one of cultural identity and nationalism seeking authentic roots, as it was one of challenging the foreign-dominated economic order.

As in the first period of nationalism, this event was an overwhelmingly black expression, and on those islands where cosmopolitanism and multiracial agendas existed, the same kinds of ethnic anxieties and fears showed signs of surfacing. In Trinidad, however, where signs of internal class tensions within the Indian community had been surfacing since the mid-1960s, a minority of the Indian youth and trade union leadership responded positively to the new social movement, even though the overwhelming community response was one of defensive and baffled rural ethnic conservatism, not to mention the hostility of the middle class. V. S. Naipaul pronounced the 1970 Black Power rebellion to be irrational and senseless because Trinidad already had a black government, thereby missing the entire meaning of the social protest.[46] He was not alone. Williams himself was not so naive, historian that he was.[47] The entire decade of the 1970s saw him making substantial programmatic concessions to the amorphous demands of the protest movement, evolving a de facto mixed economy (and in the process going much further than even the 1966 WFP program) while simultaneously repressing the more violent elements within the opposition. By the late 1970s, relative calm had returned to the island. Dissatisfaction with the government had continued to spread, even to the middle classes, but no longer in an atmosphere of radicalism. Similar social forces in the rest of the region attracted greater (and more hostile) metropolitan attention. Trinidad remained a low-keyed but decisively altered economic order from the one that had existed between 1956 and 1970, proclaiming no ideology or doctrine but concretely achieving far more than many of its more high-profile radical neighbors, and in a social atmosphere that mixed pragmatic left liberalism with rampant corruption and opportunism. All this had been possible by the political flexibility of Williams and the affluence of the oil boom decade (1973–82).

Leftist political formations in the region, sometimes at the center of events (like Grenada between 1979 and 1983), were more often on the fringes of decision-making power and serious political life. They formed and reformed themselves, agonized over their doctrinal perspectives, and tried unsuccessfully to establish new electoral mass parties on many islands.[48] It was in this context that the New Left Marxist writings and theories of C. L. R. James often came up (along with other theories) for debate and discussion to assess their "relevance" to the new social movements of the 1970s. This was the first time that James's New Left metropolitan ideas ever took root within the region, even for discussion. Before this, even James himself was not concerned to suggest that his metropolitan ideas were relevant to a semi-industrialized and non-industrialized milieu like the West Indies. Indeed, strong evidence suggests that even during this period he did not really believe them transplantable to the region, except as part of the general heritage of socialist thought on which younger West Indians were educating themselves. Outside of the series of lectures he gave on Marxism to the Trinidad public in 1960 (published under the title *Modern Politics*) James himself never pressed the point. If he had any concrete Marxian perspectives for the Third World, they were perhaps closer to Lenin's New Economic Policy perspectives of the 1920s (Russia being in his view a "backward" underdeveloped society in that period) than they were to his *Facing Reality*-type prescriptions for advanced industrial economies.[49]

Nevertheless, the debates (for and against) went on, regardless of what James himself thought about their usefulness, with many groups (including the Grenada revolutionaries) skeptical of his post-1950 New Leftism, although not his earlier ideas, and often preferring to opt for an eclectic blend of traditional Old Left Marxist ideas of one trend or another. Walter Rodney's Working Peoples' Alliance (WPA) tried to evolve a new form of New Left socialist vision relevant to Guyana and away from the traditional "socialisms" of both Burnham and Jagan. However, the ideological difficulties with James's later ideas continued to exist. Tim Hector's Antigua-Caribbean Liberation Movement (ACLM), discussed in chapter 12, exemplifies many of these problems. Trinidad's New Beginning Movement (NBM), a small post-1970 group on the fringes of the battered radical movement of the 1970s, evolved a worldview that was an eclectic blend of Jamesian and non-Jamesian New Left ideas. This group produced a few solid publications during its period of activism and was (like others) always on good terms with James himself. The old man always kept a discreet silence on the viability of "direct-democratic" visions in the context of little Trinidad.[50] Throughout the region, idealistic youth attempted, individually and collectively, to evolve a social vision that would transcend the ideological importations of the 1960s.[51]

Many found inexhaustible inspiration in the writings of James, incorporating his insights with varying degrees of individual acceptance. As a Trinidadian writer put it recently, "Every one has his own C. L. R.," and this was even more true in the 1970s and 1980s.

With the publication in London between 1977 and 1984 of three volumes of his selected writings spanning his entire life's work, plus his study of the Ghana nationalist movement under Nkrumah, the richness and depth of C. L. R. James's fluid and original worldview became available to an even wider readership in Trinidad and the region as a whole. More than just the small leftist groupings of the 1970s became exposed to the full range of his thought beyond his standard classics *Black Jacobins* and *Beyond a Boundary*. This new public appreciation has transcended (and indeed ignored) philosophical disagreements with some of his specific views. It reached new heights in 1988 when the new post-1986 government in Trinidad, led by a man who had been one of the PNM's elite figures bitterly opposed to James in 1960–61, offered him the country's highest award, the Trinity Cross.

When James died in May 1989 in London, Trinidad's government offered to give him a state funeral, with the fullest ceremony accorded to its most prominent citizens. But James's final request was that he should be buried, simply and without religious ceremony, by the Oilfields Workers Trade Union, whose president-general had befriended him in 1965 and whose collective leadership had stood loyally by him since then. On June 12, 1989, the Third World's most high profile radical writer since Frantz Fanon, the metropolitan New Left's most original non-white theorist and "guru," the British Caribbean's most distinguished radical man of letters, and Trinidad's controversial intellectual activist and native son, came home to rest in the neighborhood he first left fifty-seven years earlier, the district of Tunapuna in North Trinidad.

In death, as in life, he was surrounded by controversy, with both the workers and the government establishment arguing publicly over who should have the right to bury him, both claiming him as their own.[52] In death, as in life, C. L. R. had the final say, and he remained faithful to those who had been the original source of his creative inspiration way back in the 1930s, those whose vibrant lives had helped to enrich his social vision and insight into infinitely more complex and world-important societies far removed from little Trinidad.

Notes

1   See Ivar Oxaal, *Black Intellectuals Come to Power* (Cambridge: Schenkman, 1968), ch. 8.
2   Eric Williams, *Inward Hunger: The Education of a Prime Minister* (London: Andre Deutsch, 1969), 143.
3   Oxaal, *Black Intellectuals*, 136.
4   *Nation*, January 29, 1960, February 5, 1960.
5   C. L. R. James, *The Black Jacobins* (New York: Vintage Books, 1963), 38–41. See Oxaal, *Black Intellectuals*, 74–76, for a good discussion on the relationship between James's original insight and Williams's own focus of concentration. Oxaal maintains that there were crucial differences in perspective.
6   See, for example, *Trinidad Guardian*, May 21, 1965, for a report on a lecture by Williams at the University of New Brunswick in Canada.
7   C. L. R. James, *Party Politics in the West Indies* (Port of Spain: privately published, 1962), 110.
8   The distinguished Caribbeanist Gordon Lewis, for example, was one extreme among several, as is obvious from the many caustic comments on James in his books and articles over the years. His comments ranged from attributing "an unpleasant aroma of personal vanity" to James (1962) to charges of "egocentrism reaching almost paranoic dimensions" (1968). As late as 1984, he was still at it, describing James not only as a "self-educated revolutionary more at home in the art of the public platform than in the art of the academic classroom," but also as "a battleship attempting to turn around in a duckpond." See Gordon Lewis, "The Trinidad Elections of 1961," *Caribbean Studies* 2 (July 1962):2–30; *The Growth of the Modern West Indies* (London: Monthly Review, 1968), 222; and his review of James's *Spheres of Existence* in *New West Indian Guide* [The Netherlands] 58, nos. 3–4 (1984):205.
9   James, *Party Politics*, 89.
10   Ibid., 171.
11   Andrew Salkey, *Georgetown Journal* (London, 1972), 55.
12   James, *Party Politics*, 4.
13   C. L. R. James, "The Making of the Caribbean People," in *Spheres of Existence* (London: Allison and Busby, 1980), 190; also "A National Purpose for Caribbean Peoples," in *At the Rendezvous of Victory* (London: Allison and Busby, 1984), 143.
14   C. L. R. James, "Every Cook Can Govern," in *The Future in the Present* (London: Allison and Busby, 1977), 160; also *Modern Politics* (Port of Spain: PNM Publishing Co., 1960), 2–4.
15   C. L. R. James, "The Artist in the Caribbean," in *The Future in the Present*, 187.
16   James, *Party Politics*, 122, 125, 155.
17   Much has happened in Trinidad since the 1960s to this class, and an updated social analysis is perhaps overdue. In many respects, however, it continues to be a largely professional and bureaucratic class, and although closer to the private sector than formerly, still remains a bit on its fringes. Its entrepreneurial skills are more dominant in the state-controlled productive sector, itself largely a creation of the 1970s.

18 James, "Artist in the Caribbean," 188–89.

19 Within the Workers' and Farmers' Party of 1965–66.

20 *Nation*, Editorial, March 18, 1960; the *La Religion* article was reprinted in the *Nation*.

21 Strictly speaking, this trend can be traced back to the 1930s, and to the social movement led by Uriah Butler, but the conscious theoretical formulation of the need for such unity, based upon an appropriate social reform program, began with the Workers' and Farmers' Party.

22 James, *Party Politics*, 149.

23 See Eric Williams, *History of the People of Trinidad and Tobago* (London: Andre Deutsch, 1964), 279.

24 Selwyn Ryan, *Race and Nationalism in Trinidad and Tobago* (Toronto: University of Toronto Press, 1972), 192–94.

25 Winston Mahabir, *In and Out of Politics* (Port of Spain: privately published, 1975), 78.

26 James, *Future in the Present, Spheres of Existence, Rendezvous of Victory*.

27 See, especially, "Dr. Eric Williams: A Convention Appraisal," *Nation*, March 18, April 8, April 22, 1960; see also *Nation*, September 25, 1959.

28 Another sketch of Padmore's life, given in a speech in Britain, has been reprinted in James, *Rendezvous of Victory*, 251–63. The account serialized in the *Nation* in 1959–60 is much richer in detail and should be republished.

29 Quoted in Oxaal, *Black Intellectuals*, 128.

30 *Nation*, August 7, 1959.

31 Williams, *Inward Hunger*, 267–68.

32 The resolution was moved by Una Mohammed, a delegate from San Fernando; see *Nation*, October 7, 1960.

33 Mahabir, *In and Out of Politics*, 70.

34 James, *Party Politics*, 110.

35 *Trinidad Guardian*, March 23, 1965.

36 Ibid., April 10, 1965, for a summary of the Mbafeno Report and reactions from public figures.

37 *Trinidad Guardian*, June 22, 1965.

38 Ibid., August 5, 1965.

39 Lewis, *Modern West Indies*, 224.

40 *Nation*, November 4, 1966.

41 Ibid., September 19, 1966.

42 Ibid., July 15, 1966.

43 Basdeo Panday, *Trinidad Express*, June 2, 1989.

44 Quoted in Ryan, *Race and Nationalism*, 406.

45 Quoted in ibid., 407.

46 *New York Review of Books*, September 3, 1970, 32.

47 Eric Williams, "P.N.M.'s Perspectives in the World of the 1970s: An Address to a Special Party Convention on November 27–29, 1970." See also Ryan, *Race and Nationalism*, 415–28, for a critique of these policy shifts.

48 Throughout the 1970s and 1980s, despite the vibrant left activism of the youth groups, the formal politics of the West Indies remained dominated by the liberal-

democratic parties founded in the first nationalist period. Grenada and Guyana opted for left-authoritarian regimes, the former progressive but problematic, the latter almost Stalinist in its use of repression, electoral fraud, and murder to keep itself in power. The impact of the radical groups was generally felt more widely on the cultural plane, at the level of reinvigorated black consciousness and self-pride throughout the society.

49   See C. L. R. James, *Nkrumah and the Ghana Revolution* (London: Allison and Busby, 1977), pt. 2, essay no. 4, "Lenin and the Problem," for a highly original discussion of Lenin's views on underdevelopment and social transformation in backward, peasant Russia, as expressed in three of his last articles. This piece was originally written for a Ghanaian readership in 1964.

50   See, especially, Bukka Rennie, *History of the Trinidad and Tobago Working Class, 1919–1956* (Port of Spain: New Beginning Movement, 1973); and Franklin Harvey, *The Rise and Fall of Party Politics in Trinidad and Tobago* (Toronto: University of Toronto Press, 1972). Bukka Rennie's unpublished "Strategy for Working Class Power" summarizes the group's New Left analysis of Trinidad's society in the early 1980s.

51   Also outside the region, the best-known instance being the black youth collective in London known as the Race Today Collective (named after its news journal, *Race Today*), which was largely responsible for looking after James in his last years (1982–89).

52   The government eventually held its own separate memorial tribute.

Eleven

*The Question of the Canon:
C. L. R. James and Modern Politics
Kent Worcester*

▼▼▼▼▼

*What is the good life? An individual life cannot be comfortable and easy
or creative unless it is in harmony to some degree with the society in
which it lives. The individual must have a sense of community with
the state. That is where we began. And that today is impossible. We
tend to think of the good life in terms of individual well-being, personal
progress, health, love, family life, success, physical and spiritual fulfillment. The whole point is that far more than we are consciously aware
of, these are matters of our relation to society.—C. L. R. James,* Modern
Politics

Introduction

In 1960, at the age of fifty-nine, C. L. R. James gave a series of six lectures
on the topic of "modern politics" under the auspices of the Trinidad Public Library's Adult Education Program. Each lecture attracted an audience
of several hundred, which above all testified to the public's interest in
what the renowned black activist–intellectual had to say on the eve of
national independence. That James had resigned from the editorship of
the newspaper of the Peoples National Movement (PNM), *The Nation,*
only three weeks prior to giving the first lecture, may have added to the
sense of anticipation that the series generated. Some in the audience may
have perceived that a personal and political break was coming between
the peripatetic radical dignitary and his former student, PNM chairman
and future prime minister, Dr. Eric Williams, over the nature and future

of Trinidad's independence. As if to confirm this rupture in relations, Dr. Williams ordered that the printed compendium of the 1960 lectures be suppressed.[1]

James later stated that "*Modern Politics* means a lot to me personally. I did not prepare but faced a home audience, so to speak, and just spoke as I felt and as they responded."[2] While internal evidence suggests that his lectures were in fact organized on a relatively systematic basis, his mode of delivery was clearly relaxed, informal, perhaps even slightly idiosyncratic. We must nevertheless recognize James's dedication to his audience and to the ideas presented in the lectures. Behind a playful speaking style lay a concerted effort to explore some of the most consequential and liberating ideas ever generated by men and women on the nature of the good society and the value of political commitment. By virtue of both its subject matter and the exceptional and in many respects inspiring conditions under which it was produced, *Modern Politics* constitutes one of the most personally revealing and intellectually representative texts in the entire Jamesian oeuvre.[3]

In addressing the topic of modern politics James had in mind two related concerns. The first was to highlight the historical, intellectual, and cultural contributions of classical, Renaissance, and liberal thought to humanity and their contemporary relevance for a West Indian audience. The second was to articulate a variant of socialist politics that was both grounded in philosophy and uniquely equipped to illuminate social movements in an age dominated by American imperiousness and Soviet bureaucratism. The purpose, then, of the lecture series was to "investigate, from every possible point of view, the realities and probabilities of the world in which we [i.e., Trinidadians] shall soon be a constituent part" (*Modern Politics*, p. 1). As the text makes clear, this investigation was informed by a democratic Marxism that owed a great debt to the political theories of Plato, Aristotle, Rousseau, Hegel, and other thinkers, as well as to the "great masses of people" and their intermittent attempts to "establish a society of equality, of harmony and of progress" (p. 42).

A close reading of *Modern Politics* may thus be justified on two principal grounds. First, the book reveals something of the revelatory impulse guiding James's first direct intervention in West Indian affairs after a voluntary absence of some two and a half decades. Second, and for our purposes more significant, it makes explicit the profound impact of Western canonical traditions on James's own political identity.[4] As such, it is a provocative work unjustly neglected by interpreters who are at the very least ambivalent regarding its author's "Eurocentrism."[5] Through an analysis of the lectures that comprise *Modern Politics* we may bring into focus the Jamesian vision of a post-capitalist world order predicated on principles established in ancient Athens.

Politics in the West Indies, 1958–62

As his biography makes plain, the very concept of modern politics was for James inconceivable without literary, emancipatory, and even utopian dimensions. Having left Trinidad in 1932 to pursue a literary career in Europe, C. L. R. James was radicalized during the Depression and penned a number of works on Pan-African and Marxian themes, including *The Black Jacobins* (1938), and *World Revolution 1917–1936* (1937), as well as a novel, *Minty Alley* (1936). From 1938 until his expulsion in 1953 he worked in the United States as a left-wing journalist, collaborating with Raya Dunayevskaya and other Trotskyists and independent radicals to develop Marxist ideas and promote the notion of an inherently militant American working class. He spent the bulk of the 1950s in England writing on a variety of topics and corresponding regularly with his U.S. comrades.

For a period of nearly four years (1958–62), James immersed himself in the cause of Trinidadian independence.[6] Invited to attend the opening of the federal parliament, Selma and C. L. R. James arrived in Port of Spain only to find a "nationalist whirlwind"[7] in motion. Postwar growth and the decline of the British empire engendered political ferment, symbolized by the PNM's formation in 1956 and its program calling for self-government, state-led investment in the private sector, extensive social services, and encouragement of trade unionism.[8] By 1958 the PNM had secured seats on the colonial office's legislative council and had inaugurated the "University of Woodford Square" where Eric Williams and others spoke to crowds of many thousands. It was with high hopes that C. L. R. accepted Dr. Williams's offer to stay and work for the PNM; he told the famously self-possessed party chairman that "With a movement like this, you can do anything."[9]

Although at first the PNM chieftain sought counsel from his old tutor, their relationship quickly soured. The locus of what was in retrospect an inevitable rift centered around *The Nation*, and the so-called "Chaguaramas Affair." Launched in December 1958, *The Nation* was the

PNM's recruiting tool and political journal. Boasting a print run of 11,000, C. L. R. James, Selma James, and a sizable staff created a brash radical news weekly that walked a thin line between promoting PNM policies and pushing the movement forward. As Dr. Williams and his associates began to trim their political sails in order to legitimize their claim to power among business and international elites, James's position as editor-in-chief became untenable, and on July 14, 1960 he tendered his resignation from the newspaper.

The Chaguaramas Affair symbolized some of the underlying pressures involved in the Williams-James dispute. During World War II the British leased the Chaguaramas district to U.S. military forces. In order to highlight colonialism's undemocratic character, PNM organizers called attention to Chaguaramas's status. A 1960 demonstration against U.S. occupation (known as the "March in the Rain") was perhaps "the militant high point of Trinidad nationalism."[10] Negotiations soon followed; in September 1960 it was announced that the U.S. would release 21,000 acres, keep the rest for seventeen years, and provide a $1.1 million aid package. The bargaining process was no doubt smoothed by Dr. Williams's declaration in May 1960 that Trinidad was "west" of the "Iron Curtain." At this time "Williams was turning away from close personal contact with his old mentor," according to Oxaal.[11] "There is a strong suspicion that the Americans demanded James' 'scalp' as part of the Chaguaramas settlement," writes another historian.[12]

Modern Politics contains several oblique references to these developments. Calling attention to Williams's right turn, the preface to the suppressed 1960 edition pointedly states: "whoever, for whatever reason, puts barriers in the way of knowledge is thereby automatically convicted of reaction and enmity to human progress" (p. iii). Elsewhere James says "If I may venture a prediction based on historical experience, the exhilaration based on successful anti-imperialist struggle [i.e., independence] rapidly declines and a far more solidly based new social movement begins."[13] These and other allusions speak to a deepening disenchantment with the PNM and its leadership. Overall, however, the accent is on the positive. In striving for national self-determination, Trinidadians were marching in step with other Third World peoples.[14] West Indians were about to "enter into the great big world outside as an independent force" (p. 1). Above all, James emphasized to his listeners, "it is not size, it is not strength, it is not power; it is what you do with what you have that matters."[15]

This reluctance to spell out his differences with Williams reflected the fact that the elder radical-statesman had not yet publicly broken with the PNM. It was also not James's style to personalize what he saw as political matters. But the more significant point is that *Modern Politics* was not aimed at party-political types; rather, it was targeted at a mass West Indian audience. Because of the rich historical opportunities being opened up by the movement for independence, this audience could go far beyond what the PNM had to offer. The book's sweeping reappraisal of Western thought through a Marxian filter communicated its author's faith not in an imperfect anti-colonial political party but, as Anna Grimshaw has written, in the "unleashing of creative energies in the Caribbean":

He saw the approach of independence in the Caribbean as a unique historical moment, one leading to the creation of a new society in which the fundamental question of political life, the relationship between individual freedom and social responsibility, was posed anew.[16]

In a sense, all of James's various activities in the 1958–62 period— editing *The Nation*, promoting the cause of West Indian federation, keeping the issue of Chaguaramas alive, giving speeches, etc.—were aimed at making "the population aware of its history and potential for independent action."[17] The guiding rationale of these activities was the belief that the campaign for self-government could stimulate wider interest in cultural advancement, democratic participation, and international affairs. *Modern Politics* may thus be described as the most fully developed of a series of Jamesian intercessions in Trinidadian affairs on behalf of the time-honored quest for an honorable and just society.

Some critics have suggested that the preoccupation of the lecture series with the question of "the good society" was largely irrelevant from the standpoint of West Indian realities. "Considering the audience to whom they were addressed," argues Patrick Gomes, "the lectures dealt insufficiently with the colonial experiences and historical factors that were pertinent to the Trinidad and general Caribbean situation."[18] But James had his own, neo-Platonic understanding of the question of "what you do with what you have." His investigation was intended to help lay the groundwork for a new consciousness—and, eventually, a new mode of social life—that could emerge out of the struggle for national self-determination and self-awareness. What was described as "undoubtedly the most difficult course in any theme of politics or similar matters that I have ever given" (p. 94) was meant to inspire great political and aesthetic attainments, to encourage listeners to raise their historical sights. By its very nature it was a very different sort of project than that reflected in the PNM's pragmatic reformism, or even in more explicitly leftist programs for Caribbean renewal.

Western Canonical Traditions

The project's ambitious scope and canonical remit was clearly reflected in the range of material covered in the six-part series. The first lecture introduced the concept of direct democracy, as practiced in Athens and other Greek city-states, favorably contrasting it with liberal representative government. The second traced Marxism's roots in French and German philosophy, emphasizing the democratic character of Marx's thought (in sharp contrast to many of his *soi-disant* followers). The third and fourth lectures covered a wide array of topics related to contemporary history, such as the emergence of a world market, the threat of fascism, the "failure of the nation-state," and the promise of a better way of life as symbolized by the Hungarian workers's councils of 1956. The final two lectures concerned leading artistic figures of the twentieth century and their complex relationship to "crises in intimate relations" which originate in "a dislocation of society" (p. 119) under modern capitalism. In keeping with the series's essentially pedagogical thrust, the printed volume offers an impressive list of supplemental readings.[19]

The thesis tying these variegated topics together is a statement of the masses's creativity across history, and the closely related parallel—to James—of individual, artistic genius. For him, the formation of modern democratic principles must arise in practice, the practice of medieval craftsmen and English Levellers; just so, the rise of socialism as a potential reality rather than mere intellectual vision comes with the Paris Commune's practical demonstration of economic egalitarianism. Only a sweeping reconstruction of public and industrial life at large, on an international scale, could avert the disintegration of modern society.

As in any survey of "Western civ.," *Modern Politics* opens with the Greeks. In this survey the city-state's virtues—particularly its capacity to integrate individual wills—is a recurrent theme. One reason for this emphasis on classical civilization, as we have seen, is that James believed that small nations with meager economic resources could achieve grand results in the spheres of politics and culture. A more fundamental justification, however, had to do with the intrinsic value of classical Greek culture and the "remarkable" character of Athenian civilization. The ancient city-states

> formed, in my opinion, the most remarkable of all the various civilizations of which we have record in history, including our own. . . . And it is not only that we today rest upon their achievements. It is far more wonderful than that. If today you want to study politics, it is not because Aristotle and Plato began the great discussion, not at all; in order to tackle politics today, fundamentally, you have to read them for the questions that they pose and the way that they pose them; they are not superseded at all.[20]

Building on prior research,[21] James ascribed the exceptional character of social life in ancient Greece to two main factors: mass participation in the institutions of the city-state, and the dense emotional and political bonds harmonizing the individual with the wider community. Since male citizens (but not, of course, foreigners, slaves, or females) had an authentic voice in the polity, they felt an intense attachment to the city-state. This attachment itself constituted "the basis of a good life" (p. 97). In appreciating the need to reconcile communitarianism and free individual expression, Athens attained a more or less rational balance between the "individual citizen and the City-State . . ." (p. 5). Despite two thousand years of scientific and technological progress, humanity never recaptured the organic equilibrium of the city-state. It is with a considerable sense of melancholy that James announces that *"people have lost the habit of looking at government and one another in that way."*[22]

In the domain of politics, philosophy, and the arts, denizens of the ancient city-state created the foundations for a meaningful life for the enfranchised citizenry. But recapturing the spirit of the ancient city-state's communal solidarity—and extending its benefits to all members of society—involved something more elaborate than simply harking back to the past. It required a global movement toward the realization of a radically democratic, non- or post-capitalist order where the alienation of modern individuals from the public sphere, and from the tyranny of political economy, meaningfully could be addressed. This in turn necessitated an engagement with the socialist and Marxist traditions, since these traditions offered the most fully developed analyses of capitalist society and the struggle for its transcendence. As socialism basically represented an industrial era restatement of the philosophical values "of freedom, of equality, of democracy . . . and the desire to make them real" (p. 155), its meaning was assumed to be relatively straightforward. Explaining Marxism required a little more effort, if only because its meaning had become so distorted by the calamity of Stalinism—that which "absolutely opposed any revolutionary struggle for power . . ." (p. 57).

Marxism's meaning is a central issue for the 1960 lectures, and yet little attention is paid to such doctrinal issues as crisis theory, the state, modes of production, etc.[23] What *is* emphasized is the reasonably optimistic account of human nature that Marxism allows for—in stark contrast to secular and theological theories of "original sin"—where ordinary people have proved themselves capable of reorganizing society along progressive lines. At "critical moments," he says, "when the great masses of people, who usually are not particularly active in politics, see an opportunity to shape the course of political events, they usually, or they have often attempted to establish a society of equality, of harmony and of progress" (p. 42). This emphasis on the self-activity of the "great masses of people" is what distinguishes Marxism from classical and liberal political thought. Indeed, for James the central contribution of the Marxist tradition is in recognizing that "the great political discoveries, the actual discoveries of actual policy, come as much by the instinctive actions of masses of people as by anything else" (p. 12). This recognition enables Marxists to pose a practical solution to the difficulties involved in instituting democracy at a time when "this mass of machinery and scientific knowledge . . . is running away with us" (p. 103). That solution may be summed up in a single phrase: workers's self-management.

Drawing on the classical Marxist tradition, the lectures stressed the capacity of ordinary workers effectively to intervene in revolutionary situations and otherwise defend their autonomous interests. The social power of workers is memorably expressed in the following passage:

When ten thousand school teachers, bookkeepers, the writers and talkers like myself, and editors and so forth, vote, that is ten thousand votes; and they can have one thousand extra and have eleven thousand votes and defeat ten thousand workers, in votes. But the moment a revolutionary struggle is on, the workers—this group takes the railway, the other one the waterfront, the other one turns off the electricity, and the other one stops the transport; the teachers, etc., can only make some noise but they cannot do anything;

they can send the children back home or bring them back or something. In all struggles of this kind it is the proletariat that is master of the situation. (p. 61)

This mastery of the revolutionary conjuncture reflects the structural power of the working class as constituted in the sphere of production. The working class not only is a powerful social group, however, but also is seen as a key component to the creation of a new global order based on an enlightened form of workplace and community-based councils. History's forward march clearly points toward the possibility and desirability of reorganizing society from below: "There has been a development; the development is along the lines that I have tried to show. Man is ready for great strides forward today" (p. 154).

James explicitly saw these "great strides forward" in terms of his immediate audience, Trinidadians (and West Indians, in a more general sense) on the eve of independence. For their sake, as he makes clear several times in the text, he had interpreted the philosophical and historic backdrop to twentieth century political life, and ruminated upon the complexities of liberal democracy, fascism, Marxism, and Stalinism. For them, he suggested that the vaunted triumphs of Western culture were closing in a cycle of growing barbarism. Now they, the West Indians, were about to cast their own shadow upon "modern politics." In doing so, he urged them to recognize the immense risks and to consider the value of Marxism for the possibilities at hand.

As presented in *Modern Politics*, the lesson of Marx's historical dialectic is that the inherent contradictions of capitalism unleash forces that are capable of resolving these contradictions. At the same time, Marxism is "the doctrine which believes that freedom, equality, democracy are today possible for all mankind" (p. 155), with the proviso that the proletariat must play a decisive part if these values are to be realized. Despite the reference to "mankind," the lectures explicitly address the status of women "from a political point of view as to the relation between the traditional society under which we live and the new society which I believe is necessary if society is not to collapse completely" (p. 116). In contradistinction to most revolutionary socialists, then, James employs Marxist theory so as to grapple with issues that go beyond those of working-class politics, or the critique of the labor-capital relationship. The fifth lecture's discussion of "the exploitation of sex" highlights the recusant—yet ultimately workerist—nature of a Jamesian Marxism.

The passage on women's role in society is one of the most inventive in the entire compendium. Its recognition that "discrimination breeds a fury in the women who are submitted to it of which you have little conception" (p. 117), reflected James's longstanding interest in the condition of women in society, as well as, in all likelihood, the intellectual contribution of Selma James, who later played a prominent role in the feminist "second wave" of the 1960s and 1970s.[24] The discussion of the condition of women's lives in the U.S. is particularly acute:

> Middle class women in particular go to universities and live a life of complete freedom. They have their own latch keys; they drive motor cars about; they go to school; they take exams, they don't take exams; they go to Europe; they do exactly as they please. When they come out of the university they marry and then, almost automatically . . . from the sheer weight of the tradition of society, from the functions that men perform, from the conceptions that men still have in their minds of the relationship of men to women—they find themselves at twenty-three, twenty-four, twenty-five, in a position of subordination to which they have not been accustomed from the time that they went to school until they left university. (p. 117)

"But there is more," James says. Working-class women entered factories during World War II only to be expelled once the war effort was over. Like their college-educated counterparts these women found considerable incongruity in their ambiguous status as ancillary members of a liberal society. "[A]s in so many other things, the old standards have gone but new standards have not been established . . ." (p. 118).

What sort of standards should govern relations between the sexes? While James clearly advocates full legal and social equality for women, he nevertheless argues that "women in their physical and mental qualities are not inferior to men, but different" (p. 119). The primary difference involves "the immense burden of bearing children," which requires that society give women "extra privileges, in order to be able to maintain themselves in the work they are doing" (p. 120). The solution to the problem of integrating work and family necessitates a kind of affirmative action for women, particularly in the workplace. Such a solution is unrealizable under capitalism, however: "The beginning of a truly satisfactory relationship in personal lives must begin with a total reorganization of labor relations in every department of life" (p. 120). Some readers might find this emphasis on "labor relations" (as opposed to, say, familial, or sexual relations) faintly productivist. James's claim that working-class self-emancipation is the key to the liberation of women is emphatically argued[25] but perhaps slightly problematic from a feminist perspective, given the uneven level of consciousness among male workers.

The inferior status of women in even the most advanced market economies is for James yet another indication of the extent to which the entire global system is in deep crisis. Having reached the lofty heights of the polis, humanity finds itself reeling from the horror of twentieth-century fascism, Nazism, and Stalinism. As he argues in the fifth lecture, the only innovation on offer from the liberal democracies—or the Soviet leadership—is the welfare state, which fosters dependency and bureaucracy rather than collective empowerment. As the superpowers assemble military arsenals, and as creative artists mirror in their work the world's insecurities and miseries, the collapse of civilized values becomes a real potentiality. James calls this his "main theme": "the consciousness of total breakdown—return to barbarism, the possibility of suicidal self-destruction . . ." (p. 69). This breakdown is rooted, finally, in capitalism's rapacious, destructive nature: "it is capital that rules, and it is capital that dictates the manners and morals of those who submit themselves to it" (p. 74).

James saw in Trinidad's independence the opportunity of challenging the logic of capital through popular mobilization and education, of creating a new type of society that nevertheless shared certain features in common with the ancient city-state. That a connection is drawn between the new society and the city-state is surely not accidental. In his informative biography Paul Buhle writes that in *Modern Politics* "world history assumes a spiral upward which recapitulates the original in many ways, albeit at ever higher stages."[26] Patrick Gomes argues that James's philosophy of history had distinctly evolutionary and optimistic overtones: "Rather than Marx, the influence of [English historian Arnold] Toynbee is clearly evident and an accumulative tradition enriches the development of human civilization."[27] At the same time, there is the barely concealed fear that the future could prove profoundly retrogressive. "The world will choose between hydrogen bombs and guided missiles, and some form of Workers Councils. In 1960, the Marxist doctrine: either socialism or barbarism, seems to me truer than ever before."[28]

In *Modern Politics*, the movement for Caribbean self-determination has the potential for playing a critical role in the development of a new global order. By setting out along the path of self-organization laid out by the city-state, West Indians could break with the colonial past and even ignite flames of regional rebellion. But the revolutionary capacity of the West's industrial proletariat to avert the collapse of world civilization is emphasized as well.[29] As paradoxical as it might seem to some, Trinidad's most famous Marxist and Pan-Africanist maintained an abiding commitment to the prospect of First World working-class insurrection coming to the aid of Third World nationalist forces, a commitment he combined with a profound respect for classical and Western intellectual traditions. Unconventional and forward in both aim and method, *Modern Politics* testifies to its author's nonconformist blend of neo-Platonism and populism, idealism and ruefulness, radicalism and canonical reverence.

Conclusion

Gregory Rigsby is one of a very small number of commentators to have written on *Modern Politics* in a sympathetic and insightful manner. He writes:

> In *Modern Politics*, James examined all of Western civilization as one action. The beginning is Greece; the middle comprises the complication and conflicts of major movements and thinkers; the end is in the beginning. Since James sees history as evolving toward a world society similar to what existed in the Greek city-states, he concludes that the political structure which the law of relationship demands exists in its essential form in the Greek city-states. The form of government which existed in these city-states was called direct democracy.[30]

In the thirty years since its first, aborted publication, *Modern Politics* has barely registered among students of the writings of C. L. R. James, let alone the mass audience for which it was intended. While the original lectures no doubt generated considerable enthusiasm, there is little evidence to suggest that those who attended the lecture series attempted to put James's Marxian-canonical ideas into practice.

Now may be a good time for interested readers to discover *Modern Politics*. This is especially true given the controversies that are currently raging throughout American academia over whether the traditional literary and philosophical canon has a place in a multi-cultural society. The iconoclastic perspective that James's 1960 lectures may bring to bear on these disputes may be of considerable interest. Unlike many black intellectuals who grew up under the shadow of colonial authority, James was basically positive about his formal education and the circumstances of his childhood; and while he acknowledged the pain caused by imperialism and capitalism, he did not in any way reject or scorn the contributions of classical and Western culture to world civilization.

Notes

1   "[F]or many years," Martin Glaberman reports, "the printed volumes lay in a warehouse in Port of Spain under guard. Ultimately, Williams relented to the extent of letting a New York book dealer buy the lot and take it out of the country." "Introduction," *Modern Politics* (Detroit: Bewick Editions, 1973), p. i.

2   C. L. R. James, *At the Rendezvous of Victory* (London: Allison and Busby, 1984), p. 129.

3   Like *Beyond a Boundary* (1963), *Modern Politics* connects the lessons of James's formal education with his mature revolutionary politics. At the same time, it represents a popular restatement of the anti bureaucratic, pro-spontaneity arguments developed in *Facing Reality* (cowritten with Grace Lee, 1958).

4   James's insistence that in historical and cultural terms West Indians were essentially Westernized may be worth noting in this context. Asked "Should Shakespeare and Rembrandt and Beethoven matter to Caribbean people?" James replied: "The Caribbean people are *people*, and Shakespeare, Rembrandt and Beethoven should matter to *all* people who are living in the world today, and who are able by means of their language or by means of information and communication to understand or get some insight into what Shakespeare, and Beethoven mean. I don't like that question at all . . . if it means that Caribbean writers today should be aware that there are emphases in their writing that we owe to non-European, non-Shakespearean roots, and the past in music which is not Beethoven, that I agree. But . . . fundamentally we are a people whose literacy and aesthetic past is rooted in Western European civilisation." "An Audience with C. L. R. James," *Third World Book Review* 1 (1984):7. Cf. "Discovering Literature in Trinidad: the Nineteen-Thirties," *Spheres of Existence* (London: Allison and Busby, 1980), p. 244.

5   Having found scant reference to *Modern Politics* in the secondary literature, I can only conclude that some critics find its stance disreputable. "Classical Marxism is as much a trap in Eurocentricity since it is a close critique of European Industrial capitalism and Imperialist expansionism . . . I lament that C. L. R. James had not found his . . . African roots and heritage and still cling[s] to European culture and civilization. . . ." Aldrie Henry, "On Cricket," in Bishnu Ragoonath, ed. *Tribute to a Scholar: Appreciating C. L. R. James* (Mona, Jamaica: Consortium Graduate School of Social Sciences, 1990), p. 90. Cedric Robinson complains: "The residues of James' 'Victorian' upbringing remain until this day. . . . Witness: 'The Greeks

were the most politically minded and intellectually and artistically the most creative of all peoples.' Hardly a considered or even possible judgement." *Black Marxism: The Making of the Black Radical Tradition* (London: Zed Press, 1983). See also John Gaffar La Guerre, *The Social and Political Thought of the Colonial Intelligentsia* (Mona, Jamaica: Institute of Social and Economic Research, University of the West Indies, 1982), chaps. 1, 7, and 8; and Tony Martin, "C. L. R. James and the Race/Class Question," *Race*, XIV (1972).

6   For a biographical overview see, *inter alia*, my monographs "C. L. R. James and the American Century: 1938–1953" (Puerto Rico: Inter-American University of Puerto Rico, CISCLA Working Paper no. 12, 1984); and "West Indian Politics and Cricket: C. L. R. James and Trinidad, 1958–63" (Puerto Rico: Inter-American University of Puerto Rico, CISCLA Working Paper no. 20, 1985).

7   Basil Wilson, "The Caribbean Revolution," in Paul Buhle, ed. *C. L. R. James: His Life and Work* (London: Allison and Busby, 1986), p. 121.

8   See Selwyn D. Ryan, *Race and Nationalism in Trinidad and Tobago* (Toronto: University of Toronto Press, 1972), pp. 120–127.

9   Ivar Oxaal, *Black Intellectuals Come to Power* (Cambridge, Mass.: Schenkman, 1968), p. 128.

10   Oxaal, *Black Intellectuals Come to Power*, p. 133.

11   Ibid., p. 134.

12   Ryan, *Race and Nationalism in Trinidad and Tobago*, p. 231.

13   *Modern Politics*, p. 100. The implication being that this new movement would push the PNM leftward or break with it entirely.

14   "The newly independent states are . . . in the very vanguard of the progressive forces of modern society." *Modern Politics*, p. 88.

15   *Modern Politics*, p. 6. The next sentence reads: "And Greece showed that you can have very little and still achieve the things which stand out as among the greatest achievements of humanity."

16   Anna Grimshaw, "Popular Democracy and the Creative Imagination: The Writings of C. L. R. James, 1950–1963," *Third Text*, no. 10 (Spring 1990), p. 22.

17   Ibid.

18   Gomes, "C. L. R. James' Marxian Paradigm on the Transformation of Caribbean Social Structures," p. 253.

19   On the list were: Aristotle's *Politics*; Rousseau's *The Social Contract*; *The Communist Manifesto*, and *Capital* Vol. 1; Lenin's *The State and Revolution*; selections from the *New Testament*; Hannah Arendt's *The Origins of Totalitarianism*; *Facing Reality*, and all "collections of documents on the Hungarian Revolution . . ." *Modern Politics*, pp. 156–57.

20   *Modern Politics*, p. 3. He later stated: "I am very much aware of the vast distance that lies between the original, seminal work of Plato and Aristotle and what I have been able to do at the present time." See "An Audience with C. L. R. James," p. 8.

21   See "Every Cook Can Govern: A Study of Democracy in Ancient Greece" (1956), reprinted in C. L. R. James, *The Future in the Present* (London: Allison and Busby, 1977). Grimshaw reports that by 1954 "he was immersed in studies of the ancient

world." See "Popular Democracy and the Creative Imagination," p. 20. James was first exposed to classical Greek and Roman thought as a secondary school pupil at Queens Royal College.

22 *Modern Politics*, p. 4. Emphasis in the original.

23 However, both the fourth and fifth lectures take up the capital-labor relationship in some detail; see pp. 74–81, 101–3.

24 Selma James (nee Weinstein) coauthored the prescient pamphlet *A Woman's Place* (1952), and later became actively involved in the international Wages for Housework campaign. *A Woman's Place* is reprinted in Ellen Malos, ed., *The Politics of Housework* (London: Allison and Busby, 1980), pp. 188–94.

25 "People react violently against the idea that workers, as a class, can manage anything, when in reality it is they who organize most of the work of the world." James, *Modern Politics*, p. 121.

26 Paul Buhle, *C. L. R. James: The Artist as Revolutionary* (London: Verso, 1988), p. 166.

27 Gomes, "C. L. R. James' Marxian Paradigm on the Transformation of Caribbean Social Structure," p. 229.

28 "Books to Read," *Modern Politics*, p. 167.

29 "[T]he passing of colonialism . . . is a sign of the weakness of the capitalist bourgeois state and at the same time it provides ammunition for the breakdown of these imperialist states which dominated them before. Nevertheless there is no question about it: the basic opposition to imperialism must come from the proletariat of the advanced countries" (p. 90). As sympathetic as he was to the cause of Third World national liberation, James clearly remained committed to something approximating the Trotskyist theory of permanent revolution.

30 Gregory Rigsby, "The Gospel According to St. James," in Buhle, ed., *C. L. R. James: His Life and Work*, p. 226.

Twelve

C. L. R. James and the Antiguan Left
Paget Henry

▼▼▼▼▼

For little over half a century, C. L. R. James was the Caribbean's most distinguished socialist writer and theoretician. His towering figure moved influencially over the region's political scene, helping give coherence and direction to movements for social change. For the last twenty years the Antigua-Caribbean Liberation Movement (ACLM) has been Antigua's best known left organization. For most of these years, the direction in which it has steered the Antiguan left has been Jamesian. This in no small measure has been due to the work of the ACLM's chair, Tim Hector, a student and great admirer of James. Consequently, the ACLM has become well known throughout the region for its close following of James's ideas concerning social transformation in the modern period.

My purpose in this chapter is twofold. First, I will assess the implications for James's thought of its adoption by the ACLM. Second, I will examine some of the practical consequences for the ACLM that have followed from this adoption. Both issues will be discussed within the context of the problems and complexities of socialist transformation in peripheral or Third World societies.

With regard to James's thought, four important findings emerge from the analysis. First, in his theory of modern politics there is a clear but implicit distinction between the conditions for socialist transformation in the center and periphery. Because it is not systematically worked out, this distinction can be easily overlooked. Second, in this dichotomous model of socialist transformation, an unnamed intermediary stage is implicitly hypothesized for the case of the periphery. This notion is even less explicit, but I shall argue for its existence. Third, in the mirror of the ACLM's experience, James's model, while politically comprehensive, appears in need of economic supplement. Fourth, because of the limited degree to which the peripheral model was developed, James often did not get close enough to concrete peripheral conditions. This problem was further reinforced by the presence of interfering themes from his more developed model for the advanced countries.

With regard to the ACLM, I will show that its practice has been ensnared by some of the paradoxes that have followed James's failure to make more explicit important distinctions and crucial postulates. The history of the party's development can be read from the point of view of a process of local contextualization that amounts to a disengagement from James's model of socialism for the advanced countries to that for peripheral countries. This movement has wider implications for the practice of socialism in the periphery. The study of the ACLM can be divided into three broad phases: the Black Power years, the Jamesian years, and the party years. In each, I will examine the sociohistorical factors precipitating contextualization, and the changes in the model of transformation produced.

James's Theory of Modern Politics

Although James can definitely be described as a Marxist, the key to his political thinking is a principle that he brought to his reading of Marxist texts. In the principle of the creativity of masses, James sums up his belief that the masses, acting collectively in response to life's problems, often produce solutions that equal in originality those of the individual genius.[1] This view had its roots in James's profound involvement with the working class of his native Trinidad. His fictional writings make clear the organic nature of this involvement. It was their lives, the houses they lived in, the work they did, and the relationships they formed that he attempted to recreate in such works as *Minty Alley* and "Triumph." These texts approached and developed characters through the creative projects they formed in response to the challenges of barrack-yard life in working-class Trinidad. This approach to character development was maintained even in cases where projected solutions constituted lives that fell outside established social norms. The "triumph" of Mamitz, heroine of the short story with the same name, is not only the triumph of a creative but also a morally ambiguous projection of self. It was in this manner that James's fiction established his view of the masses as capable of creative solutions to social problems.

As James exchanged the world of fictional narrative for that of political theory, the creativity of Trinidad's working class that he had so carefully photographed became the basis for his claims concerning the ability of the masses to govern themselves. This extension of the notion of the creativity of the masses into the realm of political theory can first be clearly seen in *The Life of Captain Cipriani*, which contained James's case for West Indian self-government. James showed the ways in which racism, classism, and crown colony rule had so perverted local forms of representative government that the state was still an instrument used by small expatriate elites "to choke down the natural expansion of the people."[2] In this context, politics was not a challenge to mass creativity, but rather an exercise in submission. Crown colony rule in James's view was a hollow ritual whose primary function was celebrating and reaffirming the power of the governor. Such a form of government had no place among Caribbean people, given their level of learning and culture. Rather, "a people like ours, should be free to make its own failures and successes, free to gain that political wisdom and political experience which come only from the practice of political affairs."[3] It was upon the ability of the West Indian people to find creative solutions to political problems, and to learn from their mistakes, that James rested his case for self-government.

James's political experiences in England after 1932, and later in the United States, deepened his involvement with workers and further reinforced his belief in the ability of masses to be creative and self-governing. His encounter with Marxism during this period had a similar effect. However, it was no longer just the workers of Trinidad that were James's concern, but workers the world over. He now sought to formulate the political implications of their capacities for creative self-projection as a group into the language of political theory—in particular, their implications for the organization of a modern state.

As James's fiction was grounded in the personal spaces that ordinary men and women were capable of creating, his political writing is linked to the public spaces that the self-projections of organized workers can create. Concern with the political forms that would result from such self-projections is the key to his search for an adequate political theory. It helps us to understand why he rejects the works of some theorists and uses that of others. It explains why spontaneous mass action and its careful interpretation are so important to James. Mass actions such as strikes, insurrections, and revolutions are the media through which the masses sometimes express and formulate their solutions to pressing social problems. They are the books, the stages, the canvases upon which the masses inscribe creative solutions and sign their names on public documents. Hence these actions must also be read as texts along with those of creative individuals. James searched for a political theory that rested on such foundations.

Further, the seriousness with which he takes this textual reading of mass action is the distinguishing mark of his thought, the source of its longevity, and its visionary qualities. Particularly among theorists of post-colonial revolutions, it has made James unique in the extent to which his focus is beyond the seizure of power and upon the forms of mass organization that will characterize the post-revolutionary period. Here, he stands in sharp contrast to Fanon, the supreme theorist of the insurrectionary moment of decolonization.

James's search for a form of political organization that could accommodate the event of an organized projection of self by workers is most clearly seen in *Modern Politics*, the result of a series of public lectures that he gave in Trinidad. Starting with the Greek city-states and ending with the workers' councils of the Hungarian Revolution, James goes through what he considers to be the major political breakthroughs that have opened the door to modern politics. The significance of the Greeks is twofold. First, they showed that it was possible to move beyond representative to direct democracy. Second, in doing this, they demonstrated that ordinary people can participate effectively in government. James had already made this assessment of Greek democracy in his essay "Every Cook Can Govern." There, he noted an important limitation of Greek democracy: "One notable feature of Athenian democracy was that, despite the complete power of the popular assembly, it never attempted to carry out any socialistic doctrines."[4] The management of the economy was kept out of the public life of the polis.

After dealing with the Romans and the Italian city-states, James continues his quest with a look at the birth of modern representative government in England. Given his interests, this event is important for two reasons. The first is the insurrectionary context in which British parliamentary democracy emerged. This breakthrough occurred during the course of the struggle of the Levelers and Presbyterians against the king and aristocracy.[5] British parliamentary democracy emerged in the strategic movements of collective action before its theoretical formulation and systematization by Locke and others. Consequently, James views it as another important instance of the creativity of an organized mass. The second reason for the importance of the emergence of representative government is that it marked a significant advance in the search for political forms that could accommodate mass demands for freedom. The development of the political party, the secret ballot, the notion of sovereignty resting with the people—all these were important although incomplete steps toward that goal.

As a political form, representative government is incomplete for two reasons. First, as Rousseau had pointed out, the practice of delegating authority often turned representative government into a farce. Delegates have a tendency to pursue their own interests, not those of their constituencies. Consequently, Rousseau was extremely important for James's view of post-representative politics. His critique of the rationalism of the European Enlightenment and of representative government pointed to the unsolved problems of modern politics. Second, the Greek two-hundred-year experiment with direct democracy suggested that a move beyond representative government was indeed possible. In James's view, it was such an alternative that Rousseau sought in his flawed notion of the general will.

From Rousseau, political theory inherited an extremely important problem, Can the modern state surpass its representative form? This critical question is at the heart of James's political theory. He thinks it can. Hence it is possible for him to describe the aim of *Modern Politics* in the following way: "Much of our study of modern politics is going to be concerned with this tremendous battle to find a form of government which reproduces, on a more highly developed economic level, the relationship between the individual and the community, that was established so wonderfully in the Greek City-State."[6]

After showing the failure of Kant and Hegel to respond adequately to Rousseau's critiques of rationalism and representative government, James sees the next significant breakthrough in the works of Marx. Marx was significant because, taking up Rousseau's challenge, he moved beyond both Greek democracy and the notion of the general will. In Marx's socialist solution, James saw a political form that could accommodate the event of a projection of self by groups of organized workers.

Like Rousseau, Marx made a definite break with philosophical rationalism. In James's view, he opted for a more open notion of reason that was always beyond the confines of particular disciplinary formulations and more immanent in the historical process. James also suggests that in Marx, reason ceases to be philosophical reason and becomes "the developing consciousness of mankind seeking to establish a harmonious society."[7] This reworking of the principle rationality displaced the philosophical imagination as the home of reason and relocated rationality in the organized activities through which human beings have reproduced and transformed their societies.

It was upon this collectivized conception of rationality that Marx's socialist solution to the problems of modern politics rested. This solution reflected Greek influence in its call for direct political democracy, but moved beyond it in the demands for direct economic democracy. The events of the French Revolution, by putting the question of mass poverty on the public agenda, made a simple return to Greek political democracy impossible. Consequently, Marx's peculiar contribution is the claim that the problem of freedom for the masses will be resolved only with direct mass involvement in both the reproduction and governing of social life. In his view, only a solution to these problems at the mass level would make freedom and material well-being available to all.

As in the case of representative government, this breakthrough to socialism was not simply the result of Marx the creative individual working out a solution. In addition to his own creativity, the texts of Rousseau, and others, James includes the original solutions implicit in the new forms of mass organization that emerged during the French Revolution. These concrete manifestations of worker self-organization gave Marx's later systematization of the socialist solution both relevance and legitimacy.

This, in essence, was the solution to post-representative government that James inherited from Marx. It was a form of social organization in which political and economic power came to rest on such organizations as the councils into which the workers of the Paris Commune had quite spontaneously organized themselves. Such councils would then become the primary bases of mass consent and sources of legitimacy for both political and economic decision making. Politics and economics would then be less removed from popular control and from each other. This solution is important because it was the foundation upon which James would continue to build. At the same time, it helped to reinforce his prior organic ties with the working masses, to strengthen his belief in the importance of the active life, the creativity of the masses, their ability to govern themselves.

To get to James, the original political thinker, we must move beyond this inheritance and observe how he used it to analyze important political events that occurred both before and after Marx wrote. In many of these analyses, James's focus is on an insurrectionary event. However, the violence or seizures of power that often accompany these events seldom interest him. Rather, he seeks to extract less visible creative elements. Insurrectionary events often contain suppressed alternatives that have been forming in the language and imagination of the insurrectionists. Such positive, creative elements, new projections of self, and new forms of collective organization are the apples of James's imagination.

Ironically, one of James's earliest original moves as a political theorist was his use of this Marxian solution to modern politics against the Marxism of his early years. Between 1938 and 1948, James had been an active Trotskyist, a form of Marxism that stressed the importance of a vanguard party, state ownership of the means of production, and opposition to Stalinism. Given James's pre-Marxist views of workers, the increasing uneasiness with the classic notion of a vanguard party becomes quite understandable. However, the emergence of shopfloor organizing, as well as the growth of shop stewards and shop committees inside postwar factories, gave James the evidence he needed to challenge the notion of the vanguard party and reestablish that of the creativity of workers. The result was a comprehensive critique of Trotskyism and a turn to a form of socialist politics that relied less on the indirect or representative participation of workers and more on their direct involvement. This critique was given its most succinct statement in *State Capitalism and World Revolution*.

However, James does not restrict these participatory capabilities only to workers who have reached the stage of wage labor. Here he differs from less original Marxists. With great fictional skill, he sees the distinct creative actions of each particular group of workers he studies individually. James lets his textual readings of these actions determine his assessment of their capacity for creative self-projection and the forms of social organization implicit in these projections. In this manner he approached the study of the Haitian Revolution in *The Black Jacobins*. It was also his approach to popular revolts in Africa and to workers' movements in the United States and Britain. Further, the nondogmatic nature of this approach allowed James to deal successfully with the issue of race in the cases of African, Afro-American, and Afro-Caribbean workers.

Among the many insurrectionary events James analyzed, the Russian and Hungarian revolutions are particularly important for his theory of modern politics. In the Soviets of the former and the workers' councils of the latter, he saw additional evidence of the new forms of self-organization taking shape in the consciousness of modern workers. These forms were seen as concrete expressions of an alternative form of social organization that contained better answers to the problems of modern politics.

The Hungarian Revolution in particular confirmed James's belief in the possibility of moving beyond representative democracy, the vanguard party, and the totalitarianism of state socialism. In it, James saw "a completeness of self-organization that distinguishes this revolution from all previous revolutions and marks it as specifically a revolution of the middle of the twentieth century."[8] This completeness of self-organization indicated that workers can achieve a mastery that enables them to run the production process on their own initiative. When this occurs, a new stage in the development of society has been reached. In this stage, the approaching ability of workers to manage production makes it possible to redefine the democratic bases that secure consent and legitimacy for economic and political decision making. In turn, these possibilities for redefinition call into question existing justifications for delegating decision making to such elites as party leaders and business managers. In the language of Marcuse, the level of "necessary repression" that sustained the old order appears to contain a "surplus" in the light of the new. Thus from the Hungarian experience James concluded that worker mastery of the production process was an important indicator and precondition for the move beyond both state socialism and representative democracy.

Such a worker-based move is extremely important to James. It is necessary for overcoming the problems left unsolved by these two forms of social organization, in particular, the problems created by increased bureaucratization and delegation of decision-making power. This growth of economic and political bureaucracies suppresses the growth of the participatory aspects of public life. As a consequence, the active life is drained of substance. Politics become professionalized on the model of the doctor–patient or lawyer–client relationship. Such models rest upon the assumption that clients cannot do for themselves, an assumption contrary to James's deepest beliefs. Hence his opposition to existing forms of economic and political organization.

In his assessment of the modern political situation, James can be compared to a number of other political theorists such as Michels, Arendt, Marcuse, Lukács, Gramsci, and Habermas. Unlike Michels, James did not capitulate before the problem of bureaucracy. Unlike Arendt, he did not retreat before the problem of bringing mass poverty within the hallowed walls of the polis. And unlike Marcuse or Habermas, James did not abandon his belief in the ability of the masses to find creative and revolutionary solutions to modern political problems. The degree of complete self-organization achieved by workers during the course of the Hungarian Revolution is the evidence upon which James rested his case. That achievement points to the real possibility of reducing and deprofessionalizing the gap between leaders and led, thereby returning substance to the active life at the mass level. For James, such an active life is the key to the continued humanizing of the masses and the furthering of the civilizing process. It is the key because the majority of humans are not great artists, neither do they write nor read great books. Consequently, in a meaningful public life, politics and culture meet.

This in essence is James's theory of modern politics. It is a critical theory in that it projects a participatory socialist alternative based upon the crisis tendencies within existing forms of social and political organization. Compared to the analyses of most of the theorists mentioned earlier, it is rather hopeful. The key to James's steadfastness is that, unlike many others, his theory rests not so much on the revolutionary as the creative potential of the working class. His central focus has never been on working-class tendencies for a violent seizure of power, but on the ability to quietly spawn new forms of social organization.

James and Caribbean Politics

In 1953, on the basis of a passport violation, James was expelled from the United States for his political activities. He returned first to Britain, and then, in 1958, to Trinidad to work with the newly formed PNM, which was led by Eric Williams. This venture was short-lived, ending with James's resignation after two years. In spite of this outcome, the conflicts and writings produced by the experience are extremely important for an understanding of James's place in Caribbean politics. In preparation for his work with the PNM, James began a report on the party; together with a variety of others, this report is the basis of *Party Politics in the West Indies*. In this work we see clearly the tensions between James's political theory and the realities of Caribbean politics, along with the implicit distinction between conditions of socialist transformation in center and periphery.

As expected, James's barometers for assessing the political situation in Trinidad were the major insurrectionary events of the recent past—in particular, the movements surrounding Cipriani, Butler, and Williams. According to James's readings, these movements indicated that Trinidadians wanted a modern way of life and were ready to assume the responsibilities that accompanied it. Politically, James read into these mass events a readiness and an eagerness for the most advanced forms of representative government. Economically, he saw no signs of a readiness for a worker-controlled economy.[9] Rather, there was a desire for a more modern and productive economy that was still predominantly capitalist in nature. The creative/insurrectionary tension was between a dying colonial society and the emergence of a modern representative democracy that was basically capitalist in nature.

This assessment of the sociopolitical situation in Trinidad was similar to James's reading of events in a large number of other Third World societies. In these countries, the miseducation produced by the heritage of colonialism and racism, along with little or no mastery of modern production processes, made it impossible for workers to reproduce the Hungarian experience. A significant process of historical development stands between these countries and the move beyond representative forms of social organization. Hence James concluded that "the people of the underdeveloped countries cannot themselves form the governments." At the same time, he was confident that further along the road, the people of the Caribbean will encounter the problems of representative government that Rousseau articulated. Getting beyond these remains was the hardest and "the last hill that the people of the West Indies will have to climb."[10] This assessment shows that James grasped the region's transformative capabilities of mass consciousness with fictional concreteness rather than imposing overly general or external categories and expectations upon it. Further, in it James makes an implicit distinction between processes of socialist transformation in the center and periphery.

Given this general unavailability of the historical conditions for socialist or worker-controlled forms of social organizations, James focused his efforts on the problems of facilitating the move toward a modern capitalist democracy. In the projecting of such a goal was also the implicit positing of an intermediary stage for Caribbean socialism. For James, the insurrections of the recent past were indicators of the region's readiness for a modern society, but not of the socialist variety. Hence the ambiguities concerning this transitional phase of Caribbean society.

In spite of the region's readiness for modern life, James argues that its colonial experience created a number of special problems for this phase. Of particular importance is the absence of an indigenous civilization whose public bodies (journals, town councils, newspapers) are capable of politically educating the masses through responsible participatory activity. Thus in his essay "The Artist in the Caribbean," James points to a lack of institutional support for creative artists.[11] These institutional weaknesses summarize his attempt to situate the Caribbean in relation to modern and pre-modern societies. Caribbean society is modern in that it has been separated from its traditional past. For example, colonial domination nearly destroyed all pre-modern forms of political organization such as the chiefdoms and kingdoms that enslaved Africans brought with them. Thus, in contrast to many African countries, such political organizations are less likely to reappear in post-colonial Caribbean societies. However, in spite of this erasing of the past, the institutional foundations of Caribbean modernity are weak. Breakdowns or the emergence of pre-modern elements in hybrid formations (political tribalism, Duvalier in Haiti) are real possibilities. The supportive social structures of Caribbean modernity are rudimentary when compared to those in advanced countries. This peculiar nature of modernity in the Caribbean and other peripheral societies led James to hypothesize implicitly an intermediary stage for Caribbean socialism. It also led him to reject the view that the roots of democracy were deep in the Caribbean. On the contrary, it shared the region's general institutional weakness with regard to modernity.

At this stage, modern politics in the region would be primarily representative politics. James further suggested that the practice of representative government would have to address the problem of its fragile roots among the masses. Such an undertaking would require a special kind of party—a mass party. By a "mass party," James meant a party whose internal activities would provide "the means by which the developing consciousness of the people can be translated into such forms as to make the people themselves conscious of what it is they want, of the possibilities and the limitations of their desires." This modification of the election-machine view of the party was a necessary innovation to meet the special institutional needs of the region. It was the basis of his critique of the internal life of the PNM and an important factor in the break.

In the context of pre-independence Trinidad and a triumphant PNM, the issue of the latter's fragile institutional roots seemed unreal and far away. Compared to the authoritarianism of the colonial period, the party was sure that although representative, its democratic alternative was the harbinger of freedom. A critique of this alternative without popular experience of its limitations was premature and unreal for many. Nonetheless, focusing upon what would happen after the quest for power, James continued to push the issues of internal party organization.

James was deeply concerned with the poor quality of the PNM's internal life. Like other regional parties, internal organization followed largely from the dominance of the political leader. Through charisma, oratorical skill, or mobilizing ability, leaders were able to gather many loyal supporters. These informal networks, not active participation in the intermediary bodies of the party, determined the party's internal life. There were "no ordered grades of Party activity with leadership at every stage, . . . so that at the summit there is a body of persons known to the party membership and exercising an independent authority based on party activity."[12] Without such internal organization, the party would betray its promise of modern representative politics.

To avoid this betrayal, the PNM would have to abandon its reliance on a dominant leader and center itself more around internal mass organizations. These would have to be developed more systematically and should be the primary responsibility of the general secretary. In James's view, the general secretary's face should be turned toward the various constituency organizations and away from the governmental functions and concerns of the legislative and executive councils. These should be his concerns only to the extent that they effect the internal life of the party. James wanted active political leadership to be completely relieved of the problems of internal party organization.

Under the leadership of the general secretary, constituency and other intermediary organizations should not be just electoral mechanisms. They should serve as structures for mass education through participation in party decision making. This will require that party leaders shed the practice of "taking over every important task." Such practices are sure ways to keep the masses democratically illiterate and destroy "the confidence of the second and coming layers of the leadership."[13] James insists that the inexperienced be allowed their first mistakes so the party can advance as a whole. Relations between leaders and led should be communicative rather than authoritative. Leadership "is not only to tell them [the masses] but to see to it that they are able to tell you."[14]

These were the special participatory activities that the internal life of the PNM needed in order to meet the particular conditions of political modernization in Trinidad. Through the figure of the general secretary, the activities would be brought into harmony with the governmental functions of the party via his membership on the central committee. "I cannot," said James, "conceive any other way of developing a sense of the rights and duties of a democracy in an inexperienced and untutored population. Making speeches to them is useful up to a point. But they cannot live on that. They must have experience, experience of organization and of action. Organizing only to seek votes is a form of degradation. It is only by independent organization and independent action that people discover their needs, discover their capacities."[15]

Without these increases in mass political education through internal party organization, James was certain that the post-colonial period would be one of degeneration and disappointment. He had little faith in Williams's charisma and the anti-colonial solidarity of the pre-independence period to sustain post-colonial politics. Sensing the corruption and in-fighting that might overwhelm the party, James argued that good internal organization would be a "solvent" for such party problems in the post-colonial period. Given conditions in Trinidad, he offered the model of a participatory mass party as the appropriate instrument of post-colonial transformation, rather than a vanguard party or a small revolutionary group. The model followed from the proletarian standpoint of his general political theory but did not incorporate all of the theory's advanced transformational possibilities.

These differences in models of party organization indicated some of the tensions between James and the practice of Trinidadian politics. On a more general level, they pointed to basic differences concerning the virtues of middle class as opposed to proletarian rule. On more specific levels, they pointed to significant differences in defining relations between leaders and led, in assessing what constituted the strength of the party and the ultimate goals of political activity. Thus, James's views on the creativity of masses conflicted with current assumptions about the necessity for middle-class rule.

A second set of tensions arose from the relationships between James's theory and the realities of the Trinidadian situation, in particular, the theory's ability to be absorbed by the consciousness of the masses and the extent to which it was in step with the pace of events. Because of its critical nature, Jamesian theory tended to stay too far ahead of Caribbean actualities. Although the theory was carefully historicized when applied to the Trinidadian case, it is clear that James did not get close enough. Given local perceptions of the unfolding pre-independence events and the absence of experience with self-government, James's concerns must have seemed rather distant. In contrast, much more assimilable at the time were political theories (e.g., those of Hugh Springer, Archie Singham, and Vaughn Lewis) that focused on such things as decolonization, elections, and constitutions. The region was fully caught up in the process of establishing liberal forms of representative government and could not see beyond the mechanics of the endeavor. Although much more limited in their scope and vision, it was their greater closeness to events that gave these theories a more practical appeal. Without losing the advantage of its critical vision, Jamesian theory needed to get closer to regional events. At its initial distance it functioned admirably as a critical standard, but at the same time it was too far ahead to be practical.

A third and final set of tensions derived from the incompleteness of James's reworking of his theory to meet the Trinidadian situation. He never got around to being as systematic about the economy as he had about the party and state. But given the greater emphasis placed on economic development in the region compared to party or mass development, James was here again somewhat out of step. From Arthur Lewis through Alister McIntyre to the New World Group, the importance of this economic problem is evident. James, however, in spite of his notion of the institutional weakness of Caribbean modernity, made few meaningful contacts with this body of literature and its concerns with external economic dependence. The closest he came was in his essays on the West Indian federation, and his polemic against the Caribbean middle class.[16] In the latter incisive attack, no weakness of this class was left unexposed. However, because of the attack's polemical nature, James missed the opportunity to be explicit about the institutional foundations and economic activity in the region, in a way that paralleled his institutional analyses of the artist and democracy. Such a formulation would have given James the opportunity to do for the economy what he had done for the state. It would have forced him to formulate more systematically his position in relation to current economic policies as he did in the case of the party. All he indicated at the time was his intense dislike of the policy of industrialization by invitation that was being put into place, and to counter it with a peasant-led strategy of development.[17] This failure to develop the economic aspects of post-colonial transformation more adequately increased the gap between his theory and the practice of Trinidadian politics.

The ACLM (Antigua)

The ACLM began its political career as the Afro-Caribbean Movement (ACM) in 1968. It was a small political group formed by a number of predominantly middle-class men and women who had been strongly influenced by the struggles of African Americans in the United States and the revolutionary struggles in southern Africa. The group included such well-known Antiguans as Lesroy Merchant, Robin Bascus, Venetta Ross, Barry Stevens, and Tim Hector. Throughout these early years, the ACM remained a rather informal group. It met regularly to discuss ideas and problems, but its central concern was the publication of its journal, Outlet.

The emergence of the ACLM as a Jamesian political party out of this movement was a long and complex process that can be divided into two broad phases: the pre-party years (1968–79) and the party years (1980–present). The former was a phase of ideological formation that can be further divided into two distinct periods: the Black Power years (1968–72) and the Jamesian years (1973–79). The party years have been dominated by efforts to make Jamesian ideology concrete and put it into practice.

The Black Power years (1968–72)

As the problem of the political direction of the ACM came more into focus, it produced a split in the leadership. A more radical group began to form around Hector, including Jerome Bleau, Everett Christian, and Ellerton Jeffers. This group quickly grew in prominence, resulting in the subsequent departure of such earlier leaders as Bascus and Stevens. It was also the start of Hector's leadership, an event that would eventually take the ACM in a Jamesian direction.

Hector's introduction to James occurred during his student years at McGill University in Canada. There, he was part of a James study group that included such Caribbean notables as Rosie Douglas, Bobby Hill,

Franklin Harvey, and Bookie Renna. The last three were members of New Beginning, a Jamesian group formed in Trinidad. It was to this Canada-based circle that James retired for a short while after the 1966 defeat of his Workers' and Farmers' Party in Trinidad's general elections. From this circle and his conversation with James, the experience that Hector considers most valuable was a history of Marxism from James and his subsequent ability to look at Marxism historically.

Hector returned to Antigua in 1967, strongly influenced by both James and the Black Power Movement that had emerged in the United States and later spread to Canada. In Antigua, the political scene was dominated by two events: the split within the ruling Antigua Labor Party (ALP), which would result in the formation of the Progressive Labor Movement (PLM), and the identification of Afro-Antiguans with the struggles of Afro-Americans and Africans abroad. Hector became active in the two key organizations produced by these political currents: the PLM and the ACM. However, as the centrist faction of the PLM, led by George Walter, consolidated its hold over the new party, the left wing, which included Hector and Stevens among others, was forced out in 1969. Consequently, their efforts were now more focused within the ACM.

Hector's assumption of the leadership gave rise to a number of ideological challenges. The dominant ideology and language of political protest was clearly that of Black Power, while more conventional politics moved within the liberal idiom. The dominance of these ideologies left only little room for the Jamesian position. Thus, not surprisingly, the ideology of the ACM during this period was an uneasy mix of Black Power and Jamesian elements, and the former were dominant. A good example of this synthesis can be found in the party document *The Caribbean: Yesterday, Today and Tomorrow* written by Hector. This work provides a portrait of the yesterdays of the Caribbean from the point of view of what the working class has done to change basic social relations. From this perspective, the most significant actions have been the various insurrectionary upsurges in which attempts were made to overthrow slavery and colonialism and establish forms of self-rule. The document analyzes several of these uprisings, including the 1831 insurrection in Jamaica. Concerning this event, the governor of Jamaica reported that house and field slaves clearly joined in a quest for acquiring both freedom and property. Commenting on this specification of the object and purpose of the insurrection, Hector makes the following connection with Black Power ideology: "such object and such purpose was to overthrow once and for all the property relations . . . , and thereby to create a new society. That in my view is Black Power, and what the struggles of the twentieth century are all about."[18]

In addition to this insurrectionary perspective, a number of other Jamesian elements were also a part of the synthesis with the Afro-centric ideology of Black Power. The most important of these was the rejection of representative party politics and the definition of Black Power as "the cooperative and collective control of resources by the people." The two ideologies synthesized around these issues of representative government and white economic control.

In spite of these points of agreement, the synthesis remained an un-stable one in which the Black Power elements were dominant. This dominance was clear from the externally oriented and Afrocentric nature of the ACM's political practice throughout this period. The major event on its political calendar was the annual African Liberation Day solidarity march. These marches were extremely successful, attracting thousands and at the same time Africanizing the consciousness of many. The un-easy nature of the synthesis was mirrored in the following comment by Hector on one of his earlier meetings with George Weston, Antigua's most celebrated Pan-Africanist: "I was then too Anglo-Saxon, he too African. So we thought of each other."[19]

In sum, the period between 1968 and 1972 was one of formation and ideological definition for the ACM. Within the confines of the Antiguan political milieu, these attempts at self-definition produced an ideologi-cal formation that was an uneasy mix of Jamesian and Pan-Africanist elements. The dominance of the latter resulted in a political practice that was Africa oriented with Antigua as a secondary focus. These would all change quite dramatically in the next period.

The Jamesian years: Widening the gap between theory and practice
Two important developments separated the period between 1973 and 1979 from the Black Power years. The first was a more intense concern with getting beyond the colonial institutions of Antiguan society that were still being reproduced in spite of formal decolonization. This turn toward the crisis of post-colonial society in Antigua gave the period a more internal focus. The second important development was a much more conscious turn toward James out of a need for a clear alternative

to the declining but reluctant colonial order. Thus to the Jamesian elements already in the ACM's ideology, a carefully elaborated "eschatology" was newly added.

With these new elements in place, orientation was less toward Africa and more toward the "New Society," a society controlled by workers, that would be established in Antigua. Afrocentric concerns were by no means completely eclipsed. Rather, they were more comfortably incorporated into new ideology. The easier nature of this relationship would later be reflected in the fact that the movement named its headquarters George Weston House. This marked shift in a Jamesian direction can be most clearly seen in the important party document, *Independence: Yes! The Old Mess: No!*, by Hector, Jeffers, and Michael. At the same time, the turn toward a workers society opened a sharp cleavage between theory and practice.

Several factors contributed to the closer focus on the post-colonial crisis of Antiguan society. Among these, three events of 1973 are particularly important: a strike by workers at the Public Utilities Authority (PUA), the banning of the African Liberation Day marches by the PLM government, and the merger of the ACM with another radical organization, Youth Forces for Liberation (YFL).

The PUA strike was important because for the first time a group of unionized workers engaged in an industrial dispute openly sought the assistance of the ACM. This not only reinforced the ACM's image as a worker-oriented organization, but it also elicited a level of hands-on involvement that was new for the organization. Because the conflict was with the government, it was also a lesson in how local labor governments were treating local labor.

The decision of the PLM government to ban the African Liberation Day marches was another rude awakening to the continuities between colonial and post-colonial state in Antigua. As these marches were so central to the political practice of the ACM, resisting the ban was crucial for the survival of the movement. Not surprisingly, a decision was taken to defy the ban. The result was the largest demonstration ever organized by the ACM. It was a major victory, and it also marked a definite shift in how the two established parties regarded the ACM. From here, they ceased seeing it as an organization that was primarily concerned with the oppression of Africans overseas, but rather as one with the potential to replace them at home. These changes in relations with the major parties also helped heighten the ACM's awareness of the local context.

The third and final event that aided this inward turn was the merger with the YFL, a working-class Black Power organization that operated in The Point, a "ghetto area" of the capital city of St. Johns. Because of their strong class orientation, YFL members had up to this point distrusted the ACM, and labeled its activities as "bourgeois Black Power." However, in the context of growing repression that the PLM government directed at both groups, class difference was buried in the interest of mutual survival. This merger produced the Antigua Caribbean Liberation Movement (ACLM), replacing both the ACM and the YFL. Given the YFL's focus on urban unemployment, this development increased the pressure on the movement to look within.

To understand the turn toward James, we must grasp more clearly the change in the perception of Antiguan society that emerged from these three developments. From the conflicts with the government and the interactions and alliances with workers came a more concrete and precise conceptualizing of the crisis of post-colonial Antiguan society. This crisis—the persistence of colonial institutions in the post-colonial period—was linked to three basic sources. First, in agriculture, new political leaders carried out the peasant land-settlement schemes that had been recommended by various colonial policymakers to keep the old plantation economy going. Second, in the area of such new industries as tourism and in light manufacturing, organization was neocolonial, with high levels of foreign ownership and control. Third, in the area of politics, mass organizations—parties and unions—were rapidly being transformed into instruments of middle-class rule. This rested upon accommodations, not only with the old planter elite but also with new centers of foreign capital. In this milieu of competing interests, the mass organizations were being converted into instruments of mass control that restrained the working-class dynamic for change. The crisis of post-colonial Antigua was linked to these three primary sources.[20]

Conceptualizing this crisis more clearly made a number of limitations explicit that had remained implicit in the Black Power ideology of the previous period. These limitations emerged from the growing recognition that a replacement of whites by blacks without a change in social organization would only result in the continuation of old patterns of domination and repression. Recognition of this fact was reinforced by the experiences of other Caribbean territories, particularly the 1970 uprising in Trinidad that almost overthrew the Williams regime. This classic insurrectionary event burst the framework of existing notions of Black

Power and called for a process of transformation that moved beyond replacing whites with blacks. It was to James that the leaders of New Beginning in Trinidad turned for a more appropriate framework to interpret this event. Similarly, by 1973, the time was right in Antigua for such a turn toward James within the ACLM.

This shift toward James was part of a larger effort to do more reading within the movement. Members were encouraged to read at least one hour a day, and particular individuals were asked to speak on specific topics at weekly study meetings. The study of James produced a stronger focus on *Facing Reality* than on *Party Politics in the West Indies*. The latter was important primarily for its critique of the middle class and not for James's incomplete attempt to rework his general theory of modern politics to meet the specific conditions of modernity in the Caribbean. Consequently, it was the Hungarian and not the Trinidadian model of transformation that the ACLM used to supplement and replace the receding Black Power ideology.

Using this model, the creative/insurrectionary tension established by the movement was not that between a persistent colonial capitalist order and a modern capitalist society as James had asserted in Trinidad. Rather, it was between the former and a socialist, worker-controlled society. The ACLM projected this particular tension on the basis of what it perceived to be "the fundamental conflict" of Antiguan society—"the conflict between modern labor and the old colonial system."[21] The importance of this conflict was reinforced by its eruption in other Caribbean societies, and by James's 1977 visit to Antigua, when he addressed ACLM members on "The Impending Confrontation." Thus, it was readily assumed that the inner structure and dimensions of the insurrectionary consciousness of the Antiguan working class were such that their projection of a sociohistorical alternative would be of the modern, worker-controlled variety. On this assumption rested the closely related claim that the Antiguan working class was ready for a move beyond representative government, which, it was argued, had been clearly compromised as a result of the increasing exposure of its class nature. This bourgeois nature of Antiguan democracy was made obvious by the state's alliances with foreign capital and its conflicts with workers and the ACLM—hence its illegitimacy in the eyes of the working class. On the basis of the conflict between modern labor and the old colonial system, along with its representation in the consciousness of workers, the ACLM proclaimed a revolutionary alternative: "The organization and direct intervention of the mass of workers, unemployed, women and youth must of necessity produce a new and higher form of democracy. A new democracy wherein the worker at work, discusses and decides on the industrial plan. Likewise the farmer on the land, organized collectively and in Communes, formulates and decides on the agricultural plan. . . . Therefore in 1976 we in Antigua must strike out on a new road, towards mastery of production and politics, in a new democracy. That is the historical mission of the great masses of the people. *Forward to a New Life.*"[22]

Adoption of this sociohistorical alternative based on James's general theory of socialist transformation in the center had a number of important consequences for the political practice of the ACLM. On the positive side, it provided the party with a powerful standpoint from which to analyze both the deepening crisis of modern politics in Antigua and the legitimacy costs of the models of dependent development in use. On the negative side, it opened a gap between theory and practice as it left the ACLM without clear functional and organizational goals for itself and an unrealistic assessment of the capabilities of the Antiguan working class.

From its earliest years to the present, one of the major strengths of the ACLM has been its capacity for ideological projection. In this it has surpassed all other Antiguan parties and political groups. Its paper, *Outlet*, has dominated the print medium since 1980, not only because of the movement's tendency to attract intellectuals, but also because the turn toward James coincided with a worsening of the crisis of modern politics in post-colonial Antigua.

Between 1967 and 1971, elite accumulation of power within the ruling ALP resulted in oligarchical formations that forced Antiguans into their first major confrontation with the problems of representative government. The solutions they decided upon included greater institutional differentiation between unions and parties, a more clearly defined two-party system, and a change of regime. These reforms, while important, reinforced the liberal/representative system without a full awareness of the complexity of the problems that had generated the crisis. There was not a sufficiently profound recognition of the uniqueness of the Antiguan experience with modern forms of political power, and why it had plunged so rapidly into what Fanon has labeled "the pitfalls of national consciousness."[23] In a very real sense, leaders and party members found themselves swept up in a crisis that they could neither fully understand nor resolve.

It was precisely in regard to these problems that James's critique of representative government and his alternative of direct democracy gave the ACLM an ideological advantage. By providing a point of reference outside of the representative system, it enabled the party to see the crisis more completely and to offer more penetrating analyses. The power and appeal of these critiques became major weapons and major sources of competition and conflict between the ACLM and the dominant parties. At this level, the ACLM has been able to keep the latter on the defensive, either in the form of having to save face or to cover up exposed corrupt practices. Consequently, prolonged court battles over attempts to close *Outlet* have been a persistent feature of the relationship with the major parties. These, however, have not been successful in destroying the movement's capacity for ideological projection or the added strength it has gained from adopting James's theory of post-representative politics.

Using James's theory without adequately reworking it to suit Antiguan realities opened a significant gap between ACLM theory and the locus of its practice. One important area in which this became evident was that of the spontaneous activity of workers. Here, the Hungarian model became the basis for determining the form and content of future working-class uprisings. In my view, this imposition produced a misreading of the nature of working-class insurrectionary activity in Antigua. The basis for this imposition was the claim, reaffirmed by Hector, Jeffers, and Michael, that the Antiguan people were "totally modern."[24] This modernity made a worker-controlled society a present sociohistorical possibility. However, from James's view of Caribbean modernity, this would appear to be an exaggerated claim. The exaggeration obscures the specific nature of modernity in a neocolonial society like Antigua's, as well as its impact on the content and structure of working-class consciousness.

The classic description of the consciousness of the insurrectionary masses in colonial societies remains Fanon's essay "Spontaneity: Its Strength and Weakness" in *The Wretched of the Earth*. If we compare the inner structure and dimensions of the consciousness described in this essay with James's account of Hungarian workers, we immediately observe a very important difference. In the latter case, workers surpassed the state socialist order, including a technical and organizational mastery of the productive process that is present in that order. Implicit in this mastery is the awareness that society in its economic aspect is collectively manageable, and not just the repressive state apparatus.

In Fanon's account, little suggests that the consciousness guiding in-

surrectionary upsurges in colonial societies is capable of a similar awareness. The description does not suggest that the consciousness has the
capacity to destroy the naturelike appearance of society and reveal it as
a collectively manageable entity. On the contrary, it suggests that the
consciousness guiding these mass actions destroys only the legitimate
and natural lawlike appearance of the immediate structures of political
domination. Dereification is limited largely to the political arena. It does
not extend to the economy and other areas of society, which continue
to be seen as external entities whose fixed laws govern the behavior and
fate of members. Insurrectionary consciousness in colonial societies is
essentially a political consciousness. The totality mirrored and creatively
transformed in it is that of political society. The fixed, natural appearance of society in its economic and cultural aspects is not dissolved and
surpassed by this consciousness. Neither does it radically reconstitute
them beyond the removing of the political dominance of the colonizer.
Although the social system as a whole may include deeper sources of oppression, this insurrectionary consciousness tends to frame liberation in
terms of the overthrow and replacements of governing elites and existing
political structure. Thus, spontaneous mass action in colonial societies
is often capable of significant political revolutions, but less so of social
ones. The failure of Greek democracy to socialize the economy suggests
that the preceding may be true of preindustrial societies.

It is clear that Antigua has had less of a premodern tradition than
the African societies upon which Fanon's description was based. Hence
there should be observable differences distinguishing the consciousness
of Antiguan workers from that of their African counterparts. However,
in spite of these differences, it is my view that the insurrectionary consciousness of the Antiguan working class is closer to that described by
Fanon than that described by James in *Facing Reality*. That is, although
the insurrectionary consciousness of Antiguan workers is not identical
with its African counterpart, it, too, is unable to dereify the social totality
and reveal society as a collectively manageable entity. At the same time,
it has never displayed the technical and organizational mastery of industrial production evident in James's description. However, time and
time again it has demonstrated the ability to dereify and reconstitute the
political order of society. Its inner categorical structure is such that social
oppression is reproduced and negated in largely political terms. Thus, it
shares the political dimensions of the consciousness Fanon described,

despite the lesser presence of premodern traditions. This peculiarity can be related to James's argument concerning the institutional weakness of Caribbean modernity.

This political orientation helps to explain the success of such actions as the ALP mobilizations against the colonial state, PLM mobilizations against the ALP, and ACLM mobilizations against both of these parties. Of these, the 1968 uprisings that were mobilized by the PLM are particularly instructive. These uprisings produced the complete capitulation of the ruling ALP regime led by Premier V. C. Bird. However, no clear systemic alternatives spontaneously emerged from these uprisings. There were, however, political ones. A revolution in terms of the overthrow of the capitalist system, its classes, and its forms of class rule was not the categorical framework that guided this uprising. Rather, it was an upsurge whose categorical framework consistently translated social oppression into political terms and sought to address the problem at the political level. Jeffers, a participant in the uprising but not yet a member of the ACLM, describes his categorical framework as follows. "At that point in time, I will tell you, there was no such thing as revolution in my head. I was in opposition to Bird. My consciousness at the time was not at the level of demanding any kind of revolution."[25] This, in my view, was indicative of the political, not the systemic, nature of the insurrectionary consciousness that guided the movement. By imposing the more advanced Hungarian reading on worker insurrectionary activity, this early use of James's ideas opened a significant gap between the ACLM and Antiguan workers. Ironically, the specific creative alternatives of the workers were not grasped with James's fictional concreteness. As a result, the movement was led to expect a comprehensive social transformation from workers whose insurrectionary practice was primarily political in nature.

Closely related to this misreading of worker insurrectionary activity was the tendency to underestimate the importance of organizing both within and without the party. This underestimation was directly related to overestimating workers' capabilities for insurrectionary activity. Because it was assumed that the new worker-controlled society would be brought about by the insurrectionary activity of this class, the precise role of the ACLM in this transformation remained unclear. Would it be the articulate voice of the workers, the scribe of their actions, or a vanguard party of some sort? Only clear answers to these questions could give the ACLM the definite political identity it needed.

The clearest conception that the ACLM had of its role in the transformation process was that it would be the organization that workers would turn to in the event of an insurrectionary upsurge. The precedent for this was the case of the PUA workers. Given this self-definition, organization essentially meant being ready to support the workers whenever the upsurge came. This readiness was important because, as ACLM Vice-Chairman Conrad Luke often says, the upsurge "may come upon you as thief in the night."[26] Thus organization was largely equated with readiness, a view that complemented the advanced reading of worker insurrectionary activity.

However, if the preceding analysis of the nature of spontaneous working-class activity in Antigua is correct, this view of organization is inadequate for the Antiguan context, especially if the goal remains a worker-controlled society. Realization of such a goal would require much more vigorous leadership on the part of the ACLM and organization to enable masses of workers in participatory activities to acquire the educational and organizational experience necessary for such advanced forms of self-rule. Political practice would have to go beyond both readiness and the educative work done through the newspaper and organized classes. A number of organizing drives would also have to be undertaken.

A number of such drives were undertaken. For example, as early as 1969, ACLM members organized a drive to help peasants cut their sugarcane. This movement brought clerical workers, construction workers, and individuals from the lumpen sector into voluntary groups that did Sunday work with peasant farmers. The drive came to be known as the Pen-pushers' Movement. In 1972, two ACLM members, Jerome Bleau and George Goodwin, initiated two distinct attempts at organizing. The first was among workers at an airline company, Leeward Island Air Transport, and the second was at the local branch of the Bank of Nova Scotia. Other important organizing drives included setting up cooperative farms, attempts to form a union of the unemployed, and the civil service and Teachers Union struggles of 1975.

None of these drives succeeded in producing a permanent mass base for the ACLM, however. Hence the primarily ideological nature of its linkages with the working class and the small size of the organizational base despite the merger with the YFL. It was primarily through this merger that workers came into the movement, which so far had been dominated by radical petit bourgeois intellectuals. Jeffers later noted the paradox in which these advanced but unrealistic notions of organization and worker insurrectionary capability had trapped the ACLM's political practice: "It meant that the kind of organizational and attitudinal work that was necessary in an underdeveloped country was not being done, because you mistakenly believed that you had a developed working class which was not the case. So perhaps you could have accused us of idealism—of not being down to earth."[27]

For the ACLM, the Jamesian years marked an important formative period that produced rather mixed results. The move toward James solved a number of problems but opened some new ones. In particular, this turn gave the ACLM the clearest grasp of the economic and political crises of post-colonial society in Antigua, crises that substantially reinforced its already powerful ideological presence. However, at the same time the turn led to imposition of an overly advanced reading of the insurrectionary capabilities of the Antiguan working class. The organizational and leadership work that was especially necessary in a society like Antigua's was also minimized. Hence the "idealism" of these years. In spite of such problems, the Jamesian years were an important formative period in the development of the ACLM, and in understanding the party years to come.

The party years

Two important developments separate the party years from the Jamesian years in Antigua. The first was the decision to engage in electoral politics. The ACLM was forced to redefine itself as a party and develop a number of practical policies oriented toward an electoral rather than an insurrectionary mandate. Particularly in the area of economic policy, this decision pressured the ACLM to confront a number of technical and organizational issues left unsolved in James's general theory.

The second important development is the ongoing attempt to close the gap between theory and practice, which events and the passage of time have made more evident. Most significant in this regard has been the introduction of an intermediary period—the national democratic stage—between the present neocolonial order and the projected worker-controlled society. In both the development of party policies and the introduction of this intermediary stage, a process of contextualization can be observed that has forced the party to rework the ideology of the Jamesian years. However, in spite of significant advances in these areas, basic organizational problems remain.

Into the Stream of Electoral Politics

Although Jamesians were the ACLM's dominant faction, theirs was not
the only ideological position within the party. Because of the strong tendency to attract petit bourgeois intellectuals, some in the movement
primarily sought a party that was more progressive than either the PLM or
the ALP. However, this progressivism did not embrace rejection of electoral politics and its replacement by a direct democracy. Consequently,
the intellectuals continued to raise the issue of gaining power elector-
ally. This position was pushed rather strongly by Hendy Simon, who
saw in African Liberation Day marches popular support for the ACLM.
However, at the formal party discussion of the issue in 1975, the position of the Jamesians was reaffirmed. Hence, the categorical rejection of
"conventional politics" in *Independence: Yes! The Old Mess: No!*, which
was written on the eve of the 1976 elections. Between 1976 and 1979, a
number of events produced a gradual reversal of this position. The most
important were the party's loss of members, the suppression of the 1979
teachers' strike, and the emergence of a regional trend toward electoral
socialism.

Since the merger with the YFL, there was a marked tendency to place
workers in such important positions of authority as committee chairs,
heightening the class tensions within the movement and making many
middle-class intellectuals uncomfortable. This discomfort, the closing
of the electoral option, and the belief that Antiguan workers would not
deliver the needed insurrectionary mandate led to the departure of a significant portion of the middle-class element. Of particular note were the
withdrawals of Hendy Simon, Yvette Davis, K. D. Williams, and Bernard
Lewis. Although these departures weakened the pro-elections faction
within the movement, it also revealed the need for the middle-class
members' oratorical and technical skills. Thus, it would not be long before the ACLM would experience another middle-class infusion to help
change the movement's position on electoral politics.

The new influx of petit bourgeois elements was closely related to the
teachers' strike of 1979. Executives of the Antigua Union of Teachers
included individuals who were members of both the PLM and the ACLM.
As they sought the support of their respective parties, the PLM and the
ACLM were required to work together for the first time since the split in
1969. Support for the teachers was to take the form of calling out other

workers controlled by the Antigua Workers Union (AWU), the union affiliated with the PLM. However, the ACLM and PLM had different goals. The
ACLM had hoped that such a call by the AWU would have been the start of
an insurrectionary upsurge. The PLM's hope was that, with ACLM's ideological support, this conflict could be translated into an electoral victory.
Consequently, the decision to call out workers was repeatedly delayed.
When it finally was made, much momentum had passed. In the meanwhile, the ALP, carefully watching this merger of the forces that virtually
overthrew it in 1968, decided to "meet steel with steel" and forcefully
suppressed the strike.

The suppression destroyed high hopes for an insurrectionary mandate,
which made the upcoming 1980 election a more attractive option. At
the same time, it brought a number of teachers into the ACLM who were
interested in electoral politics. Many would assume important positions
and be candidates in the election. This new influx included Chaku Waku,
Radcliffe Robbins, and Adlai Carrot. The dominance of this new element resulted in tensions with the YFL faction, which eventually left the
movement. It also helped to precipitate the departure of Jeffers, a major
contributor to the ideological strength of the ACLM. The 1979 teachers'
strike produced some important changes in the ACLM, including a strong
push in the direction of electoral politics.

The third and final factor affecting the turn toward electoral politics
was the growing trend among left parties in the region to enter electoral
politics. This they did either singly or as part of a coalition. In Grenada,
Bishop's New Jewel Movement (NJM) had benefited from such an alliance
before their well-known seizure of power in 1979. In Jamaica, Manley's
Peoples National Party (PNP) won the 1976 elections on a democratic
socialist platform. In St. Vincent, there was the alliance between Yulimo
and the Peoples Democratic Movement, while the coalition that replaced
the Patrick John administration in Dominica included a left wing. Thus
the winds of change had been blowing electoral politics leftward, making
it all the more reasonable for the ACLM to declare itself a party and join
the stream in 1980. This leftward turn would soon be reversed by a mobilization of the right, spearheaded by the coming to power of Edward
Seaga in Jamaica and Ronald Reagan in the United States. In late 1979,
the full dimensions of this response were far from visible. Consequently,
the ACLM joined the stream of electoral politics.

Defining party policies

The transition from a socialist movement waiting for an insurrectionary upsurge to a party competing for an electoral mandate has been complex and difficult for the ACLM. Sometimes the two identities appear to be reconciled, and at others they appear to conflict. One occasionally gets the impression that the insurrectionary identity has been forced upon a party still committed to an electoral vision. Yet these changes signify much more than that. They have forced the ACLM to rework its basic policies and introduce an intermediary stage in its ideological projections. These constitute a contextualizing of Jamesian theory that is important for transitions to socialism not only in the Caribbean, but also in other, peripheral areas.

The shifts in ACLM's attitudes toward itself and the transformation of Antiguan society are most clearly visible in the party's 1980 manifesto, *Towards a New Antigua*. Without complete erasure, the framework of this document displaces the earlier opposition between the persistent colonial order and a projected worker-controlled society. In place of this opposition is the creative tension between a neocolonial order and a modern, nationally controlled society that would still be basically capitalist in nature. Mediating this new opposition in a transformative direction would be an elected ACLM government. Thus the new framework within which the manifesto is written approaches the Trinidadian model of *Party Politics in the West Indies*. Consistent with the manifesto's parameters, specific policies are laid out in a variety of areas including economics, politics, education, health, and culture. Important shifts are reflected in the areas of politics and economics.

The more immediate goal of gaining an electoral mandate forced the ACLM to articulate a set of political policies that assumed the continued existence of the system of representative government rather than its transcendence. In doing this, the party took as its point of departure James's analysis of the crisis of modern politics in the post-colonial Caribbean. In particular, the tendencies toward accommodations with old and new imperialist forces, toward corruption and oligarchy that made up the state capitalist thesis, were attributed to the Antiguan case. The ACLM focused upon the corrupt practices of the ALP and the PLM, the repressive consequences of the competition between them, and the deep division the competition produced in the working class. The competition resulted in a number of repressive laws such as the Public Order and Newspaper Amendment Acts, which significantly curtailed basic constitutional rights. Thus, the new challenge for the ACLM was to come up with policies that could address these problems without radically altering the basic premises of the representative system, without the projected transition to a system of direct democracy.

In responding to this challenge, the party produced a political platform that rested upon three basic pillars. The first was establishing a Human Rights Commission made up of government, opposition, trade unions, workers, women, and business representatives to ensure the restoration and protection of basic human rights. The second was an anticorruption code, which would require all elected members of government to declare their assets annually to be "scrutinized by the Public Accounts Committee headed by the leader of the opposition."[28] Third, there would be an end to victimization, the practice of job discrimination based on party affiliation. This was also a part of the party's larger commitment to the rebuilding of working-class unity. This political agenda was directed toward a representative democracy that would be closer to the expected norm and depolarizing the party-based split in the working class. The crisis of modern politics in Antigua would have to be addressed within its existing representative framework.

In economic policy, the adoption of more short-term goals brought a corresponding set of changes. Displacing the goal of a modern, worker-controlled economy was that of a national economy. In the words of the manifesto: "ACLM is clear that what is required now in Antigua is not a socialist economy for which Antigua does not have the pre-conditions. ACLM is loud and clear that what is required is a *national economy* with the public sector working along with the private sector, with the co-operative farm working in alliance with the private farm, foreign capital in partnership with national capital."[29] In this economy, there would be a planning council that would represent all sectors. This council would be responsible for the basic goals and problems of the economy.

Within the framework of this three-sector national economy, the manifesto outlines a series of policies for tourism, agriculture, commerce, and marketing. In developing these policies, the party was forced to move beyond the Jamesian inheritance and to draw upon the work of the New World economists, which analyzed the externally dependent and often enclave nature of major Caribbean industries. Thus, tourism policies were outlined to increase national ownership and establish linkages with other sectors of the economy. Among these were incentives for Antiguans to enter the hotel industry, attracting middle-income tourists and establishing linkages with the reorganized handicraft industry and agricultural sector.

The restructuring of agriculture reflected not only the influence of James's Caribbean writings, but also that of New World economics. At the center of this body of thought is the plantation economy, its dynamics and its propensities for generating underdevelopment. Maintaining this economic system by both ALP and PLM leaders was one of the major factors the ACLM identified as contributing to the crisis of modern economics in post-colonial Antiguan society. Thus, to finally get beyond the inertia of this reluctant colonial order, this policy had to be reversed. That is, the plantation economy had to be uprooted and replaced. To do this, the ACLM proposed a program of land reform to break up plantations into state farms and cooperatives. In these cooperatives, farmers would have substantial units of land, which would "guarantee a standard of living equal to that of the best commercial and industrial workers."[30] Traditional products such as sugar, cotton, and vegetables would be grown largely for local consumption and as inputs for a variety of related agro-industries. Policies in the areas of fishing, marketing, and commerce followed a similar pattern and were oriented toward the deinstitutionalization of the neocolonial economy and establishment of a national structure in its place.

This model of a three-sector economy and the policies based upon it have been adopted by other socialist parties that have either approached or gained power. It was the case with both the Manley and Bishop regimes and with the Sandinista regime in Nicaragua. These changes represent, in my view, an important adjustment and scaling down of existing models of socialist transformation in order to meet the dimensions, contexts, and capabilities of small peripheral societies. More specifically for the ACLM, the model revealed the significant gaps in its Jamesian heritage that it had to fill on becoming a party.

Reworking party ideology: the National Democratic stage
The experience of competing in the 1980 elections left its mark on the ACLM. Policy shifts and adjustments became a permanent feature of the life of the party, as its 1989 manifesto makes clear. Consequently, their implications for the process of socialist transformation in peripheral countries emerges as a central question. Are these shifts and adjustments

simply pragmatic adaptations to the exigencies of electoral politics, or do they have a deeper significance? Their appearances in Grenada and Nicaragua, countries that experienced insurrectionary upsurges, suggest that they go beyond the exigencies of electoral politics and are related to necessary contents of socialism in the periphery. If this is indeed the case, then existing theories of socialist transformation in the periphery (Baran, Thomas, James, and Ulanovsky) must be appropriately modified. These theories can be divided into two groups. Those (Baran's and Thomas's) that assume the possibility of an immediate transition to socialism; and those (James's and Ulanovsky's) that presuppose an intermediary stage. The experiences of the PNP, the NJM, and the ACLM suggests that the planning dimensions and capabilities presupposed by Baran and Thomas are by far too large; that Ulanovsky's intermediary stage underestimates these dimensions and capabilities; and that James's deals adequately with only the political conditions of the transition. Thus, the presentation of the contents of these intermediary stages by parties such as the ACLM is important for both the theory and practice of socialism in the periphery.

The ACLM's reading of the changes brought by the party years is contained in another important party document, *Antigua for Antiguans, Barbuda for Barbudans*, an attempt to synthesize the heritages from both the Jamesian and the party years. This synthesis takes the form of a projected national democratic stage between the existing order and a more distant socialist society. The synthetic aspects of this stage are evident in the approaches to institutional reform. With regard to political reforms, elements from the Jamesian years can be seen in the document's reaffirmation of the party's commitment to direct democracy: "ACLM is irrevocably committed to the idea that the people must govern themselves not just by representative but, through change and changes, by direct democracy." However, this is no longer an immediate sociohistorical possibility. On the contrary, the institutionalizing of such direct participation "proceeds by stages and is a function of the economic, political and cultural development" achieved by the people.[31] At the present stage of Antigua's social development, only the first step toward such a goal can be taken. Village, community, and parish councils can be introduced with authority over a variety of social services and utilities. Once these have taken root, then the process can be extended to other areas or nationally. Thus, in political terms, the national democratic stage would aim not only at an optimally functioning system of representative democracy, but also at the introducing of areas of direct popular participation.

Likewise, the reforms that aim at building a national economy also embody a comparable synthesis within the context of this intermediary stage. This would be a state-led economy with a substantial private sector. However, the commitment to workers' control was retained through the cooperative sector and its representation on the planning council. The national economy would also be a mixed, transitional formation containing elements from the Jamesian and the party years. Thus, in economic terms, the national democratic stage aims not only at the localizing and expanding of the existing economy, but also at the introducing of elementary structures of workers' control.

Earlier, I noted some of the more important implications of these intermediary formations for theories of socialist transformation. Equally important questions have also arisen from the practical side. The most important of these is, How solid a practice can be based on these intermediary formations? It remains particularly urgent because the premature ending of both the Grenadian and Jamaican experiments did not allow resolution of important difficulties. For example, would the state be able to subject foreign capital to the logic of nationalist accumulation, or would foreign capital continue to dominate the accumulation process? Would the dominance of the state sector lead to new forms of statism? Would the private sector maintain its dominance over workers despite their organization into cooperatives? Would the foreign and capitalist factors in the synthesis suppress and contain the nationalist and socialist elements? These are difficult questions to answer and will vary from country to country. However, the best clues are still to be found in cases such as those of Grenada and Jamaica.

Unsolved Organizational Problems

In contrast to the changes at both the ideological and policy levels has been the inability of the party to solve corresponding organizational problems that go with projecting its intermediary stage. The small organizational base of the ACLM has already been noted. The weakness resulting from this was clearly revealed in the party's dependence on the PLM for mobilizing workers to support the teachers' strike of 1979. It is also reflected in the ACLM's poor showing at the polls, only 1.2 percent of the popular vote in 1980. The party did not contest the 1984 elections, which the ALP called early to capitalize upon the mood following the collapse of the NJM in Grenada. As Hector said, "certainly Grenada would have adversely affected us at the polls. But . . . ACLM had said it would not contest the 1984 elections unless there was a United Front."[32] Such a united front among opposition parties failed to emerge before or after 1984; consequently, the ACLM contested the 1989 elections on its own. Because of irregularities, official results have not yet been published. However, the ACLM did not win any seats, and there is little indication of a significant increase in its popular base.

Several attempts at mass organizing had been made by the ACLM: the cooperative farms, the Pen-pushers' Movements, and the union of unemployed being the most significant. These, however, were not successful in that they did not generate a mass support base for the ACLM. A major obstacle to the success of these drives was, of course, the dominance of the two major parties and their affiliated unions, which have established a strong hold over the needs, aspirations, and loyalties of workers. This hold has been further reinforced through labeling the ACLM as communist by the major parties and unions. However, this dominance is not sufficient to explain the small organizational base of the ACLM. The highly publicized leadership crisis within the ALP, the fatal collapse of the PLM, and the regrouping of its members under the United National Democratic Party (UNDP) are clear indicators that other factors are also at work. Thus, in addition to competition from the other parties, at least two factors internal to the ACLM contribute to its small organizational base. First, the party has not adequately reworked its view of the transformative capabilities of Antiguan workers in the context of its national democratic stage. Second, the party has also not worked out a clear view of the kind of instrument it needs to be in this intermediary stage.

Throughout the Jamesian years, the ACLM adopted an overly advanced view of the insurrectionary consciousness of Antiguan workers, a view changed by the adjustments of the party years. Recognition of the fact that the capacity for self-management is affected by stages of sociohistorical development has forced abandonment of the earlier, Hungarian reading of worker insurrectionary activity in Antigua. According to Luke, the model applies "in terms of our general analysis. But its relevance to our particular situation is another question."[33]

This shift has been an important step toward redefinition of the insurrectionary role of workers in the national democratic stage. However, it has not been supplemented and completed by a positive reformulation.

At present, an ambivalent view of workers can be observed. On the one hand, there is a tendency to see and embrace workers solely in terms of their insurrectionary capabilities. On the other hand is the tendency to see them in terms of their everyday consciousness, as they appear manipulated and controlled by the major parties and the North American culture industry. Under these influences, patronage and consumerism rather than a new society appear to be the primary goals of workers. In this incarnation, the party has been reluctant to embrace workers openly. As Hector has observed, if the ACLM opens its doors, "the old consciousness (patronage) comes into the party."[34] An inner tension would be set up between the politics of participation and the politics of patronage. This is a risk that the party has refused to take. Thus the earlier view that when the people are ready for a change they will turn to the ACLM still lingers.

Given the short-term pressures of this stage, such a position, with its underlying ambivalent stand toward workers, needs to be changed and reformulated. Reaching out to masses more actively, particularly in their cloaks of patronage and consumerism, must replace this ambivalence. Because of the more stable nature of this everyday consciousness, the ACLM cannot afford to mobilize workers solely on the basis of their more fleeting insurrectionary consciousness. Workers fall from the lofty normative heights of this consciousness as often as the religious convert falls from the normative heights of the moral consciousness. This division within the totality of the consciousness of workers must be embraced by the ACLM, theorized, and linked to the national democratic stage.

To achieve such a reformulation, the ACLM must confront at least three critical issues. First, it must recognize the essentially political nature of the insurrectionary consciousness of Antiguan workers and grasp it in terms of the real creative alternatives forming within it. This is important if the party is to embody this consciousness and not impose external meanings upon it. Second, the ACLM must acknowledge the unpredictable nature of the upsurges of this consciousness. As this unpredictability points to the need for readiness as a strategy, it also points to its limitations in relation to more short-term and predictable events. Third, the ACLM must actively engage the everyday consciousness of workers, a consciousness with active religious categories and strong tendencies toward clientelism. Moral or ideological rejection of this consciousness will only make workers feel unfit to be members of the party. This important communicative obstacle must be removed if the mass base of the party is to be increased.

Finally, there are the problems arising from the failure of the party to redefine itself clearly as an organization oriented toward the goals of its new intermediary stage. This failure is closely related to its un-resolved ambivalence toward workers. Thus, despite the turn toward electoral politics, there is still a real sense in which the party continues to see itself as the small revolutionary group of the Jamesian years. As in the case of worker insurrectionary activity, the foundations of this position have been shaken, but the party has not been able to replace it with a positive alternative. However, its commitment to a national democratic stage makes such an alternative an urgent necessity. As an organization, the ACLM must be able not only to win elections, but also to take the lead in introducing elementary participatory measures and securing them against dominant, opposing forces. As the party leaders themselves recognize, such measures "can only be created by a truely socialist party. . . . Without a socialist party, the capitalist characteristics in the public, private and cooperative sectors will predominate and rob of all meaning the organs of popular control and power."[35]

Such transformational tasks, particularly at the national democratic stage, require leadership and organizational capabilities beyond those of a small revolutionary group. A party with a mass base and cadres of experts becomes a necessity. Thus, a more appropriate organizational model for the ACLM is that of the mass party James outlined and attempted to build in Trinidad. Such a party would be of a synthetic transitional nature, combining representative and participatory features like other political structures of the national democratic stage. Given the experiences of the PNP and the NJM, it is clear that it is now historically possible to go be-yond what James specifically attempted to do. However, it is also clear that although more advanced socialist moves can be made, the political culture of the Antiguan working class requires that this party have real electoral access to state power, and that it can deliver real material bene-fits as well as the higher virtues of active political life. The increased importance of James's *Nkrumah and the Ghana Revolution* during this period suggests that the ACLM is aware of this problem. However, this awareness has not produced an all-out effort to transform the party from a Jamesian small revolutionary group to a mass party of the Jamesian variety.

Conclusion

The most obvious implication of the ACLM's experience with James's ideas, particularly his view of the transition to socialism, is the definite manner in which the ACLM experience points to the power of James's thought. James's celebration of the creativity of workers; his analysis of representative democracy; his bold call for direct democracy as part of a modern solution to the problem of working-class domination; and his promise of humanization through popular participation all constitute a vision of politics at its best—and a hope for a modern Caribbean.

However, for a socialist party in a peripheral country like Antigua, the ACLM experience suggests that important modifications will have to be made in James's general view of modern politics. First, as he himself recognized, the models of socialist transformation for the periphery must be different from those for center. These divergences are related to differences in the level of development and in the creative alternatives forming in the consciousness of the masses. Thus, projected institutional changes and appropriate organizational instruments of transformation will also be different. In confronting these issues, the young socialist party will find James's model of a mass party, as opposed to the classical liberal or vanguard model, very useful. However, in sorting out corresponding economic problems, the party will find that it has to turn to additional sources. Despite such limitations, taken as a whole James's thought constitutes a vital legacy upon which current and future attempts to modernize and change Caribbean societies can build. The importance of this legacy for Caribbean socialism has increased since the tragic rise and fall of Coardism in Grenada. One clear implication of this awful but crucial failure is that a stronger affirmation of James's model of the political aspects of transformation, and working out its specifics for the periphery more clearly, is a theoretical injection that Caribbean socialism desperately needs at present.

Notes

1   C. L. R. James, *Modern Politics* (Port of Spain: PNM Publishing, 1960), 8.
2   C. L. R. James, *The Future in the Present* (London: Allison and Busby, 1977), 40.
3   James, *Future in the Present.*
4   Ibid., 173.

5   James, *Modern Politics*, 10.
6   Ibid., 15.
7   Ibid., 22.
8   Ibid., 179.
9   C. L. R. James, *Party Politics in the West Indies* (San Juan: Vedic Enterprises, 1962), 90.
10   Ibid., 4.
11   James, *Future in the Present*, 183–90.
12   James, *Party Politics*, 48.
13   Ibid., 16.
14   Ibid., 33.
15   Ibid.
16   C. L. R. James, *At the Rendezvous of Victory* (London: Allison and Busby, 1984), 85–128; James, *Party Politics*.
17   For a more detailed analysis, see chapter 9.
18   Tim Hector, *The Caribbean Yesterday, Today, and Tomorrow* (St. Johns: ACLM), 6.
19   Tim Hector, "George Weston," *Outlet*, May 12, 1977, 6.
20   Tim Hector, Ellerton Jeffers, and Vincent Michael, *Independence: Yes! The Old Mess: No!* (St. Johns: ACLM, 1976), 3–7.
21   Hector, Jeffers, and Michael, *Independence*, 6.
22   Ibid., 14–15.
23   Frantz Fanon, *The Wretched of the Earth* (New York: Grove, 1968), 148–205.
24   Ibid., 5.
25   Interview with Ellerton Jeffers, November 24, 1987.
26   Interview with Conrad Luke, August 22, 1987.
27   Interview with Ellerton Jeffers.
28   *Towards a New Antigua* (St. Johns: ACLM, 1980), 7.
29   *Towards a New Antigua*, 6.
30   Ibid., 20.
31   *Antigua for Antiguans, Barbuda for Barbudans* (St. Johns: ACLM, 1980), 7.
32   *Journal 2* (May 1984):4.
33   Interview with Conrad Luke.
34   Interview with Tim Hector, August 24, 1987.
35   *Antigua for Antiguans*, 28.

Appendix

Excerpts from

The Life of Captain Cipriani

▼▼▼▼▼

The following selections[1] from *The Life of Captain Cipriani: An Account of British Government in the West Indies* present key elements from James's first sustained nonfiction writing of any kind, and his first exposition of anti-colonialist Caribbean nationalism. Published by a small firm in Nelson, Lancashire in 1932—presumably at the expense of James's friend and noted cricketer, Learie Constantine—*The Life of Captain Cipriani* was drastically reduced (and the following sections among those eliminated) in *The Case for West Indian Self-Government*, published by Leonard and Virginia Woolf's Hogarth Press the following year.

The political insurgent Cipriani knew of James as a cricket reporter and a sympathetic schoolteacher. James obviously admired Cipriani (according to his own account, James was asked by a colonial official what would happen if Cipriani were arrested, and warned the official that the island would go up in rebellion—Cipriani was not arrested). But recognizing the vulnerability of his public position, James spoke publicly for Cipriani only once, and did not write for Trinidad Workingmen's Association newspaper, *The Labour Leader*, except a few essays on sports. Gaining Cipriani's eager approval for writing this pamphlet, James finished it before he left Trinidad in 1932. Significantly, he only published it abroad. Through that act he had more than made up for his earlier lack of public solidarity. He had become Cipriani's biographer.

As a literary document, *Captain Cipriani* is a curious mixture of legislative excerpts, military race-relations history, almost incidental island detail, biography, and antiracist or protonationalist arguments. Some critics have suggested that it can be read as a preparation for *The Black Jacobins*: searching for a protagonist through which to see the West Indian experience, James used the smaller figure of Cipriani before approaching the larger figure of Toussaint. It might also be read as James's first nonfiction approximation of Caribbean life and culture, in daily life as well as public events. The barely glancing observation of the actual Trinidad Workingmen's Association, with its core of fifteen thousand labor and socialist supporters, is the most striking negative feature—all the stranger because James never returned to the subject again.[2]

In any event, James's insistence upon "fair play" within the empire is voiced through Cipriani's own effort. English colonial administrators, James wrote in a passage reprinted in *The Case for West Indian Self-Government*, could be better suited for their responsibilities, but "the more efficient they are, the more do they act as a blight upon those vigorous and able men whose home is their island and who, in the natural course of events, would rise to power and influence." Britain *could* contain the Trinidadians through force of arms. But in doing so, they defeated the spirit of their responsibilities, for "we remain without credit abroad and without self-respect at home, a bastard, feckless conglomeration of individuals, inspired by no common purpose, moving to no common end." Cipriani had, more than anyone, set out to right the course, to persuade Trinidadians of their own potential and the British of their obligation to accelerate political emancipation.

James the Marxist and Third World revolutionary would find other formulas and words to express these hopes. But certainly his feeling for the life of the subjects, and the obligations of the West toward them, had not changed so much at all.

On Captain Cipriani

Many West Indians (and a few Englishmen, too) have worked for the emancipation of the West Indies. Their story will be told in time. But none has worked like Captain Cipriani. That is why his biography is presented here. His work is at a critical stage. That is why it is presented now.

Arthur Andrew Cipriani was born on the 31st January, 1875. His father was Albert Henry Cipriani, a planter of Santa Cruz. The Ciprianis are a family of Corsican descent, closely related to the Bonaparte family. They came to Trinidad over a hundred years ago, and have their place in the history of the Island. One of them, Eugene Cipriani, made a large fortune, but the most distinguished member of the family has been the Captain's uncle, Joseph Emmanuel Cipriani. He was a solicitor and Mayor of the city of Port of Spain for seven years. He played a great part in the lighting of the city and the laying out of Tranquility, and it is after him that the Cipriani Boulevard is named. He not only spent time on Port of Spain, but also much of his personal fortune, giving largely to charitable causes.

Captain Cipriani, one of three brothers, lost both parents early, and at six years of age was himself very nearly lost. He, his mother and his two brothers were all struck down with typhoid. Old Dr. de Boissiere passed through the rooms and examined them.

"The mother is improving," he said, "but this one (pointing to the future legislator) will die."

The boys lived and it was the mother who died. His father was already dead, and he was brought up by one of his father's sisters, a Mrs. Dick. He went to a little school carried on above the Medical Hall by a Miss Jenkins, and there he stayed until he was seven, when he left for St. Mary's College. At College with him were Gaston Johnson, the Lasalle brothers (Charlie and John), Dr. Pollonais, Napolean Raymond and many other good creoles. Young Cipriani played cricket well and was a good runner. The boys were not coddled in any way. They fought vigorously and often, but Father Brown, the Principal, gave them a chance, and though always willing to hear and settle when disputes did reach him, never interfered unduly. . . .

School-life had its politics, which after all is nothing but the art of people living well together. Now and then among the priests there were some hot-headed Irishmen who would be inclined to take advantage of the boys. But the boys kept together and stood up for their rights; and Father Brown was one who always realized that boys had rights as well as masters.

Arthur Cipriani left St. Mary's College at sixteen in the Senior Class. He had not done badly, but was handicapped by an atrocious hand-writing which he preserves unimpaired to this day.

His father had trained his uncle's horses and he had grown up in racing. As soon as he left college, some of his richer relations offered to send him away to qualify as a veterinary surgeon. But his immediate family did not wish him to accept the offer, and he refused it. Already he knew horses, and he started to ride and train. He had his trainer's license at eighteen, and regularly made the round of the different racing centres, Trinidad, Barbados, British Guiana. In between he worked on the cocoa estates of his relations and friends.

He was nearly shot dead one night at "La Chaguaramas," the cocoa estate of Mr. Leon Centeno at Caroni. He was sleeping in the estate-house when he was awakened by a noise outside. He got up and opened one half of the window, and saw a man walking towards the cocoa-house. He called out to him, and the man turned and fired a revolver, the shot going through Cipriani's forearm. He still wears the scar.

The incident is still a mystery. Many people thought it was no other than Centeno himself, who was known to be a practical joker. It was believed that he had intended merely to frighten his friend, but that the shot, as revolver shots will, had taken an unexpected course. Centeno, however, originated a theory that Cipriani was not quite right in his head, and had shot himself. His theory did not find acceptance, and some time after he left the island, to which he never returned.

For years Arthur Cipriani divided his time between racing and cocoa estates. Increased weight made him give up riding, but he trained regularly, besides which he had and still has a passion for horse-racing. He thinks that racing in those days was of a better class than it is to-day, and there was more sport. Although the stakes were smaller, owners were very keen to win. But there was more good feeling between them then than now. They fraternised more, and successes were celebrated with big dinners and receptions. There was not so much gambling, there were no sweepstakes, but among those who went to see, much innocent enjoyment on the merry-go-rounds and swings, while among the real racing men there was not so much question of gain, as honour and distinction for the various colonies. . . .

So for twenty years he went about his business, working on estates and training horses. He became Secretary of the Breeders' Association, but though well-known in racing circles, was on the whole a solitary man, going about in his khaki trousers and khaki tunic open at the neck, an inconspicuous figure of no particular importance.

The course of his life seemed settled. He saw his thirty-ninth birthday, and was only a few months short of forty when in 1914 the War broke out.

The Contingents

The earnest appeal just made to you by the lecturer appeals to me, as well as to most of you who are in the hall, with a peculiar force. It is those of you who, like me, are British subjects not of English parentage, but of alien descent, and owe their protection to the British flag, that the appeal comes with greater force. It is true the Colony has offered £40,000 worth of cocoa, which has been accepted. Putting it at five cents per inhabitant, is that all we are going to offer in return for the protection of our homes and children which we are receiving? . . . I think it is practicable for us to send one hundred cavalry horses, and there can be no doubt about it that having secured a hundred horses there would soon be secured a hundred riders to go to the Front and fight side by side with the other Colonial troops. . . . The very best we can do is to try to attain that end, and if we fail we will still have the satisfaction of knowing that we had tried to do our duty.

It was his first public speech. The occasion was a lecture, "Sayings on the War," delivered by Mr. Algernon Burkett, at S. Ann's Hall, Oxford Street, to help the Trinidad Breeders' Association in their effort to buy a hundred cavalry horses for the English Army. The War was not yet two months old.

There followed a long struggle by the people of Trinidad, led by Mr. Cipriani and the "Port of Spain Gazette," to be allowed to play their part in the War as members of the British Empire. At the very beginning of the War, many felt that the services of Trinidadians should be offered to Britain, but they had not forgotten the opposition and ridicule of the official English section in the colony to a similar proposal during the South African War, and the curt refusal of the Home Authorities. As time passed, however, it seemed to Mr. Cipriani that unless someone took the initiative, any chance of raising a local contingent would disappear, "a condition of things I was prepared to frustrate at all costs." . . .

Early in December the first batch of eleven Trinidadians at their own expense left for England to enlist. The local government contributed nothing to the enterprise, and the concession in regard to the passage rates made by the Mail Steam Packet Company known as royal was so small as to be almost negligible. But the send-off given to these young men was perhaps the most remarkable ever witnessed in the history of the colony, and was a very fair index of the feeling of the Trinidadian people. . . .

Mr. Cipriani asked permission of the local government, and on its being granted, convened the first public recruiting meeting in Marine Square, under the chairmanship of Dr. Prada, the Mayor of Port of Spain. . . . At [t]his recruiting meeting Arthur Cipriani spoke to the people:

> If the West Indies claims a place in the sun, we must do our duty as unit of the British Empire. It is true that we here form the weakest link in the chain. But it is said that the weakest link is the strength of the chain. (Cheers). I am one of the people. I was born and bred in this colony, was reared in it from childhood to youth, and from youth to manhood. I have shared your sorrows and your joys, and I appeal to you to-day in the name of the King to enlist, and I do so irrespective of class, colour or creed. . . . The game has not been played in many quarters, it is not being played now.

It was not, for Mr. George F. Higgins, a member of the recruiting Committee, was the chief mover in raising and sending to England a Merchants' Contingent for which dark-skinned men were rigidly excluded. In Trinidad, the fairer-skinned, in some mixed communities, enjoy greater advantages and have better opportunities, and thus the Public Contingent was deprived of some of the best material available. Mr. Cipriani protested without result. But the aim had been achieved. By ten o'clock on the morning after the meeting, the first contingent of men had been recruited. In September it left for England. Mr. Cipriani helped to recruit the second contingent, the third and fourth, but then decided to go to the Front, refusing the request of Sir John Chancellor to stay and continue with recruiting work.

There was some trouble about his commission, for he was already forty. The state of his health demanded an operation. But the difficulties were successfully overcome, and on the 28th of March, 1917, Lieutenant Cipriani left Trinidad for Europe in command of the third contingent.

That is how Trinidad came to send contingents to the Front, a local man and a local newspaper playing the leading parts and having to exercise as much perseverance to overcome their English masters as the soldiers had to overcome the Turks in the field. But such is a Crown Colony. . . .

It is said that the War made Captain Cipriani. So in one sense it did, in that it gave him an opportunity. But the essential Cipriani was always there. . . .

Captain Cipriani was back in Trinidad in 1919. Before the end of the year he had started his post-war public career by accepting the post of President of the Trinidad Workingmen's Association.

This Association had been founded in the last decade of the nineteenth century, the leading spirit being Mr. Alfred Richards, now an alderman of the city of Port of Spain. It led a chequered existence, and in 1906 had but 223 members. By 1914 it had fizzled out. But 1919 was a time when new things were being born, and old things were being re-born. The Working-men's Association was resuscitated, chiefly through the efforts of Mr. W. Howard Bishop, now dead, who became in time Editor of the "Labour Leader," the organ of the Association. With him were Fred Adams, Julian Braithwait, R. Braithwaite, D. Headley and W. Samuel, most of them merchants in a small way or men in business, but all coloured men and interested in their own people.

Captain Cipriani was not one of the original group, but early in the life of the new Association he was asked to become President, and accepted.

If there is anything which can prove the fitness of the people of Trinidad for self-government it is the progress of this resuscitated Association during the thirteen years since it has been restarted.

When Captain Cipriani became President in 1919, the Association functioned only in the City of Port of Spain. By 1928 there were forty-two affiliated sections in other parts of the island, besides which others distributed among the various classes of workers in Port of Spain. In January, 1930, replying to a call from Tobago, Captain Cipriani and half-a-dozen other colleagues proceeded to the island-ward and there established thirteen sections. To-day the Association has ninety-eight sections comprising thousands of members. Each section manages its own affairs, appoints its own officers, and keeps its own funds. Delegates meet once a quarter to discuss matters of general policy. To-day as in 1919, the public meetings of the Association are assisted by plain-clothes officers busy taking notes, and doubtless the Government would rejoice to get hold of something seditious. But though Captain Cipriani gives these amateur reporters a lot to take down they get little to carry away. Meanwhile the frequent rallies of different sections, the questions which they discuss, Captain Cipriani's visits to section after section explaining to them matters of policy, the circulation of the "Labor Leader" until Mr. Bishop died a year or two ago, all these have made the agricultural labourers and the artisans, the masses of the people, alive to politics as at no other time in the history of Trinidad.

Notes

1   The diction and spelling of the original have been retained. The excerpts begin with the final paragraph of chapter one, run through large parts of chapter two, skip over the detailed treatment of the war experience in chapter three, and climax with the first two pages of chapter four.

2   As Wally Look Lai notes, James was very close in later years to George Weekes, foremost leader of the TWA's descendent labor organization, the Oilfields Workers Trade Union. And indeed, several of James's last, grand public addresses in the Caribbean were made to OWTU events. But despite Weekes's own recurrent pleas for James to write the history of Trinidad union, time and energy could not be found. Khafra Kambon's biography of Weekes, *For Bread, Justice and Freedom* (London: New Beacon Books, 1988) touches upon the legacy of Cipriani, but a full history of the TWA remains a vital task of regional scholarship.

Chronology
▼▼▼▼

1901 Born in Port of Spain, Trinidad.

1910 Precocious winner of "exhibition" (scholarship) to Queen's Royal College.

1918–19 Graduates from Queen's Royal College with "School Certificate" and begins career as teacher; joins Maple Cricket Club, team of creoles and upward-bound blacks; helps organize Trinidad literary club, the Maverick.

1920–26 Teaches, organizes school theatrical group to perform Shakespeare; speaks publicly for Arthur Cipriani, labor activist and successful candidate for Mayor of Port of Spain; writes occasionally on cricket for the *Labour Leader*, a newspaper of Cipriani's movement—the Trinidad Workingmen's Association.

1927 First short story published, "La Divina Pastora," in the British *Saturday Review*, story reprinted in *Best Short Stories* (1928).

1929–30 Coedits two issues of literary journal, *Trinidad*, with creole Alfred Mendes, future novelist; James's contributions include short stories about lowerclass life in Trinidad.

1931–32 Contributes to *Trinidad*'s successor, *The Beacon*, edited by Albert Gomes.

1932 Leaves Trinidad for Nelson, Lancashire, England, where *The Life of Captain Cipriani: An Account of British Government in the West Indies* is privately published.

1933 Moves to London, publishes *The Case for West-Indian Self Government* through the Hogarth Press of Leonard and Virginia Woolf; joins

Trotskyist movement; travels to France to study the 1791 revolution in Santo Domingo, Haiti.

1936–37   Publishes *Minty Alley*, his only novel (written in 1928); his play, *Toussaint L'Ouverture*, with Paul Robeson in the lead, is staged in London; active in the Pan-African Movement with George Padmore and others, edits several issues of *International African Opinion*.

1938   The *Black Jacobins: Toussaint L'Ouverture and the San Domingo Revolution* and *A History of the Negro Revolt* appear; leaves England for the United States, meets Trotsky in Mexico and goes on speaking tour for Trotskyist movement.

1939–52   Becomes a leader in the U.S. Trotskyist movement and own political group, living mostly in New York City; writes infrequently on Caribbean subjects.

1953   Expelled from the United States, after being confined to Ellis Island. *Mariners, Renegades and Castaways* appears from private publisher.

1954–58   Lives in London with trips to West Indies; gathers group of West Indians around him, including novelist George Lamming.

1958   Returns to Trinidad, as editor of *PNM Go Forward*, changes name to *The Nation*; confidant of Dr. Eric Williams; with his third wife, Selma James, active in People's National Movement.

1960   Breaks with Eric Williams and ceases editorship of *The Nation*; publishes *Modern Politics* in Trinidad; involved in near-fatal car accident.

1962   Publishes *Party Politics in the West Indies* in Trinidad, returns to England.

1963   *Beyond a Boundary* is published in England; *Black Jacobins* is reprinted by Vintage in the United States and gains many university class assignments and reestablishes James's critical reputation as pioneering scholar of the Caribbean and of slavery.

1965–66   Returns to Trinidad as cricket journalist; is confined under house arrest and leads formation of Workers' and Farmers' Party which unsuccessfully contests 1966 elections; lives for a time in Toronto with young West Indian intellectuals.

1968–81   Reenters the United States for lecture tours and to teach at Federal City College, Washington, D.C.

1970   *C. L. R. James Anthology*, first collection of his writings, with several essays on West Indian topics, is published as issue of *Radi-*

cal America, edited by Paul Buhle. *Anthology* circulates widely to the United Kingdom and Caribbean.

1977–83 Three volumes of selected works, also *Notes On Dialectics* and *Nkrumah and the Ghana Revolution*, are published in England by Allison & Busby.

1980 Moves to San Fernando, Trinidad, in housing of Oilfields Workers Trade Union; close to George Weekes, OWTU leader; subject of frequent comments in *The Vanguard*, organ of OWTU.

1981 Relocates to Brixton, London, in housing arranged by *Race Today* collective of James's great-nephew, Darcus Howe.

1986 The critical anthology *C. L. R. James: His Life and Work*, edited by Paul Buhle, and *Cricket*, selected writings, appear, both published by Allison & Busby; awarded Trinity Cross, the highest honor of Trinidad and Tobago.

1989 First biography, *C. L. R. James: The Artist as Revolutionary*, by Paul Buhle, appears from Verso, and is greeted by James; James dies in May; BBC television's *C. L. R. James, a Tribute*, is shown in the United Kingdom and West Indies.

1991 International Conference "C. L. R. James: His Intellectual Legacies," held at Wellesley, Massachusetts, by the C. L. R. James Society and the *C. L. R. James Journal*; C. L. R. James Education Centre opened at the Oilfields Workers Butler/Rienzi Labour College, San Fernando, Trinidad.

1992 *The C. L. R. James Reader*, edited by Anna Grimshaw, appears.

Glossary
▼▼▼▼

Age of Innocence (1958) and *Season of Adventure* (1963). Famed West Indian novels by George Lamming, the first a bildungsroman of Lamming's own intellectual and cultural origins in Barbados, the second a literary exploration of social revolution as described in modernist prose.

Babylon. A Rastafarian term for oppressive social forces, including the police, imperial government, and established churches.

Dub Poetry. A style of poetry influenced by the rhythms, rhyming schemes, and speech patterns of Rastafarians and of reggae music.

Raya Dunayevskaya. Russian-born Marxist philosopher and for more than thirty years, until her death in 1987, the foremost figure of the "News and Letters" group. She was earlier a coleader with C. L. R. James and Grace Lee in the Johnson-Forest Tendency of the American Trotskyist movement, c.1941–50.

Wilson Harris. Guyanese novelist who is the most distinguished Caribbean literary modernist after Aime Cesaire. For many years a resident of London, Harris was a social intimate of James during the 1960s and an occasional visitor in later years.

The Invading Socialist Society. A little-known pamphlet of the Johnson-Forest Tendency in 1947, by James, Dunayevskaya, and Grace Lee, outlining the argument that Stalinism was not the drastic "error" or "deformation" that other Trotskyists believed, but a necessary and inevitable, if dreadful, part of the ongoing world-historical process.

Michael Manley. Admirer of James, cricket journalist, and son of Norman Manley, James's generational colleague who led the nationalist forces in Jamaica from the 1930s until independence. A more Fabian socialist than James, Michael Manley came to power in Jamaica in 1976, and his government was received coldly by U.S. leaders. Returning to power in 1988, he has taken a more moderate and accommodating approach toward U.S. interests.

Minty Alley. James's Caribbean novel written in 1927, published in London in 1936, and reprinted in 1969 by New Beacon Press.

Non-Aligned Movement. Arising from the Bandung Conference of 1955 and the need for mostly former colonialized areas to assert a "third" position between the United States and Russia, this movement peaked in the 1950s and early 1960s. Later, its supporters fell to neocolonialist pressures.

People's National Movement (PNM). Founded by Dr. Eric Williams in 1955, the PNM emerged as the leading proindependence force, then ruled from independence until 1987.

George Padmore. Born Malcolm Nurse in Trinidad, he was a childhood friend of James's who became a Communist sympathizer during his education at Howard University in Washington, D.C. He joined the Comintern (Communist International) as a leading figure on the "Negro Question," until he broke with the Communists over their alliance with the Western democracies (and colonial powers) in the late 1930s. Often cited as the "Father of Pan-Africanism." Collaborator with James's Pan-African activities in the 1930s and 1940s, and advisor to Kwame Nkrumah, he remained until his death in 1959 an important correspondent with James.

Rastafarian Movement. Religious-radical tendency centered in Jamaica. Rooted in the historical traditions of the Marcus Garvey Black Nationalist movement, Rastafarianism became extremely powerful in the 1960s and 1970s for rebellious rhetoric and use and sale of marijuana.

Walter Rodney. Leading intellectual devotee of C. L. R. James among the political generations of the 1960s and 1970s, noted lecturer and writer on Pan-African questions, also a leader of the Working People's Alliance in Guyana. Assassinated in 1980 by assailants widely assumed to have been trained by the Central Intelligence Agency.

Season of Adventure. See *Age of Innocence.*

Garfield Sobers. First Afro-Caribbean captain of the West Indian cricket team and one of the most admired world cricketers of the 1950s and 1960s. Considered by James the "Willie Mays of cricket."

Sparrow, or **Mighty Sparrow.** Real name, Francisco Slinger. Trinidad's leading calypso singer from the 1950s to the present, and for a long time a voice of political criticism.

Trinidad Workingmen's Association. A labor-political movement launched at the turn of the century, then renewed in 1919 by Captain Arthur Cipriani; a leading force in the 1920s and 1930s for Trinidad independence and labor rights.

George Weekes. An intimate of James's in Trinidad, and James's personal link to the Trinidadian labor movement. Long a leader of the Oilfields Workers Trade Union, especially in its 1950s–60s phase of economic consolidation and political-industrial opposition to the austerity policies of the Williams government.

Eric Williams. Leader of independence movement in Trinidad and first Prime Minister. Trained by James as teacher from an early age, Williams reconnected with James in the 1930s while studying at Oxford, again in the United States during the 1940s when he taught at Howard University, and yet again in the 1950s, when he invited his old mentor to return to Trinidad as editor of the independence party's newspaper. Williams's outstanding historical study, *Capitalism and Slavery* (1959) is widely regarded as an expansion upon James's ideas. The two men broke in 1960 and remained rivals afterward. Williams died in 1981.

Woodford Square. Famous public square in Port of Spain, Trinidad, where Eric Williams and his followers lectured frequently for the PNM—so frequently that their efforts became known as the "University of Woodford Square."

Working People's Alliance (WPA). Along with Antigua's Afro-Caribbean Liberation Movement (ACLM) and Trinidad's New Beginnings Movement, the Caribbean political movement most influenced by James. It remains an opposition party to the governments in Guyana.

Workers Party of Jamaica (WPJ). A roughly Marxist-Leninist organization, long led by Trevor Monroe and considered unsympathetic to James's nonvanguardist ideals. Never in government, the wpj was nonetheless a well-organized minority movement until the Grenadan counterrevolution of Bernard Coard, supported by wpj leaders, overthrew and murdered Maurice Bishop in 1983. Since then, the wpj has struggled to maintain its presence.

Index

▼▼▼▼▼

Labor movements (continued)
163, 198, 199, 231. See also Strikes;
Trade unionism; Workers
Labor relations, 219–20
Labor theory, 146–47, 151–58, 165–71,
171
Labour Leader, 263, 269, 270, 271
Lamming, George, ix, 1–2, 5, 16, 28–36,
87–88, 112, 114, 122, 124, 146, 187, 197,
272, 274
Land reform, 163, 164, 166, 201, 243, 255
Language, 47, 137–38. See also Semiotics
La Religion, 189
Las Casas, Bartolomé de, 111
Lazarus, Neil, 61, 62, 92–110
League for the Protection of Ethiopia, 8
League of Colored People, 8
Le Blanc, Norman, 42
Leconte de Lisle, Charles Marie, 182
Lee, Grace, 274
Leftism, 189, 193, 196, 197, 199, 204, 215,
225–62. See also New Left
Legesse, Asmaron, 68–69
Lenin, Nikolai, 134, 145, 151, 153, 161,
175, 177, 205
Leninism, 6, 29, 45–46, 68, 84, 160, 184
Lévi-Strauss, Claude, 137, 139
Lewis, Arthur, 145, 146–48, 158, 159,
160–61, 171, 177, 238
Lewis, Bernard, 251
Lewis, Gordon, 199, 207 n. 8
Lewis, Vaughn, 238
Liberalism, xii, 63, 65, 67, 70, 178, 204
Life value, 72, 73–80, 85
Lipsitz, George, 38n
Lloyd, Clive, 107
Look Lai, Walton, 144, 174–209, 270 n. 2
Lovelace, Earl, 49
Lower, A. M., 71
Lukács, Georg, 93, 98, 129, 233
Luke, Conrad, 249, 258
Lyotard, Jean-François, 62

McGill University, 239–40
Machel, Samora, 84
Macherey, Pierre, 64

McIntyre, Alister, 238
McShine, Halsey, 192
Mahabir, Winston, 195
Maharaj, Stephen, 198, 199, 200
Mais, Roger, 79
Makonnen, Ras, 8
Manchester Guardian, 6
Manley, Michael, 32, 91 n. 18, 167, 203,
252, 255, 275
Manley, Norman, 275
Marcuse, Herbert, 97, 232, 233
Marin, Munoz, 164
Marley, Bob, 34
Marryshaw, T. A., 121
Marryshow, T. A., 49
Marx, Karl, 6, 45, 50, 72, 80, 145, 151,
152, 175–76, 215, 229–31
Marxism, 6, 9, 10–11, 29, 32, 51, 62, 63,
64, 65, 67, 78, 79, 80, 85, 91 n. 18, 93,
97, 98, 113, 126, 134, 143–44, 175, 179,
183, 185, 199, 204–5, 210–24, 226, 227,
240
Marxism-Leninism, 45–46, 84
Masses: basic needs of, 149–50, 168–69;
creativity of, 15, 29, 150–51, 168, 188,
217, 226–30, 237; education of, xiii–
xiv, 128, 160, 235, 236–37 (see also
Participation); empowerment of, 179,
200; mobilization of, 196; organiza-
tion drives, 258; self-organization of,
29, 128, 163, 170. See also Socialist
transformation; Workers
Mass party, xiv–xv, 183–84, 186, 204,
235–37, 260, 261
Mbafeno Report, 197
Melville, Herman, 11–12, 14, 15, 50
Mendes, Alfred, 49, 59, 271
Merchant, Lesroy, 239
Mexico, 10, 272
Michael, Vincent, 242, 246
Middle class, 73, 74, 77, 129–30, 161–
62, 204, 237, 238, 243, 244, 251; black,
185–86
Minor literatures, 118–20, 138
Mohammed, Una, 208 n. 32
Monroe, Trevor, 29, 276

Contributors

Paget Henry is Associate Professor in the Department of Sociology, Brown University. He is the author of *Peripheral Capitalism and Underdevelopment in Antigua* and, with Carl Stone, *Newer Caribbean: Decolonization, Democracy and Development.*

Paul Buhle teaches at the Rhode Island School of Design and is the Director of the Oral History of the American Left program, Tamiment Library, New York University. His books include *C. L. R. James: His Life and Work* and, with Alan Dawley, *Working for Democracy: American Workers from the Revolution to the Present.*

Selwyn Cudjoe, a Trinidadian native, is Director of Black Studies at Wellesley College, publisher of Calaloux Books, and author of *Resistance and Caribbean Literature* and *V. S. Naipaul, a Materialist Reading*, among other works.

Stuart Hall, a native Jamaican, is a former editor of *New Left Review*, and is currently Professor of Sociology at the Open University. He is author of several books including *The Politics of Thatcherism.*

George Lamming, the distinguished senior novelist of the English-speaking Caribbean, lives in his native Barbados and speaks widely on literary and political subjects in the region, the United States and the United Kingdom.

Neil Lazarus is Associate Professor in English and Media at Brown University and author of *Resistance in Postcolonial African Fiction.*

Walton Look Lai is a specialist in Latin American and Caribbean Studies. He holds a doctorate in history from New York University and was the recipient of a Rockefeller Foundation fellowship in 1990–91. He is the author of a forthcoming book on the history of Asians in the British West Indies, 1838 to 1918.

Kent Worcester, a frequent reviewer of James-related works in the British press, has a Ph.D. in Political Science from Columbia University and is author of a forthcoming biography of C. L. R. James.

Sylvia Wynter, a native of Jamaica, is professor of Afro-American Studies and Spanish at Stanford University and a distinguished novelist and critic.